Nurem

An international human rights conference marked the fortieth anniversary of the Nuremberg trials; this collection of its papers and proceedings invites the reader to share in stimulating discussions by some of the leading human rights scholars and advocates of our day.

Moving speeches by Nobel Peace Laureate Elie Wiesel and Chilean human rights activist Carmen Quintana are highlights of the collection. Also included is the dramatic free speech/group libel/pornography debate between celebrated US civil liberties lawyer Alan Dershowitz, Judge Maxwell Cohen (Canada), lawyer Ram Jethmalani (India), and feminist legal theorist Kathleen Mahoney (Canada). Other papers include those by then-Canadian Justice Minister Ramon Hnatyshyn; former US Congresswoman Elizabeth Holtzman and parliamentarians Svend Robinson (Canada) and Greville Janner (United Kingdom); South African human rights lawyer Arthur Chaskalson and UK Member of Parliament Paul Boateng; and war crimes specialists Irwin Cotler (Canada), litigator David Matas (Canada), Australian Justice Michael Kirby, and Allan Ryan Jr, former head of the US office of Special Investigations.

The conference was held in Montreal in 1987. An "addenda" to the proceedings updates issues addressed at the conference and includes the Fourth Raoul Wallenberg Lectureship in Human Rights, given by Per Ahlmark, former Deputy Prime Minister of Sweden, and a discussion of possibilities for a post-apartheid South Africa by Albie Sachs.

IRWIN COTLER is Professor of Law and a member of the Institute of Comparative Law, McGill University, and an international human rights lawyer.

Nuremberg Forty Years Later
The Struggle against Injustice in Our Time

International Human Rights
Conference, November 1987
Papers and Proceedings
and
Retrospective 1993

Edited by Irwin Cotler

Published for the Faculty of Law of McGill University
and InterAmicus
by McGill-Queen's University Press
Montreal & Kingston • London • Buffalo

© InterAmicus 1995
ISBN 0-7735-1239-x (cloth)
ISBN 0-7735-1250-0 (paper)

Legal deposit first quarter 1995
Bibliothèque nationale du Québec

Printed in the United States on acid-free paper

McGill-Queen's University Press is grateful
to the Canada Council for support of its
publishing program.

Canadian Cataloguing in Publication Data

Main entry under title:
International Human Rights Conference (1987:
Montréal, Quebec)

Nuremberg forty years later: the struggle against
injustice in our time

ISBN 0-7735-1239-x (bound). –
ISBN 0-7735-1250-0 (pbk.)

1. Human rights – Congresses. 2. War crimes –
Congresses. I. Cotler, Irwin, 1940– II. McGill
University. Faculty of Law III. InterAmicus
(Association) IV. Title.

K3239.6.I58 1987   341.4'81   C95-900008-9

Contents

Foreword

A major International Human Rights Conference took place at the Faculty of Law, McGill University, on 3–4 November 1987, on the theme "Nuremberg Forty Years Later: The Struggle against Injustice in Our Time." It was sponsored by the Faculty of Law of McGill University, in association with InterAmicus, a Canadian and McGill-based human rights centre.

The conference brought together a distinguished international group of lawyers, law professors, judges, parliamentarians, government officials, diplomats and students to discuss some of the more compelling issues of our time at a uniquely symbolic, and significant, moment. For the conference took place on the occasion of the fortieth anniversary of the Nuremberg Trials; in the fortieth commemorative year of the Universal Declaration of Human Rights and reaffirmation by the United Nations of the Nuremberg Principles; on the occasion of Canada's enactment in 1987 of "generic" war crimes legislation that would prove historic not only in Canadian terms but would have important precedential value in international terms; on the occasion of the commencement in Canada of the most celebrated hate speech litigation in the history of Canadian jurisprudence – the *Keegstra, Smith* and *Andrews, Taylor, Zundel,* and *Ross* cases, and at a critical juncture in the international struggle against racism and Apartheid, involving "Nuremberg" in the *double entendre* of that word, as both an exhortation against injustice and a place which exemplifies racism.

Accordingly, the conference was organized around six major themes. First, it recalled – and reaffirmed – the humanitarian and inspirational legacy of Raoul Wallenberg – Canada's only Honourary Citizen – that "Saint Just of the Nations," who is credited with saving more Jews in the Second World War than any government. The conference sought to convey the message that one person can make a difference – that it was possible to resist, to overcome evil, to prevail – an idea that found symbolic expression in the inauguration by Elie Wiesel of the Raoul Wallenberg Lectureship in Human Rights as the opening forum of the conference. This remarkable address, to an audience that sat transfixed throughout – and where students attending the lecture described it as the "single most important educational experience we had in law school" – continued to resonate throughout the conference proceedings; while the closing and moving words by the young Chilean human rights activist Carmen Quintana, in her first public remarks since recovering from burning by a Chilean death squad, provide a symmetrical link with the message and mood of Wiesel's remarks.

Second, the conference recalled and reaffirmed the Nuremberg Principles – the Nuremberg Legacy – as an international landmark in the development of customary international law in general and international humanitarian law in particular. Third, it analysed the Canadian "domestication" of the Nuremberg Principles in comparative perspective, including the first major paper on Canada's newly enacted war crimes or "Nuremberg" legislation by then Canadian Justice Minister Ray Hnatyshyn. Fourth, it sought to inquire into the role of the United Nations – and of UN law – in the international protection of human rights – including the juridical "dissonance" between the rhetoric and aspiration of international human rights law and the reality of continuing human rights violations. Fifth, it examined, in comparative perspective, the notion of "freedom of expression" and "freedom from expression," i.e., the competing claims to freedom of expression on the one hand and the right to protection from group vilifying speech on the other. And, finally, it examined Apartheid as involving "Nuremberg" in the double entendre of that word: the Apartheid State of South Africa as the successor state regime to the racist "Nuremberg" laws and as a case-study in the application of the Nuremberg Principles to the regime and policy of Apartheid.

Part One of this book contains the papers and proceedings of the 1987 conference, including interventions from panelists and the resource faculty for the conference, as well as remarks from members of the audience. Apart from inviting conference presenters to correct any errors in the transcription of their remarks, I have sought to remain faithful not only to the words but to the context in which they were spoken – to try to capture not only the content but the drama of the exchanges – as illustrated by the debate on free speech and hate propaganda. This has also mandated the inclusion of passages and remarks that might have been "edited out" in a more formalistic approach, but whose excision might have prejudiced the rhythm of exchange.

Part Two of the book contains a special "retrospective" on the issues raised at the conference, written five years later – in 1993 – commissioned both from the original conference participants and from two new contributors, Per Ahlmark of Sweden and Albie Sachs from South Africa. The paper by Per Ahlmark, former Deputy Prime Minister of Sweden, on "Human Rights, Anti-Semitism, and the Wallenberg Legacy" dovetails perfectly with the inaugural Raoul Wallenberg Lecture delivered by Elie Wiesel; while the paper by Albie Sachs, constitutional advisor to the African National Congress, on "Perfectibility and Corruptibility: Towards a Post-Apartheid, Non-Racial, Democratic South Africa" serves as a sequel to Arthur Chaskalson's paper on Apartheid in Part One of the book. Part Two also includes an update on the status of bringing war criminals to justice in the United States, Canada, the United Kingdom, and Australia, as well as on the free speech-hate propaganda debate.

As I write this Foreword, it is forty-five years after Nuremberg – five years after the conference – and at a critical juncture in the state and struggle for human rights in our time – a Dickensian moment of "the best of times and the worst of times." On the one hand – and particularly since the holding of the Nuremberg Conference in 1987 – there has been an explosion in human rights. Things that were thought impossible have not only happened but have already been forgotten – or are at risk of being forgotten. Democracy is on the march from Central Asia to Central America. Nelson Mandela has been liberated from a South African prison, and South Africa is being liberated from Apartheid. An International Convention on the Rights of the Child has come into effect, receiving more ratifications more quickly than any other treaty in history. The idea of "Women's Rights as Human Rights" is the clarion call for the first United Nations Human Rights Conference in twenty-five years. And human rights are being spoken of as "the new secular religion of our time."

And yet, at the same time, in a kind of Dickensian dialectic, the violations of human rights continue unabated. The homeless of America, the hungry of Africa, the imprisoned of the Middle East can be forgiven if they believe that the "human rights revolution" has somehow passed them by; while the silent tragedy of the Kurds, the horror of Sarajevo, the ethnic cleansing of the Balkans, the agony of Africa are metaphor and message of the assault upon – if not abandonment of – human rights in our time.

The unthinkable – ethnic cleansing – emerges not as a consequence of war but as the reason for waging it; mass rapes – the silent screams – emerge not as the consequences of ethnic cleansing but as the instruments for achieving it; the post-Nuremberg unspeakable – genocide – appears not as an abstraction but as advocacy. And 35,000 children die every day in developing countries from *prevent-able* diseases. And so it is, then, that the rhetoric of the human rights revolution invites the not uncynical rejoinder that human rights is so much "nonsense on stilts" – that it is rights without writs, rhetoric without remedy, semantics without sanctions.

It is perhaps useful – imperative – forty-five years after Nuremberg – to recall and reaffirm the lessons – the legacy – of Nuremberg that inspired this conference and that underlay its deliberations. That Nazism almost succeeded not only because of the pathology of hate and the technology of terror but because of the crime of indifference – of silence. That, as Wiesel reminds us, neutrality always means coming down on the side of the victimizer, not on the side of the victim. That, as the Supreme Court of Canada recalled and affirmed – as it took judicial notice of the "catastrophic effects" of racism – the Holocaust did not begin in the gas chambers, it began with words. These are, as the Supreme Court put it, "the dark and chilling facts of history." That the term "war criminal" – while appropriate as metaphor and shorthand – is still somewhat of a misnomer; for we are not speaking in the main of those who committed crimes against combatants in the course of the persecution of a war but of those who committed crimes against humanity in the course of the persecution of a race. That the presence of Nazi war criminals amongst us, forty-five years after Nuremberg, is a moral outrage, an affront to conscience, a betrayal of the Nuremberg legacy.

And more: to paraphrase the German Protestant theologian Martin Niemoller, while it may begin with Jews, it doesn't end with Jews. In a world which will not be safe for democracy, for human rights, it will not be safe for Jews, or Blacks, or Aboriginals, or any of the world's historically disadvantaged or vulnerable. But in a world which will not be safe for Jews, or Blacks, or Aboriginals – for the disadvantaged and vulnerable – it will not be safe for democracy or human rights. There are certain universal norms that oblige us all; killing, torture, rape, racism, ethnic cleansing – none of this can be respected by any faith, or culture, or people that respect humanity.

That is why this Foreword – some five years after the conference – seeks to take up where the conference left off: to make a plea today for Sarajevo – for the Sarajevos of the world. For if the Sarajevos – the ethnic cleansings – are to become the killing-field metaphors of the nineties, if the horror of the unthinkable and unspeakable – genocide – is to be matched only by the horror of our indifference to it, then I shudder to think what lies ahead of us, what the twenty-first century will hold.

And so, in the end – forty-five years after Nuremberg, we come back to the beginning – to the Nuremberg legacy, to Wiesel and the conference, to the existential responsibility for words and deeds. For if this century is not to become the century that began with Sarajevo and ended with Sarajevo; if Sarajevo – ethnic cleansing – is not to remain the metaphor and message of our "human rights" universe – of the human condition; then each person must realize that he/she does make a difference; that each intervention is indispensable to the cause of human rights and the lives of human beings; that to be indifferent to genocide is to be an accomplice to it; and that, as the conference concluded, we are each, wherever we are – by what we say and by what we do – the guarantors of each other's fate.

I would like to express my appreciation to McGill-Queen's University Press, in particular to Philip Cercone and Joan McGilvray. Indeed, Philip expressed his enthusiasm for the project right at the beginning, while Joan nurtured it through its various stages of development. Both appreciated the unique historiography of Nuremberg and its legacy, including its relevance for the major human rights issues of our time – combatting racial incitement, bringing war criminals to justice, building democratic, non-racial civil societies – and the importance of inspirational role models such as Raoul Wallenberg in an age characterized by apathy and indifference in the face of the most unspeakable of atrocities.

Ann Crawford-Benson, as my administrative research assistant in 1987–88, was especially helpful in the early stages of this project; Evelyn Cherry and Lieba Shell assisted in proofreading successor drafts of the papers and proceedings, particularly Part 2 of the book. My thanks also to Gigi Grein for diligently typing the various drafts of the manuscript and to Kathe Roth for her skilled copy editing.

Irwin Cotler

Nuremberg Forty Years Later
The Struggle against Injustice in Our Time

Remarks

Welcome

DEAN RODERICK MACDONALD

Madame Justice L'Heureux-Dubé, Honourable Ministers, Principal Johnston, guests of honour, ladies and gentlemen, welcome to the Faculty of Law of McGill University. Madame le juge L'Heureux-Dubé, Honorables Ministres, Monsieur le recteur Johnston, chers invités d'honneur, mesdames et messieurs, permettez-moi, au nom de la Faculté de droit de l'Université McGill, de vous souhaiter la bienvenue à cette conférence internationale sur les droits de la personne – "Nuremberg, quarante ans après."

Central to this faculty's vocation is the quest to sharpen our understanding of the morality of law. None of our tasks as educators, as formative influences on our students, both by our words and by our example, is more important or more difficult.

Forty years ago at Nuremberg, the whole world was led to hone its collective understanding of laws of morality. Indeed, the war criminals did not stand accused in the dark, alone. The law itself, its very capacity to have meaning, also stood accused. Was law silent when confronted with the greatest crimes, or could it articulate standards by which to judge unspeakable horrors?

Aujourd'hui, il existe une réponse au défi posé par Nuremberg. Les droits de la personne servent désormais de bouclier contre les affronts de cette nature. Depuis longtemps, la Faculté de droit de McGill compte parmi ses professeurs des gens qui se sont illustrés, par leur enseignement, leurs recherches et leur exemple dans le domaine des droits de la personne et qui en ont fait quelque chose de significatif et de concret. Percy Corbett, Frank Scott, Maxwell Cohen, mes collègues actuels, John Humphrey et Irwin Cotler, ont tous été ou sont encore des protecteurs et aussi des promoteurs zélés des libertés publiques, non seulement au Canada, mais à l'échelle internationale.

Aussi, d'avoir eu à McGill ces nombreuses figures de proue, témoigne de la vitalité des traditions de la Faculté dans le domaine des droits de la personne. C'est en même temps un hommage à Irwin Cotler, à son inspiration, à sa détermination. Dans une certaine mesure, en encourageant le débat et les discussions, cette conférence reflète le plus grand espoir qu'on puisse placer dans les valeurs morales du droit, dans sa compréhension et son utilité.

Precisely because of the moral dimension to the problems we must address here, lawyers cannot pretend to be the only ones with something to say, or even the ones with the most to say. Raoul Wallenberg, a non-lawyer, for whom we inaugurate a human rights lectureship tonight, taught us that fundamental rights can, and must be, defended – not only by the state, but also by the individual.

And Elie Wiesel, also a non-lawyer, has with unparalleled depth and clarity given voice to the humanity of all. Tonight, it is fitting that the Faculty of Law should look beyond itself to these two great teachers – one of whom we honour in name, and the other who honours us with his presence.

Les thèmes et les questions qui seront abordés au cours de ces deux jours ont autant d'importance que le droit lui-même. Cette conférence représente un pari considérable pour nous tous réunis ici. Au nom de la Faculté de droit, je vous souhaite la bienvenue à McGill et vous incite fortement à relever ce défi. Merci.

Opening Remarks

PROFESSOR IRWIN COTLER, CONFERENCE CHAIR

As I look about me, I am touched by the fact that the *témoignage*, the witness, of this evening is the presence of the moral, intellectual, political, legal and judicial leadership of this province and this country. And the presence, in such inspiring numbers, of the future moral, intellectual, political, judicial, and legal leadership of this country – the students. I am delighted, in particular, to welcome them this evening. Also, there are people representing almost every region of the world, be it Asia or Africa, Latin America or North America, the Middle East or Europe; and, perhaps more importantly, I see the faces of those who have been at the forefront of the struggle for human rights in our time – whether it be the struggle against apartheid in South Africa or the struggle for human rights in Chile and Central America; whether it be the bringing of war criminals to justice or the combatting of hate propaganda; whether it be striking out for aboriginal rights or for women's rights. Here among us are the people who have been toiling in the trenches of human rights all these years; people who, by word and deed, have shown that, indeed, one person can and does make a difference.

It is only fitting, therefore, that this assemblage come together at a critical juncture in world history, in the life of our country, our community, and this university. For we come together on the occasion of the fortieth anniversary of the Nuremberg judgments and, in a kind of symbiotic relationship, on the eve of the fortieth anniversary of the Universal Declaration of Human Rights – itself created out of the ashes of the Holocaust and as an alliance against Nazism, fascism, and racism.

We come together, as well, in terms of the *double entendre* of Nuremberg, the double meaning of Nuremberg: Nuremberg as an exhortation against injustice, as a reminder of our collective responsibility to bring war criminals to justice, but also Nuremberg as a place which personifies racism and where, in its successor form, this racism, regrettably and tragically, still finds expression today. And we come together at a time when this university is about to embark on its one-hundred-and-fortieth anniversary as a law school in this community and in this country.

We commemorate, as well, the official founding of InterAmicus, which we hope will become a counsel for the oppressed in our time. It is only fitting, therefore, that we inaugurate a lectureship in the name of Raoul Wallenberg, who saved more lives in the Second World War than any single government, and that the person who is with us this evening to inaugurate the Raoul Wallenberg Lectureship in Human Rights is a person who has emerged as the conscience of humanity, the messenger to mankind: Elie Wiesel.

I would like to thank those with whom I have had the pleasure of working and who have made this evening and this conference what I believe it will become: a historic initiative in the case and cause of human rights.

Je désire d'abord remercier le Doyen de la Faculté de droit de l'Université McGill. Je veux aussi remercier les organismes suivants pour l'appui et l'aide financière qu'ils ont apportés à cette conférence: le ministère fédéral de la Justice, le ministère de la Justice du Québec et le Secrétaire d'État fédéral.

And I want to thank, as well, the organizing committee, in

particular, professors Buckley, Jukier, Sklar, Toope, and Benson, as well as Richard Janda, Lorianne Weston, and our coordinator, Richard Golick.

And now, I would like to introduce the Secretary of State, responsible for human rights, perhaps best known in Canada under the appellate of the "tiny perfect mayor," from the time when he was Mayor of Toronto. He has now become the "tiny perfect Minister." I introduce him to you this evening, the Honourable David Crombie.

Greetings on Behalf of the Government of Canada

THE HONOURABLE DAVID CROMBIE

Most distinguished guest speakers, Principal Johnston, Mr Elie Wiesel, Madame Justice Claire L'Heureux-Dubé, Minister Marx, ladies and gentlemen: Prime Minister Mulroney asked me if I would bring to you his very sincere regrets that he could not be here tonight. But he asked me to make sure that I quoted him directly to you, and I quote:

On behalf of the Government of Canada, may I convey my warmest greetings and sincere best wishes to the delegates of the International Human Rights Conference. This Conference marks the seventy-fifth anniversary of the establishment of the McGill Law Student Association, the one-hundred-and-fortieth anniversary of the founding of the Faculty of Law, and the twentieth anniversary of the establishment of the National Law Program of McGill's Faculty of Law. This conference is indeed a significant milestone for more than one reason. The theme of this conference, "Nuremberg Forty Years Later: The Struggle Against Injustice in Our Time," tells all of us – the civilized societies – to assess our successes and failings in the area of human rights legislation and its practice throughout the world. And I trust that your discussions will be productive and I am pleased that this conference coincides with the inauguration of the Human Rights Lectureship in the name of one who stands as a landmark figure in the struggle for human rights: Raoul Wallenberg.

And I am also pleased to offer my best wishes to Mr Elie Wiesel and to each of the distinguished guests for a most enlightening conference.

Prime Minister of Canada

En ce qui me concerne, c'est pour moi à la fois un grand honneur et une gratification personnelle de représenter le Premier Ministre à l'ouverture de cette conférence. C'est aussi pour moi l'occasion de vous expliquer le rôle que mon ministère joue relativement aux engagements internationaux du Canada dans le domaine des droits de la personne. Pour remplir ce mandat, le Secrétaire d'Etat travaille en étroite collaboration avec divers autres organismes fédéraux et provinciaux.

The secretary of state is responsible for the government's interdepartmental committee on human rights. And that is why, as secretary of state, I will be chairing the Federal-Provincial Territorial Conference for Ministers Responsible for Human Rights, to deal with questions of mutual concern in this country.

We are intent on promoting and creating a wide range of awareness and understanding of basic human rights and freedoms. We also concern ourselves with the voluntary sector of the community-driven projects that safeguard human rights, with the public education and curriculum materials promoting the knowledge of human rights. I might add that our efforts to help in these matters serve to remove barriers, to allow full participation by all Canadians in the community at large.

We are, as some of you know, about to bring forward a Multicultural Act, this country's first. Its preamble will invoke the minority and racial rights provision of the United Nations Universal Declaration of Human Rights, and it will be based on the enduring principles of Canadian citizenship: equality and diversity in the community.

Our government initiative, very pertinent to the conference theme, is, of course, the establishment, on 7 February 1985, of the Deschênes Commission of Inquiry on War Criminals. Bill C-71 flowed from that commission's findings. The Criminal Code amendments received royal assent some time ago and, last week, I am delighted to say as the Minister responsible for citizenship, the citizenship and immigration provisions were also proclaimed.

And I am pleased to see, I might add, the commission's chairman, Mr Justice Jules Deschênes, who is here with us tonight. I would like to add my own applause to that of those many Canadians who want to thank you for this work.

Je ne saurais terminer cette allocution sans adresser mes sincères félicitations à la Faculté de droit de l'Université McGill d'avoir institué la série de conférences Raoul Wallenberg et d'avoir choisi monsieur Elie Wiesel pour prononcer le discours de la conférence inaugurale dédiée à ce héros, Raoul Wallenberg. Où qu'il se trouve aujourd'hui, il demeure la première et seule personne à avoir été reçue citoyen honoraire du Canada.

My friends, that was a prepared text which I thought about on my way from Quebec City to Montreal because I wanted to be clear and firm in my responsibility as the secretary of state. But, I want to say, much of it moved around in my head as I met, for the first time, Elie Wiesel, a man I have honoured in my own heart for many years, and other people, who for many years have been dedicated to the cause of human rights and to making sure that people understand these rights.

Let me say this directly and clearly: Whatever this government can do to carry on the work of those who are concerned with human rights, and that is all of us, I can pledge to you that the Prime Minister and this government, and this secretary of state, will do it. Thank you very much.

Greetings on Behalf of the Government of Quebec

L'HONORABLE MINISTRE HERBERT MARX

Les questions qui seront soulevées au cours de cette conférence témoignent d'une préoccupation peu commune pour la justice et sa promotion. La qualité des personnalités et conférenciers présents, ainsi que leur nombre, confirme sans nul doute que cette conférence sera un événement marquant. Cette conférence est d'autant plus notoire qu'elle sert de tremplin pour l'inauguration par l'Université McGill, des Conférences Raoul Wallenberg sur les droits de la personne.

Peu de gens auront tant fait que Raoul Wallenberg pour la promotion et la préservation des droits de la personne. Monsieur Wallenberg est plus qu'un défenseur des droits, il est une source d'inspiration pour tous les peuples. Je me réjouis de constater que la conférence qui est inaugurée ce soir sera désormais un événement annuel, car il s'agira d'une occasion unique de poursuivre un travail et une réflexion essentiels sur la destinée de l'humanité.

Il est très approprié que ce soit Elie Wiesel, Prix Nobel de la Paix, qui fasse la conférence inaugurale, celui qu'on appelle souvent, comme le professeur Cotler nous l'a rappelé, la "conscience de l'humanité."

I would like to take this opportunity to congratulate McGill University's Faculty of Law which, in conjunction with InterAmicus, the newly created Canadian-based human rights centre, has made this evening possible.

The theme of the conference – "Nuremberg Forty Years Later: The Struggle Against Injustice in Our Time" – is a contemporary one. As Canadians, it is safe to say that we are somewhat of a privileged society. Not only do we live in a free and democratic society, but it is also a society which is in the process of reaffirming the rights and freedoms of its citizens through the application of our Charter of Rights and Freedoms. This must, and I am sure will, continue to be an ongoing process.

Notre lutte contre l'injustice doit passer, je crois, par la lutte contre l'ignorance, voire contre l'indifférence. Je pense qu'une sensibilisation accrue des citoyens et des groupes de citoyens doit demeurer l'essence de nos préoccupations, car le changement passe par la connaissance. Et cette connaissance, elle, passe par l'existence de forums comme celui-ci.

Je remercie les organisateurs de la conférence pour leur contribution et je les invite à poursuivre dans cette voie. Enfin, je souhaite à tous la bienvenue au Québec. Merci.

Opening Plenary
The Raoul Wallenberg Forum on
Human Rights

Introduction of Guest Speaker

PRINCIPAL DAVID JOHNSTON

When the Nobel Committee awarded Elie Wiesel the Nobel Peace Prize in 1968, the choice was greeted with international acclaim. It is difficult to imagine any citizen in the world who has so commanded the attention and the respect of political leaders and common people alike. One suspects that if the Nobel Committee had awarded Elie Wiesel the Nobel Prize for literature, the acclaim would have been no less.

He writes, as the title of one of his books suggests, as a soul on fire. That flame has not only animated the literary imagination, it has ignited the struggle for peace and human rights worldwide. His eloquence is all the more remarkable because, as he has put it, the Holocaust is beyond vocabulary. In matters such as these, language mocks reality. Yet the man who felt that Auschwitz and Buchenwald were beyond communication and comprehension has not only conveyed the particularity of the horror, but also transmitted the universality of the message: that never again must this horror be allowed to be repeated, that the next time there would be no "never again."

One suspects, as well, that if Raoul Wallenberg were here – and with the efforts of people like Elie Wiesel, he might yet be with us – he would choose Wiesel to deliver this inaugural lecture. For what has been said of Wallenberg can be also said of Wiesel. Surely, it is the reverence for life, for humanity, for human rights, for peace that comes to mind when we speak of Elie Wiesel, our speaker.

"Author, Teacher, Witness – A Messenger for Humanity." These are the words inscribed on the Congressional Gold Medal presented in 1985 to Elie Wiesel "in recognition of his humanitarian efforts and outstanding contribution to world literature and human rights." The same words were repeated by the Nobel Committee in citing Wiesel as one of the foremost moral and intellectual leaders in the global struggle for human rights.

Elie Wiesel has spent his life bearing witness. As a boy, he survived Auschwitz and Buchenwald. The transformation of this experience into literature has become a great testimonial to the human spirit. With an eloquence born of the truth, Wiesel has spoken out against injustice wherever he has seen it. The world has recognized his contribution by awarding him some of its highest honours, including the Prix Bordin (Académie Française), the Eleanor Roosevelt Memorial Award, and, most recently, in 1986, the Nobel Peace Prize. But perhaps his most significant accolade is that he has become a universal metaphor, that of "conscience of humanity." Author of thirty books and the subject of fifteen others, distinguished teacher and Andrew Mellon Professor in Humanities at Boston University, Elie Wiesel is a leading spokesman for human rights in our times. It is right and fitting that Elie Wiesel inaugurate the Raoul Wallenberg Lectureship in Human Rights.

Inaugural Raoul Wallenberg Lectureship

GUEST SPEAKER: ELIE WIESEL

Monsieur le Recteur, Messieurs les ministres, Madame Justice Claire L'Heureux-Dubé, Monsieur le doyen, Ambassador Gur-Aryeh of Israel, my fellow participants in this colloquium, distinguished members of the faculty and students. Since I have heard that the topic is "Witness," I couldn't but question my own adequacy. Naturally, I do believe that it is the task of every human being to serve as witness. Unfortunately, however, I belong to a generation that has endured events of such a terrifying character that the methods, the tools of bearing witness, have been denied to it. And yet, bear witness we must.

Ne pas oublier! Ne pas oublier! C'était là notre obsession commune. Nous racontions nos expériences de guerre pour qu'elles servent d'avertissement et d'exemple. Au temps de la nuit, des hommes, des femmes et des enfants aussi, tenaient non pas à la vie mais à la survie pour déposer, sauvegarder l'écho d'un seul cri, transmettre l'étincelle d'une seule flamme, toujours la même, partout la même. Une flamme qui dévorait tout un peuple, ivre de silence et d'éternité.

My friend Irwin asked me to give the first lecture devoted to the memory of Raoul Wallenberg. How could one refuse a friend, and how could one refuse anything connected with Raoul Wallenberg?

Strange: Raoul Wallenberg was arrested in 1945. He then vanished; and yet, somehow, for reasons that remain obscure, the story of Wallenberg remained unknown until well into the 1970s. Why?

Why did it take so long for his legend to become popular? Why has there been no immediate organized struggle to assure his release, or at least to apply sufficient pressure on the Soviet government to reveal the mystery surrounding his disappearance? Why has there been no effort, not even among ourselves – I mean the Jewish community – to make the story known? What better example could there be to teach people, young and old, about the necessity of remaining human in an inhuman world?

Why has there been so much silence around Raoul Wallenberg? After all, there is, in his adventure, enough material to produce ten plays and to write a hundred books and many more films. A romantic, aristocratic man with principles and courage, he stood up to the greatest police state of our century. But why has it taken so many years for most people to as much as acknowledge his existence?

Je ne comprends pas ce mystère. Je ne comprends pas le silence autour d'un homme qui mérite qu'on s'en souvienne. Et je ne comprendrai jamais pourquoi un peu partout dans le monde, on a parlé de tout, on a tenté d'évoquer tout, sauf cet homme qui a été comme englouti dans un oubli volontaire, dans un oubli presque organisé.

One possible answer may be that he disturbed too many people. He disturbed the enemy during the war, but he also disturbed people after the war. His story became an irritant. Why? Because he demonstrated that it was possible, even under the worst and cruellest circumstances in recorded history, to oppose the oppressor and side with his victims.

In other words, the tragedy was *not* unavoidable. The tragedy was *not* a kind of inexorable endeavour of destiny to serve death to the very end. It was possible to stop, to block the machinery. It was possible to save victims. It was possible to save Jews. Indeed, it *was* possible to save, if not all of them, at least some of them, one of them, if not for an entire life, at least for one year, one month, one day, one minute ... And one minute of life is already containing, if not concealing, a spark of eternity.

It was possible to hide the victims from their assassins and offer them refuge and protection; it was possible to provide consolation to their parents, relatives, and friends. And because of Raoul Wallenberg, no person, other than a victim, may ever claim in his or her defence that he or she was powerless then. No human being is powerless.

It is not given to the individual to totally vanquish the enemy, but it is given to him or her to resist the enemy, and then, on a small but essential scale of humanity, to triumph over the enemy. André Malraux said it this way: "Bien sûr ... à la fin c'est la mort qui remporte la victoire! Mais tant que nous vivons, avec chaque souffle, c'est nous qui triomphons et non la mort!"

The story of Wallenberg marks a moment of human grandeur and offers proof of, and testimony to, man's ability to transcend his own life by sacrificing it to others. Therefore, in a way, Wallenberg is linked to the topic of our conference: Nuremberg.

Nuremberg is the story of those who did the killing, those who committed the crimes. But also – and now we must say it, although it was not sufficiently brought up during the Nuremberg trials – Nuremberg is also the story of those who did nothing. The killer killed and the victims perished – and the others stood by.

When the Jews arrived in those places that will remain monuments to death, monuments marking and symbolizing a century which, according to Hannah Arendt, was the most violent in history, when the victims arrived, what shook them up was the sudden realization that they had arrived in a parallel universe. They had the feeling that they had found themselves in a creation just like any other, just like *the* other. They had the feeling that they had landed in a world that evolved parallel to our own. Everything was there. There were princes and slaves and judges and victims, and there was a language, a totally different language, invented for that place only. They had their customs, their folklore, their legends, their fears, their obsessions. Somehow, you had the feeling that another Creator had created a different universe, and that the universe evolved alongside our own, and what hurt us was that everything in it worked. The system functioned. With incredible efficiency.

The fires were there as though they were given by their Creator for the sole purpose of consuming human beings. The enemy was powerful, the victim feeble and weak, and you asked yourself, What happened? Has creation gone mad? Was history plunged into a nightmare? The fact is that the event enveloped the totality of the human condition. Every human being who was alive then was involved in that experiment willed by the enemy; unfortunately, to our embarrassment, the experiment permeated even those who, in their lives and in their words, opposed the enemy.

So Nuremberg marks a moment of awakening when we realized that something had happened to humankind. A watershed had occurred that ensured that, from Nuremberg on, nothing would be the same any more. For in Nuremberg something was revealed. Oh, I know that afterwards there were discussions and stormy, passionate debates, among professors of law, experts in international jurisprudence, wondering whether Nuremberg was legally the proper arena for judging the criminals. Some said, "How can you retroactively judge for crimes committed before the laws had been formulated and adopted?" Others said, "How can you judge these criminals? What they have done is beyond justice." You remember Cain in the Bible? Cain was spared because his crime was so monstrous that there was no punishment fitting his crime; he was shielded by the magnitude of his crime, for he had killed his own brother, half of humanity. And whoever kills, kills his own brother and humanity.

So there were those who said, "Why bother with all this? It's a farce, because you cannot judge men who have done so much evil: a Himmler, who committed suicide, or a Goëring, who was hanged after he committed suicide. The law must not stoop to their level – that is, make them participants in a trial."

Still others said, "One must not judge them because, in judging them, you single them out and you give the impression that only they were the criminals, whereas we know that so many thousands and hundreds of thousands of other people, men and women, of all nationalities in Europe, were accomplices. So why single out the leaders alone? Why whitewash the others? Haven't they all served the Angel of Death?"

And yet, I believe – but then maybe I believe so because I am not a professor of law or a lawyer – but I believe so, because Nuremberg, to me, marks the triumph of memory. It was not only justice, but memory too, that was served at Nuremberg.

Justice was served, but, above everything else, in a strange way, in a dark poetic way, it was memory that was confronted and celebrated at Nuremberg. When hundreds and hundreds of witnesses emerged to piece together a story – a story that we all must remember, although our memory and our mind and our soul are too small to comprehend it, to take it all in. Our sanity was at stake. If we remembered everything, we would lose our minds. But then, if we don't remember everything, we also lose our minds.

Nuremberg, therefore, was the repository of testimony. Hundreds, thousands, hundreds of thousands of documents were introduced in evidence in Nuremberg. Thus, it was an important and meaningful event. For the first time, I think, it gave memory such an exposure. Now, we know that if there is one word among others that also symbolized the dark years of that tragedy that has no pertinent name, it is *Memory*.

On one hand, there was the killer who, in killing Jews, sought to exterminate the memory of the Jews. Therefore, the killer not only killed Jews, he killed their death. After they were killed and buried, the enemy unearthed and burned them: this had never happened before in the history of my people.

The history of the Jewish people is fraught with tragedy. So much so, that one historian, Louis Namier, said that there is no Jewish history, there is only Jewish martyrology. He is wrong. Because Jewish history also means a *response* to martyrology. But, although there is so much pain and so much agony and so much anguish in our history, we had never before experienced the double deaths of the victims. Never before have we heard of an era when we couldn't bury our dead.

Only once did we experience something close to this: for a short period, during the Bar Kochba Rebellion, the Romans ordered the Jewish population of Judea to leave the corpses outside, exposed to wind and sun. That was such a tragedy for us that when we finally were permitted to bury the dead, our sages and scholars wrote a marvellous prayer that is still repeated every day after the meal. We call it *Hatov Vehameitiv:* "Blessed be God," we say, "who was good and moved other people to goodness." Why? Because we were, at last, allowed to bury our dead. Now, in the middle of the twentieth century, for the first time in history, our dead were not buried. We had no more cemeteries. Imagine a generation, a people without cemeteries. The cemeteries were in us. We still carry them in our heart. In our memory.

Therefore, I now turn to the word that Irwin wanted me to meditate upon: "witness." How can you bear witness when the memory has attained such a dimension that it is broken down by language? No word will ever contain the silence of one child, when that child went to the nocturnal flames. No word can contain the prayer of an old man who, hand in hand with his grandchild, stepped forward to the mass grave. No word can contain the anguish that preceded a selection in a concentration camp. No word can ever contain the fear that descended on a ghetto at certain times, at certain moments. No word can contain the solitude, the solitude of the Jewish victim who was more alone and more abandoned and more tragic than all the other victims. Granted, there were other victims as well; we should never forget them either. But the solitude of the Jewish victims remains unparalleled. How many times must we repeat that? Everyone who was not Jewish had family outside. Thus, the non-Jewish prisoner could cling to hope: "If I die, my son will live. My parents will have more children. My sister will remarry." The Jewish prisoner knew that he or she was *alone*, maybe the last, for his or her entire family had been condemned to extinction. An entire people was sentenced to death for *being*.

Thus, the solitude of the Jewish inmate also goes beyond language.

And yet, the stubbornness of the witness, to keep his or her testimony alive, is as powerful as any other motivation in history that kept a civilization productive or creative. Just as the enemy was bent upon destroying our people, our people were bent upon remembering the destroyer.

And so they all became witnesses. Children, five-, six-, or ten-year-old children, remembered that they had a story to tell, and they grew older than the oldest of their teachers. I could spend centuries speaking in praise of Jewish children. One million or more, they were the first target of the enemy. If, from now until I die, I were to do nothing else but name them, simply recite name after name – and the least they could expect is that their names be remembered – I would die before reaching the end of the list. Those children were brave, and noble, and so generous. They would sneak out of the ghetto clandestinely, risking prison and beatings or death, to bring a potato back to their parents, a piece of bread to their friends. Itzhak Katznelson proposed to erect a monument to the Jewish child.

I could also spend centuries speaking to you about the beauty of the Jewish women who were made ugly, miserable, who were humiliated by the enemy by shaving their heads, beating them up, persecuting them. I could spend centuries speaking of their husbands, the fathers and, especially, the grandfathers, who, in their melancholy vision of the world, still found words of consolation for those who surrounded them. They all became either an object or a subject of testimony.

A man named Shimon Hooberhand, a rabbi, went from ghetto to ghetto mainly concentrating on religious life, to bear witness and testify that the religious spirit, the faith, has never deserted our people.

Emmanuel Ringelblum, a historian by vocation, created a group called *Oneg Shabbat*. How ironic! The joy of Sabbath! That group was to meet – and met – in the Warsaw ghetto. It was composed of a hundred chroniclers who would gather and record more details, more information, from all walks of life, from all areas of death.

A Hebrew teacher, Chaim Kaplan, kept his diary in the holy temple, and I will never forget the way his book ended: "And now," he said, "and now, I feel the end is near, what will happen with my testimony?"

A young boy called Moshe Flinker began writing, again in Hebrew – he learned Hebrew in the ghetto; he described a sunset in such a way that any romantic poet would be envious of his talent. Anne Frank, who gives us a lesson in optimism, how old was *she*?

There were chroniclers who bore witness not only in the ghettos, but even in the concentration camps, even in the death camps. I remember: I had heard there of the Sonder Commandos. Their tragedy was probably the deepest, the most inhuman, the most agonizing of all, for they were forced to burn their own people. Then they themselves were murdered and burned. Now, I had heard rumours for years that they, too, had written chronicles. I didn't believe it. How could they, in the shadow of flames, write and choose to bear witness? Witnesses for whom? For what? They wrote. Their words were found. When they appeared in France, *Voix dans la Nuit*, I prefaced them. I remember: everything in me cried when I read the book. Often, I stopped, I had to, I couldn't read anymore. I had to force myself; if they had the courage to write, I must have the courage to read. They, too, were chroniclers, and they, too, from under the ashes, wanted to testify.

For what? I'll tell you. Not for themselves, it was too late for them. They knew they were doomed, they were dead before they were dying. Somehow, they were convinced that the world didn't know. So was I. I was convinced that the world didn't know, because *I* didn't know. When we Jews from Hungary arrived in May, 1944, two or three weeks before D-Day, in a place called Auschwitz, the name meant nothing to us; we had never heard of its special meaning. We were convinced that nobody knew what lay behind that name. Had we known that the world knew, that Roosevelt knew, and Stalin and Churchill, that everybody in America knew – it was enough to read the newspapers – I think many of us would have yielded to despair, given up on humanity, and committed suicide. But we didn't know, and therefore everybody wanted that someone should remain to tell the story for the living.

In other words, to bear witness is not only to redeem the memory of the dead; it is to bear witness for the living. I repeat: for the dead it is too late, as it may even be for those who were their companions. For *you* it is not too late. For you who were born later. For you who are now burdened with our memories. For you who live in fear that our past may become your future. That is why we must do whatever we can to share with you what we have, not to give you sadness, surely not to create a morbid mood around you – we don't believe in that – but to speak to you of an impossible humanity that must be made possible, even as we speak of so much inhumanity. In speaking about it, we give humanity its due.

But how *does* one speak about it? Here the witness faces a dilemma. I remember when I was a child, I always admired our Prophets. I loved their words because they were great writers. They were also politicians, but we remember their poetry more than their political activity.

Jeremiah was a great politician, though nobody ever voted for him and he was never elected to any position. I always felt sorry for Jeremiah: he had predicted the tragedy. Almost like Ezekiel, he had predicted what was going to happen – literally, the whole story. I often tried to imagine what he must have felt when he realized that nobody was listening. In my mind, Jeremiah was the epitome of human tragedy.

Not so. After the war, I understood that the tragedy of the witness is much deeper than the tragedy of the Prophet. The witness, after the event, is trying to tell the tale of the event, hoping he will make a difference. But it makes no difference.

Oh, there are changes. Let's not be totally unfair. As a Jew, I must say that for me to be alive and witness the resurrection of a Jewish state is a source of extraordinary joy and pride. There *is* change. I don't link the two events. I don't like to think of one as the consequence of the other; it would be terrible to link them or to compare them. One should never compare.

But still, Israel *is* here. My father and his father and his father were not fortunate enough to experience what my eyes behold: the vision and the gift of a dream that came to pass. An ancient people has found its place in its ancient homeland. It is young and old at the same time.

Oh, naturally, there are other changes, other differences too. Nuremberg made a difference. Because of Nuremberg, other trials were held: the Eichmann trial in Jerusalem, the Barbie trial in France, your own trials here. And I think Canada is to be commended for having these trials, of those vicious, ugly, stupid people who dare to say, while we are still here, that our tragedy did not occur. They should be shamed into silence and treated as outcasts of society. So there *is* a difference.

However, when we think of the infinite sadness that is linked to that story, only the smile of a child could defeat it, at least for the moment. When we think about the victims, we cannot but choose despair. But then, when we think of what we are trying to do in their name, and for them, we must invoke some hope.

What, then, have we learned from Nuremberg? First of all, we have learned the need to discern evil. And, in times of stress, we must at least know the difference between evil and what is not evil. We cannot allow evil to take on the mask of good.

Why was the Nazi era so horrifying? Because the law itself was immoral. To kill innocent people was lawful. The killers were convinced that they were obeying the law, and indeed it *was* the law to kill children, parents, old men and women, all those who needed protection. It was the law to be inhuman. Therefore, we must know that the law must be not only legal, but moral as well. It must be founded and based on, and rooted in, ethical exigence, in a thirst for ethical behaviour.

Second, from Nuremberg we have learned that, whenever we discover evil, we must resist it, even if it is hopeless. Even if we have no chance of winning, we must fight it. For in resisting evil, we save something in our own self. We save a certain image of ourself. We save a certain sense of dignity which may be seen as a source of strength by those who live with us and who will live after us.

Third, we must realize that neutrality is wrong. When human beings are in danger, when human dignity is at stake, neutrality is a sin, not a virtue. For neutrality never helps the victim, it only helps the victimizer; it never assists the tormented, it only encourages the tormentor. Therefore, neutrality, which used to be, at one time, a high idea or ideal of nations, is wrong. Reject it! You must side with the victim, even if you both lose.

Why? Because the solitude of the victim is another vehicle, another instrument in the hand of the victimizer.

What does the tormentor say to the victim: "Come on, don't you know you don't count for anyone? Don't you know people have forgotten you? What do you think? People remember you? You are alone!" In order to break the victim's spirit, the tormentor will use solitude, isolation, as an added dimension of torture. And we must, and we can, say to the victim, "No, you are not abandoned."

We have seen it recently. Whenever victims of oppression anywhere know that they are not alone, they gain strength, they live longer, and they are triumphant. Take the noble battle of Soviet Jewry, in which both my friend Irwin and I have been so involved. I have been involved in it since 1965, before many of you were born.

I remember my first meeting with Soviet Jews, when they felt dejected. They felt that nobody cared and, indeed, nobody did care. But when they realized that here and there activists *were* concerned, that they were no longer alone, they became the first to brave the Soviet terror – before Solzhenitsyn, before even Sakharov, before all the dissidents. The first to brave the Soviet police terror were the young Soviet Jews.

There is one man here whom I also must mention, my friend Greville Janner, who has gone to the Soviet Union at least as often as I have tried to go, in order to see the dissidents and bring them courage and offer them hope. For that is what they need. They don't need money, they don't need anything but the realization that we are with them, that their isolation is not eternal. Therefore, what we learned from Nuremberg and from our history is that whenever victims are alone, it is our responsibility to break their solitude. In other words, it is our duty to interfere in other people's business.

There were times when every nation would say, "Don't mix in our domestic affairs." No more. This argument is no longer valid. Whenever a prison is opened for innocent people, whenever and wherever children die of hunger, wherever torture is being used, whenever people die before their time, it is our duty as human beings, as witnesses in the present, to interfere and stop the government's political activities or the government policy. And if governments don't do that to other governments, it is the role of individuals or of private groups, such as InterAmicus, to interfere and say, "We are now taking on the mightiest regime in the world. We are ready for it." For it is enough for one person to say no, to make a difference.

One more thing: we have learned that human rights naturally include the right to be free, the right to be together, the right to live, but also the right to remember. Memory is one of the human rights to which we are all entitled. For the enemy was also against memory. Not only the enemy in Nazi Germany, but even – and I don't compare, again, please, remember I never compare any regime to the Nazi regime, any criminal leader to Hitler or Eichmann – the Soviet totalitarian policy has tried to manipulate memory. You would open an encyclopedia and it was never the same. One year, Stalin occupied fifty pages; the next year, only one page; the year after, not even a word of praise – he was no longer a leader, but a criminal, or the other way around. A dictatorship feels that it has the right to adapt, to adjust, to mutilate memory. And we believe that every person has the human right to be remembered as he or she was.

And lastly, what we have learned is that indifference is the worst disease that can contaminate a society. I always thought that evil was, and is, the enemy. Not so. Indifference to evil is a more dangerous enemy. I always thought that despair was and is something we must fight. Not so. Despair can be a beginning. Despair can move you to creativity. You may write a beautiful poem, compose a sonata. Despair can give you the necessary impetus, the needed impulse to seek a kind of purification of words, of gestures, of encounters. And what are words or gestures, if not encounters? Despair can lead you somewhere. Not so indifference. Indifference is the end of the process, not the beginning.

What is the opposite of love? Not hate, but indifference. But then what is the opposite of education? Not ignorance – indifference. I would even say what is the opposite of law? Not crime – but indifference to law. What is the opposite of beauty? Not ugliness – indifference. What is the opposite of life? Not death – but indifference.

And there is only one weapon that can fight indifference, and that is memory. Memory can bring words and generations together, it can link human beings to one another. Memory can endow the present with a meaning that preceded it. Memory can restore the sacred dimension to everyday words. Memory can turn words into a prayer. And do we need prayers! Do we need poetry! Do we need passion! Do we need compassion!

Thank you.

Appreciation:
Madame Justice Claire l'Heureux-Dubé

Le silence, je crois, serait le plus éloquent témoignage à rendre à
Elie Wiesel après son émouvant témoignage.

Cette leçon d'histoire.

What more is there to say?
Poetry and passion,
Compassion,
Humanity and talent.
He touched our hearts.
He impressed our minds.
He said it all.

Witness he was, witness he is.
Alone he was, alone no more.
Silent no more.

To a great person,
To whom the world has given
Its greatest distinction.
To a friend of the nation,
For whom human rights is mission.
To a man with a vision,
Who deserves our admiration.

En ce jour de célébration,
De la déclaration,
C'est avec émotion,
Que nous écoutions cet homme d'action

Qui ne néglige pas la réflexion
Et à qui nous disons
Toute notre admiration.

To a person of talent,
Whose words are important
For us to hear and remember
Forty years after Nuremberg.

Avec le talent que nous lui connaissons,
Qui lui a valu tant de distinction,
Il s'est donné une mission,
Celle d'un homme de vision.

To peace and to justice, he devoted his efforts.
But there is always more for us to strive for.

Son message est vibrant
Et il est important.
Tout en nous remémorant
La tragédie des jours d'antan,
Il faut aller de l'avant
À faire il reste tant.

In this day of celebration
Of the Universal Declaration
Passed by the United Nations,
We proclaim our appreciation
To Elie Wiesel, a man of action.
We say thanks with emotion
For giving us inspiration.

Et avec émotion,
Elie Wiesel, nous vous remercions
De nous donner l'inspiration
De poursuivre la mission.

Panel One:
Nuremberg and Its Legacy

Chair

MR JUSTICE JULES DESCHÊNES

It would be wonderful if we could emulate the passion, the strength, the feelings of Mr Wiesel; at the very least we should remember how Mr Wiesel cautioned us yesterday night against both the danger of indifference and the evil of silence; how he described the devastating effects of solitude on the victims of terror and torture; how he taught us to show solidarity with the victims so that they don't stand alone in their fight for freedom and liberty.

Here in Canada, we are faced with a relatively small legacy of the past, yet considerable efforts are needed to get rid of the evil. One of our speakers this morning, the Honourable Mr Hnatyshyn, will deal with this issue.

For our neighbours to the south, the situation is, to a large extent, similar; it may be different in scale, but not in nature. Elizabeth Holtzman will also be dealing with the relevant aspects of this question.

But we must keep in mind that in many countries, people are not concerned with a legacy of the past, but with a current situation that causes them to cry for help. Let us think for a moment of the Tamils in Sri Lanka, the Baha'is in Iran, the millions of Blacks in South Africa, the Anadists in Pakistan, the Indians in Latin America, the Tibetans in China, the millions of Afghan refugees – and the list could go on. And, recalling Mr Wiesel's address, how can we be so selfish as to remain indifferent to the plight of those victims? And when will we tear down the walls of solitude and show our human solidarity?

Nuremberg, of course, needs no introduction. In 1945 and 1946, nineteen of twenty-two accused were convicted, and twelve were sentenced to death. The last of the convicted people, Rudolph Hess, died a few months ago.

Then Nuremberg again, 1946 to 1949, twelve further cases involving war criminals – doctors, judges, industrialists, generals, guards, straight killers – one hundred and seventy-seven accused persons. This time, one hundred and forty-two were convicted and twenty-five were sentenced to death. Those trials may appear to have been rather far from our own preoccupations, but Canadians, members of the Canadian Armed Forces, had themselves been victims of war crimes, and Canada was not indifferent to their fate at the time.

At the time, we investigated no fewer than one hundred and seventy-one cases of war crimes against Canadians. At the outset, the Canadian Forces launched their own prosecutions in Auschwitz. The Canadian Army – many of you who are too young to have been around at the time, may have read about this episode – tried General Kurt Meyer in Germany. He was convicted and sentenced to death by firing squad. The sentence was commuted to imprisonment, which he served here in Canada, and then he was returned to Germany, where he died a few years ago.

At that time, our air force prosecuted six accused in three separate trials. All six were found guilty; three were sentenced to death, one to life imprisonment, and the two others received long jail sentences.

What happened, however, was that by then the Canadian forces were being repatriated and no Canadian personnel remained overseas to continue the job – and the job was not finished at the time. An arrangement was reached with the British forces, which agreed to carry on with the trials. Six more trials took place, with twenty-eight accused. Fifteen were found guilty; eleven of them were sentenced to death, and four were sentenced to long prison terms. Twelve were acquitted and one was not found.

And then we arrive at the present day, because, for reasons which I need not elaborate upon now, the matter lay dormant in Canada for one third of a century. And it was only revived in this, your generation.

THE NUREMBERG PRINCIPLES

MR JUSTICE JULES DESCHÊNES Ms Holtzman was born in Brooklyn, New York. She attended Radcliffe College and then graduated from the Harvard Law School. She practised law until 1973, when she was elected as a Democrat to the House of Representatives. She was a member of Congress for nearly eight years, and she served on the House Judiciary Committee. She is probably best known as the successful promoter and author of what has come to be known as the Holtzman Amendment, which has opened the way to revocation of citizenship of suspected war criminals, which could then lead to their deportation. Ms Holtzman has returned to the practice of law, and she has been elected district attorney in King's County.

Speaker

ELIZABETH HOLTZMAN

It is a special privilege to participate in this conference on the legacy of Nuremberg. The subject has a unique resonance for Canadians, since your country has only recently begun to grapple with the thorny question of how to deal with Nazi war criminals in your midst.

Faced with the extraordinary horrors of the Holocaust, the Nuremberg trials set a new standard of justice. They created the principle that international norms of civilized behaviour would govern, that national frontiers would not insulate mass murderers from punishment, and that crimes of this enormity would become matters for international concern and resolution. Unfortunately, after the main Nazi leaders were tried, the Nuremberg Principles seemed to be forgotten.

Once the cold war gave the West a new enemy, the desire to try other participants in the Holocaust became less urgent, and the commitment to justice was gradually abandoned. When the minds and hearts of the West Germans were needed, de-nazification programs ended; they were never even started in Austria. When a rebuilt West German economy was needed as a bulwark against communism, the industrialists who profited from the slave-labour camps were forgiven. When battle-hardened anti-communists were needed to combat the new enemy, the "anti-communist" Nazi war criminals – remember, Hitler was an anti-communist – were enlisted.

Of course, helping Nazi war criminals was not likely to be popular with the people of nations that had recently fought Hitler. As a result, these shameful, immoral, unjustifiable policies of collaboration were veiled in secrecy.

Today, we know only the outlines of the role United States officials played in this collaboration, because the mantle of darkness still cloaks so much of what happened. We do know, for example, that while the Nuremberg trials were still going on, American officials snatched Klaus Barbie from the jaws of French justice, sheltered him, paid him, used him to spy, and then sneaked him out of Europe to Latin America on the so-called Rat Line – a well-worn escape route for Nazi murderers.

According to the Justice Department, US officials committed crimes to protect Barbie; because of their actions, it took almost forty years to bring him to trial.

In addition to sheltering Nazi murderers and obstructing justice abroad, American government officials brought Nazi murderers to America. One case involved Arthur Rudolph, who was a top manager at the notorious Doris Slave Labour Camp, where more than twenty thousand persons were worked to death in the development of Nazi missiles. Even though a Presidential directive prohibited any Nazi scientist or technician who had engaged in persecution from coming to America, US officials disobeyed the order in Rudolph's case – and who knows in what other cases.

Moreover, according to recent government reports, US agencies regularly deceived each other in order to bring other Nazi murderers to America. American officials also allowed Nazi war criminals who came to the United States on their own – an estimated ten thousand persons – to stay and find sanctuary.

Today, it is recognized that assisting Nazi murderers to avoid justice or to find shelter in America was profoundly wrong. As the Justice Department said in its report on Barbie, "To actually employ a man who had been the leader of the Gestapo in a city in France and to rely on him to advance the interests of the United States was incomprehensible and shameful."

A major and systematic effort has been undertaken in the United States to undo the wrongs of the past and to deny sanctuary to Nazi war criminals. A special unit, the Office of Special Investigations (OSI), was created in the Department of Justice with a single mission: to track down and investigate alleged Nazi war criminals in the United States and, where the evidence warranted it, to bring actions to expel them.

The primary objective in creating a special unit was to assure the development of expertise and the highest degree of professionalism in the handling of these difficult cases. But the unit has served another purpose; it has ensured that the mission of expelling Nazis from the United States continues to receive high priority.

In addition, we have amended our laws, strengthening the ability to expel those who engaged in persecution under the Nazis. We have also prohibited by law those who engaged or assisted in Nazi persecution from entering our country. Just recently, under this law, Kurt Waldheim, president of Austria, was barred from the United States.

Measured by the obstacles, the success of the efforts in the United States has been remarkable. As a prosecutor, I know how hard it is to amass evidence about a murder that took place only five years ago. Imagine the difficulty of bringing cases about murders that took place more than forty years ago. Memories fade; witnesses vanish or die. In Nazi war-criminal cases, the hurdles are even greater – there were to be no victims left to tell the story. The relative handful of survivors have scattered over the face of the globe. Evidence – documents and witnesses – must be painstakingly hunted in numerous countries. Nonetheless, many of these obstacles have been overcome by determination and skill: nineteen Nazi war criminals have been expelled from our country, twenty-six cases are pending in our courts, six hundred cases are under investigation, and new cases come to light every day.

But, despite the success, more needs to be done. The process of expulsion in the United States is far too cumbersome. It is burdened with duplicative, labyrinthine procedures. As a result, it takes inordinately long for the proceedings to be completed. For example, it took eight years to deport Karl Linnas, a top official in an Estonian concentration camp, and nine years to expel John Demjanjuk, a man accused of pumping gas into the gas chambers of Treblinka, where at least seven hundred and fifty thousand Jews were killed. One deportation case has been pending for eleven years, and it is still not completed.

Unfortunately, the United States Congress has taken no action to consolidate and streamline the proceedings. It must do so at once – time for justice is running out.

Another problem is that too many of those whom we expel are not subsequently punished for their crimes. Of the nineteen expelled as a result of the work of the OSI – excluding the case of one man who died shortly after being deported – only three persons have been brought to trial: in Yugoslavia, the Soviet Union, and Israel. Portugal, for example, allowed Bishop Trifa, deported from the United States for his activities in the fascist Romanian Iron Guard, to live out his days in peace there. The biggest culprit of all is West Germany, which has refused to take action against a number of Nazi war criminals, including slave-labour-camp manager Rudolph, expelled there from the United States. The inaction of these countries is reprehensible.

The countries bringing the Nazi war criminals to trial have very different criminal law systems. Some of these countries are democracies, others are not. Under United States law, a Nazi war criminal may be deported to a country regardless of the nature of its criminal law system. Nonetheless, because of the significance of these cases, and the crucial educational and moral function they serve, nations prosecuting deported war criminals ought to ensure certain minimal standards for the prosecutions. The trials should be open to the public and to the press, including, specifically, the foreign press. The defendants should have access to family members, should be permitted to choose defence counsel, and should, of course, have the right to present evidence on their own behalf.

In the United States, there is a final issue to confront respecting official complicity with Nazi war criminals after the Second World War. The whole ugly story of that collaboration must be uncovered and told. How many Klaus Barbies were helped abroad? How many Arthur Rudolphs were brought to America? How many Trifas and Linnases were allowed to remain in the United States, unharmed and untouched, for almost thirty years? Why were they helped? What did they do in return for the help? Who was responsible, and how high in our government did that responsibility reach? To discover the truth, a commission with full subpoena powers must be created. A bill has been introduced in the House of Representatives to create such a commission, but it has not yet been enacted. Its enactment is crucial.

Finding out the truth is important not just for historical purposes, but to help preserve our democracy. It is not surprising that widespread lawlessness marked the secret US involvement with Nazi murderers. As reports have documented, helping Nazi war criminals was apparently so important that US officials were willing to break the law, deceive government agencies, and flout presidential orders in the process. These officials went further. The secret policy of complicity was never put before Congress for approval, nor was the public ever informed. Collaboration with Nazi war criminals – the cynical pursuit of a policy based on the ends justifying the means – involved a direct assault on our democratic institutions.

Our only recourse against any repetition is exposure. Since statutes of limitation prevent prosecution, turning the searchlight on the officials who protected Nazis and shaming them by naming them may be the only deterrent to those who might be tempted in the future to engage in similar activities.

The process in the United States of coming to grips with the years of Nazi collaboration has been important, if not historic. It has won renewed respect for our country from its own citizens and from other nations. By correcting the immoral and shameful policies of the past, our country has purified and strengthened its commitment to justice and to human rights. We show our abhorrence of Nazism – the bigotry and evil that was at its core – and of those who carried out its murderous policies.

Since 1974, when the problem of Nazi criminals in America was first made public, my country has been working to rid itself of these people. Your country, Canada, is just beginning its own efforts. I applaud the enterprise on which you are now embarking. It is no easy thing for a country to admit its mistakes, as Canada has done by conceding the presence of Nazi war criminals. I congratulate you for your willingness to own up to the shortcomings of the past and to try to correct them.

The Deschênes Commission, created to assess the problem of Nazi war criminals in Canada, designated approximately twenty cases for prosecution and two hundred other cases for further investigation. The commission issued a report (Commission of Inquiry on War Criminals Report, or the Deschênes Report) which provides a framework for prompt and efficacious action against Canadian Nazi war criminals.

But the real question is, Where will Canada go from here? Will it build on that framework for justice and will it do so quickly, efficaciously, with determination and seriousness of purpose, and without compromise? On this score, there remain some troublesome matters and I would like to point them out and share my concerns with you.

First, the Deschênes Report opposed the creation of a Canadian Office of Special Investigations, and none has been set up. This, in my view, is unfortunate. The ability to undertake effective investigations and measures against Nazi war criminals requires the development of substantial historical and investigative expertise. Such expertise can best be built by having a corps of people who deal with these cases, learn the history, and share in the knowledge acquired by others. The expertise of such a unit can be helpful in other ways. For example, when our Department of Justice investigated US involvement with Klaus Barbie, the attorney general turned to the distinguished head of the OSI, Allan Ryan, to prepare a special report. When a decision had to be made on the applicability of US law to Kurt Waldheim, it was the OSI that was called upon to prepare the materials for the Attorney General's decision. I urge your government to create a Canadian OSI.

Second, the Deschênes Report made no specific recommendations on seeking evidence from countries in Eastern Europe, the Soviet Union, or Israel in cases where these countries did not denounce the alleged Nazi war criminals living in Canada. I find this puzzling. If there is a serious allegation of war crimes, evidence relevant to that allegation must be sought everywhere. No case should be closed unless all sources of information have been thoroughly checked. It would be unimaginable, and I cannot expect in any way that it would have been the purpose of your efforts, to exonerate those who actually engaged in war crimes because of a failure to seek the truth.

Third, the Canadian government has taken no steps to follow up on the recommendations of the Deschênes Report to improve the Canadian processes of denaturalization, deportation, and extradition. Particularly in view of the problems the United States has had with its own unwieldy procedures, this failure is especially regrettable.

Fourth, the decision to prosecute Nazi war criminals in Canada for their crimes instead of deporting them has a theoretical appeal, but it may turn out to be counterproductive in practice. Canada's misdeed was to allow Nazi war criminals to find sanctuary within its borders. Canada can undo this wrong simply by reversing that decision and denying the Nazis sanctuary and expelling them.

In choosing not to deport but to prosecute, the original wrong may be compounded. First, there is no basis for assuming – as the policy of a "Canadian solution" does – that Canada's system of justice is better than that, say, in France, Holland, or West Germany. Second, there is no compelling reason to deny the victims of the Holocaust the right to try Nazi war criminals. The evidence and the witnesses are near at hand, and the legacy of the Holocaust is part of the victimized nations' consciousness. Third, in cases in which there is enough evidence for extradition or deportation but not enough to warrant prosecution, the made-in-Canada solution would preclude deportation and the Nazi war criminals would remain in Canada. In this category of cases, the Canadian solution would provide no solution at all, and the continued presence of these Nazi war criminals in your country would make a mockery of your efforts. Finally, the Canadian solution presumes that juries will be able to properly assess the full significance of Nazi war crimes. But if the experience in the United States is any example, there are many people, particularly younger people, who are badly informed about the Second World War and ignorant of the Holocaust. For some jurors, the war crimes may be too remote in time and place to have the full weight they deserve. On the other hand, the defendant's connections to Canada might seem more vivid and real in contrast. In a way, then, the cards may be stacked for acquittal, and juries may acquit even when there is full evidence of guilt. This may well be the reason that groups in the United States that have defended alleged Nazi war criminals and opposed the OSI have clamoured for trials in the United States instead of expulsion. Acquittals of alleged Nazi war criminals in Canada, based not on the facts but on the jury's nullifying powers, could pervert history, and could be used as false evidence by revisionist historians. I urge Canada not to reject wholesale the option of extraditing or denaturalizing and deporting Nazi war criminals to face prosecution in the country where they committed their crimes or in Israel.

In the end, bringing the Nazi war criminals to justice is one of the great moral tasks of our times. We know the indifference that gave rise to the Holocaust and allowed it to have the vast scope that it did. We cannot remain indifferent to the demands of justice now and to the faces of the victims that are still with us.

Nor can we assume that the US and Canadian governments will always do the right thing left on their own. For example, both governments recently supported keeping secret thirty-eight thousand Nazi war-crime files at the United Nations. And while we have been told that this cover-up will end, the files are still not open, either to scholars or to journalists, much less to the public. We have also seen Bitburg and we have seen government officials in high places opposing our efforts.

This means that we must be vigilant; we must be alert; we must continue our efforts until the work of justice is completed. If the work is not completed, then the message to anti-Semites, bigots, and racists of all kinds is that crimes of the greatest horror can be committed and, in the end, the world will not care. We dare not allow this message to be sent. Thank you.

DOMESTICATING THE NUREMBERG PRINCIPLES: THE CANADIAN "WAR CRIMES" LEGISLATION

MR JUSTICE JULES DESCHÊNES Mr Hnatyshyn, a native of Saskatchewan, is a graduate in law from the University of Saskatchewan. Formerly president of the Law Society of Saskatchewan, he practised in that province for a number of years. He was first elected to the House of Commons in 1974. He became minister of energy, mines and resources, and later minister of state for science and technology in the short-lived Clark government of 1979. In 1984, he became a member of the current government. He was government house leader in 1984, and president of the Privy Council in 1985, before he moved into his current position as minister of justice and attorney general for Canada.

Speaker

THE HONOURABLE MR RAMON HNATYSHYN

I would like to wish Ms Holtzman welcome to Canada. Unfortunately, you have a misunderstanding of some of the initiatives of our government, which I hope to elucidate. I very much understand the principles that you are speaking about, but there are some points on which I have to take issue with you with respect to your assessment of our initiatives.

Just by way of example, in canvassing some of the points that you made at the outset, the fact is that we do have existing extradition treaties with such countries as Holland, West Germany, and France, and these proceedings are available for the extradition of suspected war criminals to those countries in the appropriate cases. Indeed, our extradition and immigration laws have, in fact, been formulated, as I hope to point out in my remarks, with sensitivity to the issue that we are addressing today.

The final point I'll make at this juncture, and just in brief response, is that we are engaging in, on an active and urgent basis, an examination of all the facts – regardless of where the facts and evidence are located, regardless of whether on this side of the Iron Curtain or on the other – in order to ensure that these matters will be brought before the appropriate tribunals for action against suspected Nazi war criminals.

Having said that by way of introduction, I now go to my prepared text, which I hope will deal with some of the matters that have been addressed by Ms Holtzman.

I wanted to begin by noting the remarkable series of anniversaries which coincide so appropriately with this conference: the judgments at Nuremberg, the Universal Declaration of Human Rights, and, of course, the three anniversaries associated with the law school here at McGill. I think that in future years we'll look back and include in that list the contributions of those here today, not least of which is the inauguration of the annual Raoul Wallenberg Lectureship in Human Rights.

I will speak to you today about the actions taken by the government to address squarely the problems of war criminals here in Canada and the extent to which the internationally recognized concepts of war crimes and crimes against humanity will form a permanent part of Canadian criminal law. I will also speak about the measures that have been taken to complete the work begun by the Deschênes Commission of Inquiry on War Criminals and to ensure that those involved in past war crimes and crimes against humanity are brought to account.

By looking back over the years since Nuremberg, we are reminded of the need to remain vigilant and committed to ensuring that war crimes and crimes against humanity do not go unpunished. This is true not only because of the horrendous crimes committed in the years before Nuremberg, but also because recent years have borne witness to the commission of other crimes, in other regions, and in the context of other conflicts.

We must also remain aware of our own history. It is important to recall that, as Mr Justice Deschênes has mentioned, Canada has held war crimes trials in the past. Under Canada's War Crimes Act, trials of war criminals were conducted from 1945 to 1948. Unfortunately, during the fifties and subsequently, as individuals and nations moved to put the trauma and horror of the Second World War behind them, the pursuit of war criminals became less of a priority in many countries. It was only at the beginning of this decade that public attention turned again to the problem of war crimes.

Reports during the early eighties suggested that the number of war criminals in Canada could reach six thousand. In the face of such a possibility, it became increasingly apparent that the Canadian government should take firm action to see that the interests of justice were served. However, there was no clear information on the scope of the problem, nor a consensus among legal authorities on appropriate remedies.

Le présent gouvernement a établi, le 7 février 1985, la Commission d'enquête sur les criminels de guerre, qui a été chargée de recueillir des données factuelles et de recenser les moyens légaux pour régler les problèmes. Le rapport de cette commission qui a été déposé le 30 décembre 1986 a permis au gouvernement d'agir résolument et rapidement.

The Deschênes Report allowed the nature and scope of the problem of war criminals in Canada to be identified with far greater precision than was previously possible. The legal avenues available to take action against war criminals were identified and explored. As a result of this work, the government has been able to respond quickly and comprehensively to the identified problems. Mr Chairman, I would like at this point to acknowledge your contribution and the contribution of those who supported your work in the endeavour that has now been set in motion. Your work was comprehensive and your report cogent and compelling, establishing a standard for all subsequent efforts.

In the course of its response, the government has kept in mind

certain fundamental principles. First, Canada will not be a haven
for those who commit or who have committed war crimes or crimes
against humanity. Second, the problem of war crimes and crimes
against humanity should, whenever possible, be dealt with here in
Canada and in a manner consistent with the standard of the Charter
and other Canadian standards of law and evidence.

In my address to the House of Commons on 12 March of this
year, I stated that, in accordance with the commission's recommendation, the government was prepared to amend the Criminal Code
to give Canadian courts jurisdiction to try war crimes or crimes
against humanity in Canada, where the conduct in question would
amount to a criminal offence in Canada. The amendments to the
Criminal Code to do this came into effect 16 September. From that
date, Canada has had the power to try, in Canada, individuals implicated in war crimes, wherever those crimes may have occurred. I
should say, parenthetically, that I am indebted not only to people
within my own party but also to the opposition parties, who, in a
spirit of unanimity, cooperated in expeditiously dealing with this
legislation.

La Commission a recommandé que le gouvernement du Canada
envisage d'allouer des ressources suffisantes aux institutions
canadiennes existantes pour qu'elles puissent assumer cette
responsabilité. En outre, elle a indiqué que le gouvernement du
Canada devait prendre les mesures nécessaires pour continuer à
mener des enquêtes et pour terminer celles amorcées.

This has been done. My department and the Royal Canadian
Mounted Police have been allocated the necessary resources, and
the necessary inquiries and investigations are well underway.

The Deschênes Report recommended that immigration into
Canada and Canadian citizenship not be available to those who have
participated in war crimes and crimes against humanity in other
countries. Measures directed to this end were included in the
legislation passed on 16 September and proclaimed into effect on
30 October.

The Deschênes Report also recommended that the government
should decide whether to request the co-operation of foreign
governments in gathering the evidence necessary to resolve cases
here in Canada. This decision has been made and the process is
under way, subject to certain specified safeguards.

It is my belief that, through these measures, the government has
responded decisively and effectively to the problem of war crimes,
in a manner consistent with the highest traditions of the Canadian
legal system. For the first time, we now have, in Canada, the capacity

to deal effectively with war crimes and war criminals, both past and future.

I would now like to take a few moments to share some observations with you about certain specific aspects of our new law.

The legislation is in strict conformity with the Charter and is not retroactive. Section 11(g) of the Charter provides that no person may be found guilty of an offence unless, at the time of commission, "it constituted an offence under Canadian or international law or was criminal according to the general principles of law recognized by the community of nations."

This provision makes these standards the reference point by which Canada must apply its jurisdiction for past and future war crimes. The definitions of war crimes and crimes against humanity in the legislation, and the jurisdiction to try them, have therefore been shaped by international standards of conduct, such as the Geneva Conventions, the Nuremberg Principles, and customary international law.

La législation n'est pas une mesure de représailles, elle accorde aux tribunaux canadiens la compétence pour juger seulement les crimes internationaux qui, au moment où ils ont été commis, auraient constitué une infraction aux droits canadiens s'ils étaient survenus au Canada. Cette législation s'applique à des crimes passés, à venir, et non pas uniquement à ceux commis pendant la Seconde Guerre Mondiale.

It is useful to consider more fully the jurisdictional basis of this law. Both the traditional jurisdiction over the nationals of warring parties and the evolving notion of universal jurisdiction have been included in the amendments to the Criminal Code. Section 7(3.71)(a) of the Criminal Code reflects the internationally recognized traditional basis of jurisdiction for the prosecution of crimes committed in the course of wartime. States that were parties to an armed conflict have the right to prosecute such war crimes.

Over the course of time, however, other bases of jurisdiction have been developed and recognized by international law. The most important is the principle of universal jurisdiction, which provides that persons who commit particular types of crimes are considered to be, in effect, international criminals. War crimes and crimes against humanity are two examples covered by this principle; torture is another. To put it another way, there is growing international agreement that certain acts are so clearly heinous that it is the right of any nation to try any offender found within its borders, regardless of where that act was committed.

Where universal jurisdiction exists, a state, its nationals, or its allies need not have participated in the war, nor is the jurisdiction altered because the crime against humanity took place during peacetime. And section 7(3.71)(b) of the Criminal Code applies the principle of universal jurisdiction to allow trials for these crimes to take place in Canada, regardless of where the crimes may have occurred. As international notions of what actions should be considered war crimes and crimes against humanity continue to develop, Canadian jurisdiction will also expand.

Because of the gravity of the crimes being considered, means to protect the rights of an accused were of great concern in the development of this legislation. Any trial conducted under this legislation will afford the accused person all the safeguards and rights that ensure fair and equitable treatment to anyone tried for any crime in our Canadian courts. In addition, any defences available under international law, both at the time of the commission of the crime and at the time of the trial, will also be available. In redressing historic wrongs, it is essential, at the same time, to recognize and preserve the traditional rights of the accused under our criminal law.

I would like to spend a few moments discussing the implementation of the legislative measures we have put in place.

The chair of the Commission, Mr Justice Deschênes, stated that if the government chose to proceed with his recommendations, "It is clear that another monumental effort will be required to forge ahead with speed, organize work, assess the results and counsel the government as each case ripens." I think that Canadians have a right to know how that work is progressing.

It is important to understand that the nature and extent of the evidence that will be required to prove individual guilt – to the standard of beyond a reasonable doubt – will require an extraordinary effort, given the age and complexity of the crimes being investigated. Evidence sufficient to allow Canadian juries to understand the social and political context of other countries, more than forty years ago, to a degree sufficient to assess guilt and innocence will also be required.

Ce processus comportera nécessairement la compilation minutieuse de renseignements et des recherches historiques approfondies dans des pays étrangers ainsi que des enquêtes partout au Canada. Des affaires aussi délicates et aussi complexes prendront plus de temps que les enquêtes criminelles actuelles se déroulant ici au Canada.

Some persons have undertaken this task within the Department of Justice and the Royal Canadian Mounted Police. They bring legal, academic, investigatory, linguistic, and other skills to this work. They will draw on the assistance of other officials in these and other departments of government, as required, to support their endeavours. I believe that this is a substantial and appropriate degree of commitment. Nevertheless, it will remain under regular review and will be adjusted as required.

I have often been asked why cases identified by the Deschênes Report have not yet proceeded to our courts. The short answer is that no case will proceed until there is sufficient evidence available to present a responsible case. Here, we should keep in mind the difference between allegations or suspicions and proof that will meet the evidentiary standards of Canadian criminal law.

Since the Deschênes Report was tabled, the tasks in which my department have been involved have included not only the marshalling and assessment of such evidence, but also the development of the necessary amendments to the Criminal Code, the careful review and follow-up of all of the commission's files, the acquisition of the necessary expertise in this new field, and the negotiation of agreements with foreign governments to enable all the necessary evidence to be obtained.

In keeping with the government's earlier commitment, this evidence will be obtained only where there are specific, credible, and serious allegations against individuals and in accordance with the six conditions recommended by Mr Justice Deschênes with respect to the gathering of evidence abroad. These conditions are the protection of reputations through confidentiality; the use of independent interpreters; access to original documents, where relevant; access to witnesses' previous statements; freedom of examination of witnesses in agreement with Canadian rules of evidence; and the videotaping of such examination.

To allow the search for foreign evidence to begin and to pave the way for Canadian authorities to do the necessary foreign historic research, negotiations have already begun with the Soviet Union, Poland, Romania, Czechoslovakia, Hungary, West Germany, Israel, and the Netherlands. Dans chacun des cas, il faut arriver à une entente non seulement afin de sauvegarder les droits de l'accusé mais aussi afin de nous conformer aux exigences juridiques de chacun des gouvernements étrangers pour ce qui est de la collecte des éléments de preuve dans leur pays.

It is the need to protect the rights of the accused that I wish to comment on in the last of my remarks today. Our legal process must continue to maintain the highest standards of law and evidence. As I am sure you are well aware, it is customary to refrain from commenting on the specifics of criminal cases under investigation. If the government has evidence concerning alleged criminal acts by individuals, there is only one proper form for its release, and that is in court, after a charge has been laid. Our Canadian criminal justice system and fundamental principles of fairness dictate that the names of suspects must not be released. Those who are tempted to publicize names should reflect upon the obstacles to a fair trial that such release creates.

It is my belief that the laws and mechanisms that we have established in Canada to bring war criminals to justice will address past evils wherever it is legally possible, and will also go a long way toward preventing future wrongs.

Questions from the Floor

Q. I have a question for Mr Hnatyshyn. You mentioned that the government of Canada would be prepared to go ahead with extradition requests in appropriate cases, in accordance with existing law. Would it also be true that the government of Canada would be prepared to go ahead with denaturalization and deportation cases, in accordance with existing law?

A. THE HONOURABLE MR HNATYSHYN: Well, that's something that has probably not been concentrated upon. There are existing laws with respect to these items and the law is available in appropriate cases for action. We have amended the Immigration Act in accordance with the recommendations of the Deschênes Report with respect to prospective cases, and with respect to establishing a procedure in immigration terms which will avoid any of the vagueness that has, unfortunately, been manifest in the past and which has posed some difficulties with respect to the processes that you have indicated. The amendments will also provide very clear guidelines henceforth with respect to the whole question of denaturalization and deportation.

Q. My name is Professor Roman Serbyn, of the Université de Québec à Montréal. Yesterday we heard Mr Wiesel's very eloquent and moving talk on the theme of "Forty Years After Nuremberg." I am wondering whether the irony of history was not lost on this audience. While Wallenberg was being incarcerated in Soviet prisons, the Soviets were playing at justice for Nazi war criminals. Mr Wiesel said that justice was rendered at Nuremberg. I agree: justice was rendered at Nuremberg. But it was selective justice; it was partial justice. Is it still up to us, forty years later, to continue with selective justice? We know that, during the Second World War, crimes were committed all over the world for which the Soviets were responsible. The communists were responsible for a good deal of that injustice and crime, and yet we continue to harp today only about Nazi war criminals. What is being done about communist war criminals? Many of them left the Soviet Union during the war and after the war.

And my second question is, do you consider it moral, today, to neglect this issue and to deal only with Nazi war criminals? Thank you.

A. ELIZABETH HOLTZMAN: First of all, with respect to Soviet war criminals, undoubtedly, you are not familiar with the immigration laws of the United States, but virtually immediately after the war it was prohibited for persons who were members of the Communist Party – not just those who had engaged in actual deeds of torture – to enter the United States. So providing sanctuary to Soviet communists was never a US policy. Second, I would like to say that the comments I made with respect to where your government is going, I do from the basis of enormous respect for your country, for your system of justice, for the fact that you have shown remarkable courage in being willing to acknowledge the problem of Nazi war criminals in your midst. No one says that there is any clear solution engraved in stone that applies to any one country, and so, as I made clear in my remarks, I wanted to compliment you on this effort. It is, regrettably, one that many nations have to grapple with.

But I would hope that you would avoid some of the problems that we ran into and that you can build on the experience of the United States, taking what was useful and what was effective and trying to avoid some of the pitfalls. I am trying to suggest some of those pitfalls to you. I sincerely hope that the solutions you have arrived at will work, because the world is watching and history is watching, and future Canadian generations are watching. How you discharge this responsibility will be something that will be noticed. Forty years from now, people will ask, "What did you do?" And what will your answer be?

With respect to the issue of "harping on" Nazi war criminals; I reject that statement. I don't think we've harped enough on the Second World War and its legacy; we are here today because we didn't finish the business of the Second World War. Perhaps if we had clearly set a standard of conduct by governments with respect to the Nazis and there was universal condemnation of the Nazis, we might have been more successful with respect to other countries in setting those standards. It seems to me there can be no "but" and no "yet" and no qualifiers when it comes to dealing with the unfinished business of the Second World War. No one who has any sense of human decency, of human justice, of morality, could listen to what Elie Wiesel said and then come to this conference and say, "But ..."

A. THE HONOURABLE MR HNATYSHYN: The Holocaust was a matter that, as I indicated in my remarks, could not be overlooked. But I think that the response of the government has been one which, on the recommendation of the Deschênes Report, has been to take a generic approach. As a Canadian, I am sorry about the fact that it took forty years for Canada to look at the question of war crimes and crimes against humanity. I am proud to be part of an administration that, after all this time, has acted expeditiously with respect to such crimes, regardless of where they took place, and regardless of the time of occurrence. I think that we, as Canadians, have to join together in a co-operative effort to ensure that Canada does proceed against all war criminals with alacrity, with effort, and with effect, to make sure that Canada is not a haven for war criminals.

Q. Mr Hnatyshyn, I'm with United Press International. When Mr Justice Deschênes released his report, there was a companion piece, prepared by researcher Alti Rodal, which looked into the postwar Canadian immigration policy and collaboration by Canadian government officials and civil servants in the resettlement of Nazis in Canada. It also outlines the collaboration between the Canadian and US governments in that matter. Why has that report not been made public and when will it be made public?

A. THE HONOURABLE MR HNATYSHYN: It has been made public. There has been criticism with respect to the fact that, as we say in access-to-information law circles, there have been, by virtue of the provisions of the Privacy Act, certain deletions in terms of personal information. But the report itself is available. It has been published and is available on application to the appropriate office.

Q. We have heard a very interesting exchange between the two panellists this morning about the need for an office of special investigations; that is, of course, something which was recommended by the Deschênes Report, which the government has considered and rejected. I suppose that it is now an issue that, at least for this moment, has gone by the boards.

But in your remarks, Mr Hnatyshyn, you did address the need for building a reservoir of experience, expertise, and talent in some entity, and that of course has been done by the construction of the US Justice Department team.

This enterprise had been done before by the constitution of the commission itself, and I wonder whether the government would consider at this moment tapping the resources of the commission by attracting to the Justice Department team, at least on a part-time basis, some of its key personnel. This might be a guide, a means of putting a reservoir of talent, experience, and expertise in the Canadian Department of Justice to deal with this matter.

A. THE HONOURABLE MR HNATYSHYN: Just two brief comments. First, the Deschênes Report recommended against the establishment of an office of special investigations. We have accepted that recommendation, but, as I indicated in my remarks, we have devoted resources within our existing Department of Justice, the Solicitor General's Office, and the RCMP. We have, in fact, put forward a substantial effort to develop the expertise. Our practice, in terms of hiring persons, is that we intend to take advantage of the expertise that is available.

Q. My name is Allan Ryan. I was formerly the director of the Office of Special Investigations in the US Justice Department. My question is directed to Minister Hnatyshyn. I listened with interest to your safeguards and precautions in the taking of evidence in foreign countries. Generally, I think they're fine. Indeed, they're the ones that the Justice Department followed for many years when this began.

My question goes to the criticism that has been raised quite vociferously, both in this country and in the United States, centring on what is known as Soviet evidence. That criticism states, in essence, that evidence from the Soviet Union is so suspect that it can never be trusted and therefore ought never to be used, regardless of what other precautions and safeguards may obtain in the judicial process.

My question is whether this government intends to take any stand on that issue, and specifically whether this government will adopt any policy or practice in its prosecutions that will treat evidence that originates from Soviet archives or from Soviet witnesses in any special way or on a different footing from evidence that originates in other foreign countries, assuming that the safeguards and the normal rules of evidence are complied with.

A. THE HONOURABLE MR HNATYSHYN: I think that a lot of people don't fully appreciate the fact that Soviet evidence has already been used in prosecutions up to this time. There was the case of Helmut Rauca, in which evidence from the Soviet Union was part of the evidence, and which led to Rauca's extradition to West Germany.

The safeguards that we have established are those that are recommended by the Deschênes Report, but, of course, under our Canadian standards of justice, evidence, regardless of the location, is always available for presentation. There is no particular stigma attached to it. What the safeguards do, though, is make sure that the method of investigation and the development of that evidence will be of such high quality that it will be taken into consideration by the courts, and that there will be no suspicion with respect to its veracity or authenticity. So the protections that we have established – and the agreements that we are negotiating now with several countries – will be in the best interests of the proper prosecution of war criminals in Canada; the safeguards will allow us to bring in this evidence effectively.

Q. My name is Leona Finkler. I am a survivor of eight concentration camps, including the infamous Auschwitz. My question is to Ms Holtzman. In the mid-seventies, there was an International Conference on Liberators. A lot of data had been gathered. Has this been compiled and disseminated in any way to the community at large, not just in the United States, but all over the world?

A. ELIZABETH HOLTZMAN: I don't know the specifics, but Allan Ryan, who's much more of an expert on this than I am, says yes. And I think that's one of the other important things about these trials which I tried to mention in my remarks, that they also serve the purpose that Elie Wiesel talked about of "memory": to create a record, to construct the history, and to refute those who, even today, would deny the reality of what happened, and the horror of it.

Panel Two
Nuremberg Forty Years Later: Bringing War Criminals to Justice in Our Time

Chair

MICHAEL MEIGHEN

Svend Robinson is the Member of Parliament for Burnaby, British Columbia, and the Justice Critic for the New Democratic Party. Mr Robinson has taken a particular interest in bringing war criminals to justice in our time and has spoken eloquently on the subject, both within and outside the House of Commons. He is the NDP spokesman on war criminals and human rights matters.

Speaker

SVEND ROBINSON

Je tiens tout d'abord à féliciter les organisateurs de cette conférence internationale sur les droits de la personne, surtout la Faculté de droit ici à McGill et surtout, je dois dire, monsieur Irwin Cotler. Sans sa contribution extraordinaire, ce congrès n'aurait jamais eu lieu et je suis très heureux d'être ici ce matin. Mais je dois dire aussi que je ne suis pas vraiment un expert, ça c'est sûr, et pour moi c'est un grand honneur d'être invité ici pour partager mes points de vue sur les questions si importantes qu'on va aborder ce matin.

I was deeply moved yesterday, as we all were, by the eloquence of Elie Wiesel and in particular by the juxtaposition with which he closed his comments. He spoke of indifference as the opposite of law, as the opposite of love, duty, education, and life. It is my belief that it is precisely that shameful indifference that has characterized

Canada's response to date on the question of the victims of the Holocaust and, indeed, of those who sought to flee the Holocaust.

Ray Hnatyshyn has given an overview of the government's response to date on this question. I would like to make a few comments, to give some historical background to the Canadian perspective. I think that it is important that we examine the government's current response in the light of the historic context.

As many of you are aware, and as Irving Abella has written so eloquently, Canada's policy with respect to those who attempted to flee from the horrors of Nazi Germany is summed up by the words "None is too many." The record is clear on that question, and I am indebted to the magnificent contribution of Alti Rodal, who set it all out in a report that has finally been made public – a rather expurgated and laundered version, with many white spaces, but, nevertheless, we read between the white spaces and what we find horrifies and shocks us.

For example, on the question of the initial policy of the twelve-year period from 1933 to 1945, we are told by Irving Abella that the United Kingdom opened its doors to seventy thousand Jews and allowed another one hundred and twenty-five thousand Jews into Palestine. Argentina took fifty thousand, Brazil took twenty-seven thousand, and Australia took fifteen thousand. Now, in this twelve-year period from 1933 to 1945, Canada found room for fewer than five thousand people. And after the war, until the founding of Israel in 1948, we admitted another eight thousand, only *eight thousand,* people. Hence, Canada's history is a shameful one. It is a history which compels us, surely, to take action today.

We also know that Canada, as a member of the Commonwealth, agreed to the position that was suggested by Britain in 1948. This position was stated in a directive which came out of Britain's Foreign Office: "In our view punishment of war criminals is more a matter of discouraging future generations than of meting out retribution to every guilty individual. Moreover, in view of future political developments in Germany envisaged by recent tripartite talks, we are convinced that it is now necessary to dispose of the past as soon as possible."

And dispose of the past is exactly what Canada, Britain, and other members of the Commonwealth did as soon as they possibly could in 1948. This was done by taking, effectively, no action. No action, but, as Elizabeth Holtzman indicated when she spoke earlier, there was extensive action when it came to assisting those who were anti-communist who sought to come to Canada, the United States, Britain, Australia, and elsewhere. But at the same time as we were throwing open the doors to those anti-communists, we were continuing to turn away Jews. Once again, the Rodal report provides an eloquent testimony to this.

Also a matter of history was our explicitly racist immigration laws. The director of immigration said, "Canada's immigration laws reflect class and race discrimination. They do and necessarily so. Some form of discrimination cannot be avoided if immigration is to be effectively controlled in order to prevent the creation in Canada of expanding non-assimilable racial groups. Many organizations have passed resolutions urging selective immigration. It is not possible to have selective immigration on the one hand and no discrimination on the other."

So that was our official policy as a nation. And lest there be any doubt that it was applied – I could give many examples, as did Rodal – I will provide only one here, that of a young Jewish man who wanted to come to Canada as a lumberworker, perhaps to my own province of British Columbia. He was accepted. He had to wait for a long time, but then, when he applied in Munich he was told by the head of the Canadian team that the instructions were to countermand the selection of Jews as lumberworkers in Canada.

So, that is our history as a nation. We slammed the door shut when Jews were attempting to flee prior to the Holocaust, and the doors remained tightly sealed after the Holocaust as well.

Also documented is the extent to which we helped some escape; Klaus Barbie, for example, went to Bolivia and elsewhere – for services rendered.

It was not until 1981 that, finally, the first action was taken in Canada. I had the honour of serving as a member of the Special Joint Committee on the Constitution of Canada, at which time an amendment was passed to the Charter of Rights and Freedoms which facilitated, or at least enabled, retroactive legislation to deal with those guilty of crimes against humanity. That was the first step.

In 1982, Robert Kaplan, then solicitor general, had a look at some of the options and struck a committee headed by Martin Low, of the Department of Justice. And basically, Martin Low came back to Cabinet, threw up his hands and said that there was nothing he could do. Martin Low, by the way, is today the head of the Human Rights Section of the Department of Justice.

And that line, "Nothing we can do," remained the line of the government headed by former Prime Minister Trudeau. And of course, not only did that remain the line, but in 1982 there was massive file destruction. Many of the files, the key files in this area, were destroyed. When we questioned this, we were told that it had been done according to normal retention and disposal schedules supplied by the Public Archives. This was not normal and those files should never, never, have been destroyed. Why was this policy adopted? And policy it was. For example, Robert Kaplan said, in a letter of September 1982, "The conclusion reached by the Low Committee, which was made public some time ago, was that domestic legislation provided no recourse and that any action undertaken against an individual, even if his war crimes were proven, would result in an acquittal or dismissal."

This, of course, totally begs the question as to why domestic legislation was not changed. Well, that was the official position. I remember asking then Minister of Justice Jean Chrétien if that was all he was prepared to do in terms of extradition. After all, we had extradited one person upon request – Rauca – to West Germany. And Chrétien said, "I do not think, personally, it would be advisable to start having trials in Canada on actions that occurred in other nations." Think of the implications of those words. Former Prime Minister Trudeau spoke of "foreign baggage," of people bringing their baggage to Canada. Well, that was the response of the Trudeau government until the dying days – and, I emphasize, the dying days – of that government. Then, suddenly, Mark MacGuigan discovered another remedy. He said, "After careful and extended reconsideration of our views, we have looked at the question of denaturalization and deportation." And he concluded, "It might well be possible for such proceedings to be successfully instituted."

And that was the position taken in those last days. Why? One can speculate. Robert Kaplan, in one of his more candid moments, indicated that he was concerned that the government would not take action because of the risk that it might, in his words, "upset people." Such comments are similar to those of an adviser to Howard Green, back in the early sixties, who suggested that it would not be a good idea to take action because West Germans would prefer that we, in his words, "let sleeping dogs lie."

So that was it until 1984. And then, following extensive pressure by many individuals and groups, the Conservative minister of justice, John Crosbie, to his credit, established a Commission of Inquiry headed by a very distinguished jurist, Jules Deschênes. And that commission, working within a deadline that was impossibly and painfully short, as Jules Deschênes himself has acknowledged and as Michael Meighen would agree, did an extraordinary job in documenting the horrors and in making recommendations to the government.

It was not easy, because no sooner had the commission been struck than attempts began to subvert its work. What sorts of attempts were they? Primarily attempts to suggest that those who wished to witness, to give evidence, to provide archival materials, wherever they might originate, including in the Soviet Union, should be denied the right to do so. Fortunately, Mr Justice Deschênes considered those arguments and rejected them. But the arguments had strong backing. Tory and Liberal members of Parliament suggested that we must not accept Soviet evidence; we must not allow those people as witnesses, despite the clear fact that, in the use of Soviet evidence in other jurisdictions, there is absolutely no record of any perjury or any doctoring of the evidence. We have even used Soviet evidence ourselves – in the *Rauca* case – as the minister acknowledged. Despite this, members of Parliament did everything they could to put pressure on the government. And what position did the government of Canada take on the question of Soviet evidence? No position at all. The lawyer representing the government of Canada went into court and said, "I have no position." At least he did not take the position advocated by persons such as David Kilgour, a member of Parliament who appeared before the commission and argued that it was somehow a breach of the Charter to hear this evidence.

I travelled to the Soviet Union just this past July – to the Ukraine, to Lvov – one of the areas in which the Holocaust was particularly devastating. I listened to the witnessing of some of those who saw the horrors: a young man who, at the age of seven, fled from the village in the middle of the night and came back and found a scene of indescribable horror; a woman who saw her father kicked to death in the town square. And this woman said to me, "Why can I not tell my story before I die? The perpetrator of this crime is in your country. He is in Canada, and why will you not let me tell my story?" By silencing these individuals, as Elie Wiesel said, we are denying their reality. Similarly, those who have survived, those who are children of victims, are being doubly victimized by the inaction of governments.

Furthermore, there have been classes of victims established. As has been acknowledged, it was not only the Jews who suffered in the Holocaust, it was communists, homosexuals, and gypsies. Some of those classes of victims still remain. The Federal Republic of Germany refuses to compensate homosexuals who were victims.

And then, after Mr Justice Deschênes reported on 30 December, with his extensive documentation and his plea for continued action, the government finally responded in June of this year with Bill C-71. This legislation permits the trial in Canada of those who are alleged to have committed crimes against humanity and war crimes – not just the crimes of the Nazis, but all war crimes. It is generic legislation. Those who are responsible for the terrible atrocities, for example, in Chile, those same murderers who are responsible for burning Carmen Quintana, who is being honoured at this conference, could be tried if they dared to appear on Canadian soil.

But there has been no change whatsoever in our policy with respect to extradition. I believe that this is profoundly wrong. I believe that we should have accepted the recommendations of the Deschênes Report with respect to changes in our law of extradition. There are just two examples that I would give. One is with respect to our treaty with Israel; as Mr Justice Deschênes indicated, the amendment that was made to our treaty, suggesting that we could not in fact deal with war crimes, was "a cruel embarrassment." I think that that is true. I do not understand why our government has failed to put that right.

The other example is with respect to the question of extradition of a man named Jacob Luitjens. Jacob Luitjens stood accused of very serious crimes in the Second World War in Holland. He was convicted *in absentia*, forty years ago, of collaboration with the Nazis. It was alleged that he was responsible for the murder of a German anti-Nazi and a member of the Dutch Resistance. Well, the Dutch have said that they want Luitjens back. He is living in Vancouver, a former professor at the University of British Columbia. The Canadian government has said, "Well, no, you cannot have him because our Extradition Act does not allow it." The Dutch replied, "Why do you not change your Act?" It seems like a sensible suggestion. Earlier today, Ray Hnatyshyn said, "We have a treaty with Holland, among other countries." And I say to Ray Hnatyshyn, "Why do you not change the Act, as was recommended, to allow this man to be brought to justice?"

I regard Bill C-71 as important, as significant, but far more significant will be the follow-up to it. And, in that regard, I want to note that even during the passage of this legislation, there were those who attempted to silence the victims once again. A member of the committee that studied the bill, a Conservative member of Parliament from Toronto, Andrew Whitter, moved an amendment to suggest that in Canada the trials of war criminals should be held in secret, behind closed doors. What does that do to the concept of witness? And how does that reinforce the concept of solitude? Shortly afterwards, he was elected by his Conservative colleagues as the vice-chairperson of the Standing Committee on Human Rights of our Parliament.

And so we continue to wait for action; we wait for the first trials; we mourn the irony that those who deny the Holocaust have had their forum – the Zundels and Keegstras have had their forum, grabbed the headlines, mocking the reality, and Zundel may get another trial. And yet the victims themselves are denied the right to bear witness. There must be follow-up in the strongest possible terms, not only with respect to the twenty people identified by the Deschênes Report as cases for prosecution, but also with respect to all of the other cases identified as worthy of further investigation. And even if the evidence does not lead to prosecution, even if there are not trials, then at least those who have been silenced for so long need be silent no longer. They will be able to witness. They will be able to shame by naming.

I would like to close by referring to a story. It is taken from *The Murderers Among Us*, the Wiesenthal memoirs. In that book, Wiesenthal talks about an incident that took place shortly after the Second World War. Thousands of Jewish prayer books had been found in a cellar of an old castle in Austria, and Wiesenthal went to investigate. There were thousands upon thousands of books that had been brought from Jewish homes and houses of worship all over Europe. The Nazis had wanted to distribute these books as historical records. And there was a young man with Simon Wiesenthal who picked up one book after another; in one of the books, on the very first page, he found in his own sister's handwriting these words: "They have just come into our town. In a few minutes they will be in our house. If someone finds this prayer book, please notify my dear brother. Do not forget us. Do not forget our murderers."

I hope that, at last, we will heed that plea.

MICHAEL MEIGHEN Mr Ryan is the former director of the Office of Special Investigations in the United States Department of Justice. He is currently general counsel for Harvard University. He is the author of *Quiet Neighbors: Prosecuting Nazi War Criminals in America*.

Speaker

ALLAN RYAN, JR

I speak to you this morning as a friend and as a co-worker for justice, and not as a critic – certainly not as a political critic. I hope that our experience in the United States, and particularly my experience as director of the OSI, might be of some use to you in Canada as you embark on a somewhat similar task.

The United States began a policy – thirty years too late – of investigating and prosecuting Nazi war criminals within its borders. It has proceeded, I believe, in a professional and effective manner. Ten years after the United States, Canada has promised to do the same.

I think that the efforts being made in this country should be applauded and supported by all of us who believe in human rights. But I think that one must not make the mistake of assuming that whatever the United States did, Canada must therefore do, or the equally fallacious argument that whatever the United States has done, Canada must therefore avoid.

I read with equanimity the recommendation of Mr Justice Deschênes that the government not establish a *Bureau d'Enquêtes Spéciales*. What has proven effective in the United States may not necessarily prove effective or appropriate in Canada, and it is of no particular issue to me whether there is an office of special investigations in the Canadian government.

What I think is critical, however, as Ms Holtzman mentioned this morning, is that there cannot be any effective program, any effective prosecution of Nazi war criminals in this country or any other country, unless there is assembled a staff of professionals who are dedicated to that task and to no other. When I began as director of the OSI in 1980, we had a staff of twenty lawyers, three historians, and eight investigators. Within a year, I had changed that around to twenty lawyers, eight historians, and three investigators. And within another year the three investigators had pretty much departed, as had three of the lawyers. Their slots were taken up by historians, translators, and other support professionals. You simply cannot prosecute the case of a person alleged to have been a member of the Latvian secret police unless you know the street plan of Riga, Latvia, in 1941, better than the Latvians knew it. Any prosecutor will tell you, I believe, whether he or she is prosecuting Nazi war criminals or other types of murder, rape, embezzlement, fraud, or crime of any kind, you have got to know the evidence better than the defence, better than the judge, better than anyone in that courtroom, or you are not going to persuade a judge or a jury to convict. That holds true for war crimes at least as much as it does for crimes that take place in the streets or in the boardrooms of our cities.

It is absolutely necessary to have historians and professionals work with lawyers and prepare the cases. You simply cannot have lawyers working on bank-fraud cases in the morning and Nazi crimes in the afternoon. You cannot have them concentrating on Toronto and Montreal one week, and on Riga and Vilna the next.

So, whatever the form that the people and the government of Canada might think appropriate, do not lose sight of the principle that you need people to learn this subject and to know it better than anybody else. I do not know what the resources are in Canada for historians of this period, but I am sure that there are more than enough qualified people for the task. The point is that they have to sit down, as we did, and learn the street plans, learn the political organizations, learn the names, learn the addresses, and learn how these crimes took place. Only then can you prosecute effectively.

I am somewhat disturbed by what I have been told and what I perceive, to some extent, to be an attitude that the OSI is the "problem" and, therefore, if Canada chooses not to have an OSI, Canada avoids the problem – the problem being taking evidence in the Soviet Union and other Eastern Bloc countries. That is a subject that could engage us for much longer than the few minutes that I am entitled to take of your time. But I want to make another point, I think equally important to the one I just made, and that is that no country can hope to have its investigation and prosecution of Nazi war criminals taken seriously, by its own people and by the people of the world, if it consigns evidence from the Soviet Union or the Eastern Bloc, or from any particular country or group of countries, to that of second-class evidence that is somehow categorically less reliable, less credible, and less worthy of a democratic society than evidence from other countries.

I have no brief with the Soviet Union or the way it runs its courts or its government. That is not the issue here. The plain fact is that many of the crimes that were committed by Nazi war criminals who are now in the United States and, I believe, in Canada took place in the Baltic countries, in the Ukraine, in Russia itself, and in other areas that we now generally call the Soviet Union. The witnesses are there and the documents are there. You are not going to investigate or prosecute these crimes unless you go to the witnesses and to the evidence. That is the only way I know to prosecute a crime. A prosecutor has no choice but to follow the evidence wherever it may lead.

Every witness must be examined in detail. A close and very scrupulous judgment must be made by prosecutors, no less than by judges and defence counsel, as to whether a witness is telling the truth and whether he has a motivation to lie; as to whether a document is reliable and credible; as to whether a document may have been doctored. All of these decisions have to be made very seriously and in the context of each witness and every document. No prosecutor in the United States, and I am sure no prosecutor in

Canada, who takes an oath seriously is going to stand up in court and present evidence that he or she might have reason to believe is suspect or unreliable.

On the other hand, I do not believe that Russians always lie. I do not believe that Latvians or Lithuanians or Ukrainians or Jews or any other nationality, religious group, or political coalition always lies. I am constrained to say that much of the criticism that I have heard emanating both from my country and from Canada concerning the reliability of Soviet witnesses makes the subtle but, I think, unmistakable and fallacious assumption that you can never trust the Soviets to do anything that might conceivably be reliable or truthful because they are, after all, Soviets – and we know what that means. That attitude, although it is seldom stated so bluntly, is largely what lies behind the sentiment in the United States and in this country to do away with, or to emasculate, these prosecutions altogether.

There is in the United States a group, or a coalition of groups, that I think has as its aim the abolition of the prosecution of Nazi war criminals and of the Office of Special Investigations. They do not often say it in so many words and it is a broad collection of individuals and groups, but that is their aim.

In the United States, the OSI was well established and well under way before these groups and these individuals were mobilized to speak in opposition. In Canada, they have a chance to strangle the baby in the crib. I believe, based on what I have seen being written and said from some quarters in this country, that that is what they intend to do. Whether they shall succeed or not is still an open question.

I applaud the undertakings of the Deschênes Commission and the promises made by Minister Hnatyshyn on behalf of the government that these cases will be prosecuted effectively and fully. Personally, I will wait and see what the results of those laudable promises might be before I draw any conclusions. But I must commend to you my deeply felt desire that those of us who share, as we all profess to share, the conviction that Nazi war criminals must be brought to justice and that the United States or Canada, or any civilized country, should not be a haven for war criminals must put aside the distracting and ultimately destructive political arguments and unite behind a program – however it might be structured, given the priorities of any particular country – to prosecute these people effectively and to bring them to justice forty years after their crimes have been committed.

While there is certainly room in this debate to discuss the standards that are appropriate and the most responsible way to proceed, do not, I beg of you, allow yourselves to be sidetracked into fruitless and bad-faith arguments that the problems in this process are so severe that we must study them forever or not undertake the task at all. The time is late, particularly here where the time is even later than it was in my own country when we began. The message that I leave with you, in all humility, is, Let us keep our eyes on the prize. Let us see the objective that maintains us and that drives us to bring these people to justice, and let us put other considerations aside.

MICHAEL MEIGHEN Mr Janner is a lawyer and Queen's Counsel and a Labour Party member of Parliament of the United Kingdom. He is the convenor of the UK Parliamentary War Crimes Group; founder, trustee, and former chair of the All-Party Committee for Homeless and Rootless People; vice-chair of the All-Party Committee for Release of Soviet Jewry; and founding member of the International Committee for Human Rights in the USSR.

Speaker

GREVILLE JANNER

I am so pleased to be here. I was here during the war, as my father, who was a leading Jew in England, was near the top of Hitler's blacklist. My father stayed in London, but he sent us across here. For four safe, good years, I was in your country, and I thank you for that.

I am glad to be back also because your country has, in some ways, changed. I remember as a youngster wanting to go skiing at Sainte-Agathe with a friend and he said, "I'm sorry, you can't come with me because you are Jewish." And I said, "I don't understand." He said, "The hotel where my family is staying has a select clientele." This was the bounce-back effect of the cause of the Holocaust, as it existed in Canada during the war. The infection from Europe had spread, irrespective of the Atlantic or the Pacific, and it is this infection with which we are still dealing, and which I believe brings us together now.

An absolutely horrific article in Monday's *Montreal Gazette* explains, again, why we are here. The headline is, "'I have no regrets,' says Nazi who refuses to repent." The story reads, "The most notorious Nazi war criminal still at large said from his home in Syria that he regrets nothing he did during the Second World War. 'All of them Jews, all of them deserved to die because they were the Devil's agents and human garbage,' Alois Brunner said in an interview with the *Chicago Sun Times*. 'I have no regrets. I would do it again.' When West Germany asked for Brunner's extradition, Syria said that he had committed no crimes that are punishable."

That is the precise position of those who are alleged to have committed war crimes in the United Kingdom: they have committed no crimes that are punishable. Not because our law, as was the problem with your law, says that punishment and jurisdiction depends upon *where* the crime was committed. We have a law that says that a British citizen may be prosecuted for murder or genocide committed *outside* the jurisdiction of the courts. But our government takes the view that this applies only to those who were citizens of the United Kingdom at the time when the offence was committed. So we have sixteen alleged war criminals in the United Kingdom, as a result of lists provided by the Wiesenthal Centre and by the Soviet Union – whose lists we treat with care but with respect. "*Chashdeihu ve chabdeihu*," they say in Hebrew – "respect and suspect." You watch with care, but you treat with respect because there is no other place where the evidence is available. So far, they have honoured their evidence, and, to the best of my knowledge, they have not disgraced their good name by forging any documentation. But you watch it, nonetheless, to see who is on the list.

We have on our list a man called Gecas, known as Antanas Gecevicius when he was in Lithuania, who is suing *The Times* for libel, I am told, because *The Times* said that he is a major war criminal. The Simon Wiesenthal Centre said publicly in London that he was personally involved in war crimes, more personally involved than Barbie. I don't say that. I repeat under the cover of complete and absolute privilege what I said in Parliament, namely, that if the evidence that is available against him is correct – and I have every reason to believe that it is – he was the leader of a Lithuanian battalion that destroyed thousands of Jews and he was personally involved. Indeed, he himself has said on television that he didn't have any personal involvement, but he was there and he was guarding the Germans while they murdered. In law, I regard that as an admission of being an accomplice, which makes you guilty of the murders themselves.

But you see, there is no current crime which he has committed for which he is punishable under British law. And if that is right, ladies and gentlemen, "the law is," as Dickens said, "a ass – a idiot [*sic*]." It is also an iniquitous law which must be changed.

I am also delighted to be here because you have had the courage and the leadership and the all-party support to change your law. And we are finding it much easier to move against our government, and I say that on a non-party socialist basis, because you have done this. The Australians have introduced a similar law into their Parliament. We shall find it much easier to do so in ours because they have done it. The critics of the Commonwealth should understand that, even in countries which do not always agree with everything the Commonwealth does, it is more difficult for a Commonwealth government, particularly our own, to withstand pressures, when it can take examples from Canada and Australia and other Commonwealth countries and be told, as we tell them, that Britain, which did, after all, stand alone in many ways against the Nazis, must not be the only country to stand alone in refusing to charge and prosecute Nazis who are within our own borders.

So, how are we doing this? For a start, we have a very powerful all-party committee which recognizes that this is not a Jewish concern. Jews, if I may use an expression used in a question from the floor, "harp on" about this because many of us lost our families in the Holocaust. And if we did not "harp on" this issue, we would be neither true to their memories, nor true to ourselves. We also "harp on" because we believe that, if others do not learn the lesson from our tragedies, they can suffer as we did.

I am pleased to be here in the distinguished company of my colleague and friend, Mr Paul Boateng, who will be addressing this conference this evening. Paul is a very good personal friend, a distinguished lawyer, newly elected to Parliament for Brent and, in my view, the outstanding leader of Britain's black community. He will tell you why he came. I am glad that he is here because I do not believe that the prosecution of war criminals in the aftermath of the Holocaust is merely a matter of bringing Gecas or anyone else to justice. I believe that we must "harp on" the issue of bringing Nazi war criminals to justice so that we will prevent this from happening again to anyone – black, white, Catholic, or Jew – anywhere in the world. Because if we do not learn from what Elie Wiesel told us last night, from what we, ourselves, have seen, and from what we can pass on to others, then what hope have our children got of living in a decent society?

To turn to the dry bones of the law, I enjoyed the argument about whether we deport or extradite or prosecute. But we do not have that choice. We have problems. Deportation can be used only for non-British citizens. These fellows sneaked in. They are British citizens, so you cannot deport them. Can you remove their citizenship? The only person who has the power to do that is the Home Secretary, who has absolute discretion to order deportation, subject to an appeal at that stage by the person to be deported. So, it is up to him. If he says no, then that is it – subject to parliamentary pressures. If he says yes, and we are applying pressures, then the next question is, *Can* he deport? The problem is that the House of Lords has held that you must not use deportation as a cloak for extradition. And so, we have to look at what deportation means. It means, send them anywhere that they want to go. We have had a marvellous case in the States, where nobody wanted the fellow, so he had to go to the Soviet Union. But our Home Secretary has said that we will consider extradition, we will consider sending people anywhere but to the Soviet Union, because of their system of justice; anywhere but the place where the people were killed; anywhere but the place where the evidence is. That is what the Home Secretary says.

And so, we turn to extradition. There is no extradition treaty, of course, with the Soviet Union. There was such a treaty before the revolution, but it no longer exists. Why do we not send them to Israel? Well, there are two problems with that. One is that the extradition treaty with Israel does not apply. The second is that the Israelis do not want them. The Israelis say that they have enough problems. They have enough trials. They have not got enough money. They want us to prosecute our own criminals in our own countries, and to get on with it. That is what they said. They are right, are they not? Don't you think they are right that Canada should do it, Australia should do it, and the United Kingdom should do it?

The Soviet Union is not an option and Israel is not an option. Where does that leave us? Would you like them here? Perhaps we can find some jurisdictional argument. But this is not dealing with reality.

So, we have this enormous problem. What are we doing about it? We have a Parliamentary committee with a former Home Secretary in the chair. We have a distinguished group of lawyers in the House of Commons, all-party lawyers, all coming into this work. We are pressing and we are hoping and we are working. We do this for a number of reasons.

First, because we believe that it is right in itself. These wicked people should be brought to justice. When they say to us, "But it was a long time ago" – and they do – we say, "So what? There is no statute of limitations that applies to murder." There is no period of limitation in murder cases, so why should there be one for mass murder? Why should a man, and it is all men as far as I know, escape justice by creeping into the country under false terms? Is that a reason for a person to escape justice? I do not think so.

Second, it is an exercise in history. And even if the trials fail – and I hope greatly that they won't – it is an extraordinary lesson. It is an extraordinary lesson, isn't it, that the French learned from Barbie, and that the Israelis learned from Eichmann, and that we are all learning from Demjanjuk. It is a lesson which in a few years time will not be available. It is a lesson in life and in death. It is the lesson against indifference. It is the lesson of the Jewish people. It is the lesson of all others who suffer. It is a lesson for the world to learn. And these trials are, in their own way, a national and an international way of reviving the memory of the past as a flare to the future.

And finally, we do this because of the words of the great Pastor Niemoller, who was himself in a concentration camp. And when he survived and came out, he wrote this:

First they came for the Jews
and I did not speak out
because I was not Jewish

Then they came for the communists
and I did not speak out
because I was not a communist

Then they came for the Catholics
and I did not speak out
because I was not a Catholic

Then they came for the trade unionists
and I did not speak out
because I was not a trade unionist

Then they came for me
and there was no one left
to speak out for me.

In the war crimes campaign, which unites us all, we are speaking out about the past as a guide to the future. I thank you so very much for inviting me to be part of this day.

Questions from the Floor

Q. First of all, I apologize for the unfortunate term that I used: "harp on." Second, I hope that I was not misunderstood; I do not deny the Holocaust. I do not deny the fact that the criminals should be brought to justice. In *The Gazette* some years ago, I was quoted as saying, "Let them be hanged, hang those who are guilty." So I go all the way. I don't even say that they should be pardoned. However, my point was that now we also have to address other war criminals. Is it moral for us, is it a sign of our integrity, to be limiting ourselves only to Nazi war criminals? When will we start dealing with the other war criminals? When will we have organizations like the OSI to seek out other crimes? I remind you that we are here today in the name of Wallenberg, who suffered not from the Nazis, but he suffered, and probably is still suffering – because we don't know if he is dead – from the *Soviets*.

A. ALLAN RYAN, JR: I think that there is a historical fact here that has to be taken into account, and that is that, in the United States, from 1948 to 1952, we had in place as our chief immigration law the Displaced Persons Act of 1948, under which four hundred thousand refugees from Europe came to the United States. Included in that number – for reasons that I think had to do with the tragic priorities of our legislation – were a large number of those who had collaborated with the Nazis. I made that estimate in my book, and since then I believe that the number has grown by ten thousand or more. I say immediately that that is an educated guess. It is not something that is susceptible of proof, but I have tried to be responsible and conservative in arriving at that figure. But the point is that we are not talking about a few hundred or even a few thousand in the United States. We're talking about a much larger number of people who collaborated with the Nazis; we're talking about very large numbers who came into the United States under what I think was one of the most tragically flawed pieces of legislation that the United States Congress has ever passed. I part company, somewhat, with Ms Holtzman in that I place much more emphasis on the immigration laws and the way that they were carried out, and quite a bit less on the overt or covert efforts of the intelligence communities to bring Nazis into the United States. I think that the latter was a minor factor in terms of numbers.

   In any event, to answer your question, Soviet criminals and criminals from other countries simply did not enter the United States to any extent that I am aware of. When I say Soviet criminals, I refer, as I gather you do, to those who committed their crimes not necessarily on behalf of the Nazis, but in the service of Stalin or other Soviet forces. If those people are in the United States today, they are certainly susceptible of being prosecuted and deported, no less than Nazi war criminals. The Holtzman Amendment, in fact, was supplemented a year or two after it was passed, in 1978, to require that any person in the United States who has taken part in the persecution of any other person based on race, religion, or national origin be subject to denaturalization and deportation. It need not be a Nazi connection. The reason that there is a special office in the Justice Department that deals with the Nazis is only due to the fact that I mentioned earlier in my remarks: it takes a great deal of specialized knowledge to put these cases together, and the number of cases justifies the expense. We would put together an office dedicated to Cambodian war crimes or Vietnamese war crimes or Soviet war crimes, but I don't think the numbers are there because I don't think the immigrants came to the United States in such numbers. At least, from our perspective, that is why there is a special office of Nazi war criminals and not for others. Others will be prosecuted if the evidence is there to justify it.

A. SVEND ROBINSON: In terms of the Canadian situation, the legislation adopted by Parliament is not restricted to a particular class of alleged war criminals. It refers to crimes against humanity and war crimes, and it doesn't matter by whom they were committed. So, what I would suggest, with great respect, is, that if indeed, you, sir, have evidence, or others have evidence that would link specific individuals in Canada to crimes that are defined in this legislation, you give that evidence to the attorney general at the earliest possible time. And I might say as well, at the same time, that I would hope that certain groups that have been "harping on" a different matter – a number of them signed a full-page ad in *The Globe and Mail* in February of this year, saying, "Protect the Innocent" – do not frustrate the cause of which you speak. The whole thrust of that ad and these groups is to deny the Deschênes Commission and to attempt to persuade the government of Canada to prohibit any access to evidence obtained from witnesses in the Soviet Union. I would therefore hope that, in the desire for justice of which you speak, a desire to bring to justice those who are guilty of war crimes, wherever those crimes might have occurred, there would not be attempts to suppress prosecution and investigation of the crimes that were committed.

A. GREVILLE JANNER: What concerns me is the way our own governments are attempting to suppress evidence by not releasing documents concerning events that happened forty and forty-five years ago, on grounds of alleged security and military intelligence. We can't get from our government the documents concerning Barbie. We can't get the documents concerning Waldheim. If you have any ways of extracting evidence from governments, I shall look forward to hearing from you.

Q. My name is Ron Sklar. I teach law here at McGill. I agree with Elizabeth Holtzman that the primary response to war criminals should be denaturalization and deportation or extradition. I also agree that if the crimes were committed in the Soviet Union, if the evidence and the witnesses are in the Soviet Union, and if the victims lived in the Soviet Union, then the deportation and the extradition should be *to* the Soviet Union.

On the other hand, what I think we have to face is the tendency in the Soviet Union sometimes to use trials for purposes other than establishing guilt or innocence. Again, I have to qualify and repeat what I said, that on balance I still think that deportation, even to the Soviet Union, is proper.

But Irwin Cotler demonstrated in a brief that was monumental in size, content, and quality, in the case of Natan Sharansky, that the Soviet Union, when it thinks it serves its own purposes, will fail to apply its own law, will fail to follow rules of evidence that it has established in its own statutes and case law.

To what extent must we take into account, on the issue of extradition and deportation, the fact that the Soviet Union does not have a good track record in trying cases that have extreme social importance to the Soviet government and the Soviet people? This is something that troubles me, even though I believe, as does Elizabeth Holtzman, that such extradition or deportation would be appropriate in the right case.

A. SVEND ROBINSON: I just want to add one point to the professor's question and that is the existence in the Soviet Union of the ultimate punishment – the death penalty. Fortunately, as far as I am concerned, we in Canada recently decided that we would not reinstate capital punishment. The question must be raised about extraditing to a country that is prepared to execute those who are found guilty, when we, as a nation, have said that we will not use this ultimate weapon.

A. ALLAN RYAN, JR: Frankly, I would have deep misgivings about sending anyone from the United States to the Soviet Union to stand trial in the Soviet Union, when that individual had not undergone a complete and thorough judicial process in the United States. For that reason, I am just as happy that the United States does not have an extradition treaty with the Soviet Union, because extradition is a quite summary procedure, and I place no reliance whatsoever on the Soviet judicial system.

However, in the case of Karl Linnas, who was deported to the Soviet Union, a case that we prosecuted when I was director of the OSI, Mr Linnas had had two complete trials in the United States: denaturalization and deportation. A federal judge found, beyond a reasonable doubt, that Linnas had taken part in the murders of many people at the concentration camp in Estonia of which he was the commandant. Therefore, when he is deported to the Soviet Union, I look upon him and say, you have been found, in effect, guilty in the United States of these crimes by standards of justice that are, to me, unimpeachable. (I would say the same, obviously, if it were Canada that was involved.) So what happens to you in the Soviet Union, sir, is not going to cause me a loss of sleep. That may be a somewhat blunt way of putting it, but I draw a sharp distinction between that situation, which I will defend and encourage, and a situation where people are sent to the Soviet Union without a close examination by a system that affords due process.

Q. My name is Jack Silverstone. I am the executive director of the Canadian Jewish Congress. I have a question for the panel, but particularly for Mr Ryan. Faced with various options for dealing with suspected Nazi war criminals and other war criminals, Ms Holtzman and, I gather, other people in the United States have taken a rather dim view of the Canadian approach of prosecution within Canada, either for philosophical reasons or for the very practical reasons of the difficulty of establishing a case so far away from the site of the original crime and the difficulty of gathering evidence. But I have a question that has been bothering me for quite some time – and I have had some involvement with this issue and it has been a personal dilemma for me. I certainly commend the OSI for its efforts, which have resulted in deportations of some suspected Nazi war criminals. But some, by Ms Holtzman's own estimation, have not been tried at all. She mentioned the *Trifa* case. There's been another one very recently in West Germany. Now, as you have just mentioned, the "reasonable doubt" test, a high standard, would be applied by the American courts, as it would be in Canadian courts. Why, then, criticize the approach of prosecution within Canada or the United States? If the objective is bringing individuals to justice, why not – while rejecting prosecution where it is not appropriate and using extradition or revocation when it may be more appropriate – have, as a general principle, prosecution within the country?

A. ALLAN RYAN, JR: Ms Holtzman can answer that question as to her own views. My views are somewhat different, and I encourage and welcome domestic prosecution if it will lead, swiftly and effectively, to a just result, including a sentence, where guilt is found. I would be delighted to be able, in the United States, to carry out criminal trials and send criminals to jail there. Due to constitutional restraints, I don't think that we are free to do that. The situation in Canada apparently is different. As I said before, I welcome the representations by Minister Hnatyshyn and by the government that it will proceed expeditiously to put criminals on trial and to see that they are sentenced once found guilty. I'm very results oriented. I want to see these people in jail. I'll leave aside the capital-punishment question. I much prefer putting criminals on trial to seeing a situation like that of Bishop Trifa, where he was deported to Portugal and spent the rest of his life lying on the beach. I certainly prefer a trial in Canada to the situation where we have deported a number of people from the US to West Germany, only to find that the government there takes no action whatever. If the alternative to all of that is swift and fair and effective prosecution in Canada, I say absolutely, I fully support that.

A. GREVILLE JANNER: There's another reason for it; it's what Napoleon is alleged to have said when he shot a deserter: "C'est pour décourager les autres!"

A. SVEND ROBINSON: Yes, in that same vein, there's another reason as well, and it was alluded to by Elie Weisel yesterday; the whole question of "memory." I have certainly found that when I've travelled, for example, to the Soviet Union, to Western Europe, and elsewhere, there is a very, very deep memory. But perhaps in Canada it's not as ingrained, particularly among younger people. I think that, for that purpose alone, trials in Canada at which people can witness and talk about what has happened are very, very important.

Q. My name is Leslie Green. I am from the University of Alberta. Two small comments before a question. One, the issue of "why we didn't act" is, I think, becoming redundant, at this conference in particular. We're talking about Nuremberg forty years after. The background and the blame are less important than what we do now and in the future.

The second short comment relates to evidence from Eastern Europe. Nobody has pointed out that the most important evidence in the *Dehring* trial came from Poland.

But what I want to ask of the panellists is this: What is the danger that we might fall into the trap of emotional reaction? That is why I personally believe that the definition in our new legislation is so terribly important, rather than wild allegations of war crimes. Nobody today has attempted to say what they mean by war crimes. The second point I would make in that connection is the definition of the accused. It is so easy to say, I saw him in a camp, therefore he was. It is so easy to say, He was on a platform keeping order, and therefore he was. The point I am making is, is it not essential that from our own point of view, even with war criminals or alleged war criminals, regardless of their nationality, we take extreme care whom we charge, what we charge them with, and the evidence that we bring forward to substantiate that charge? In other words, is it not essential that for the future, and for ourselves, we remember that even they are entitled to justice and the application of the rule of law?

A. GREVILLE JANNER: The answer to the final question is, of course, yes. Nobody is suggesting for a moment anything else, and I'm surprised that it should be suggested by a professor of law that any of us involved with justice or the administration of justice would think that anybody in our decent countries would be prevented from having that justice which they so singly denied to others.

Second, you said that the issue of "why we didn't act" is redundant. It is not redundant. It is very precise in the minds of those who refuse to provide us with the documentation that we need about why and how these people came into our countries in the first place. For some extraordinary reason, in every country, military intelligence is covering up what I regard, without paranoia, as an international conspiracy. Talk to the people concerned with the Waldheim issue and you will discover precisely the difficulties that have been placed in their way because of the hiding of documents – because somebody is trying to cover up, whether it's the Labour government in England or the Tory government in Canada, it doesn't matter. I was a war-crimes investigator as a youngster in Germany in 1948, when they packed up the war-crimes group. I've seen a little of what happened. We were absolutely appalled. There were a very few of us looking for a very large number of war criminals, but still they packed us up. It was a Labour government that did that, to the deep shame of the Labour Party, and they don't want to open up the documents either. Nobody does. It is, I'm afraid, not a matter for lack of concern.

As for the *Dehring* trial, yes, of course, we remember that. And of course, without the evidence of the Soviet Union, Demjanjuk would not be where he is at the moment. Without the evidence from the only place it exists, you cannot prove the case, and of course, Professor, we must prove it.

And, finally, "emotional reaction." We don't make wild allegations, but we don't pretend that we have no emotional reaction. Decent people recognize their emotions and control them and bring them together in order to see that people are brought to justice and that justice is done. They don't ignore the fact that it is an emotional issue for us all.

Q. My name is Sharon Williams. I teach at Osgoode Hall in Toronto. I would like to address my few words to Mr Ryan, if I may. Quite clearly, from what Ms Holtzman and you have said, and from what we all know, the United States has not been able to extradite to the Soviet Union for reasons similar to those of Canada and the United Kingdom. But you have been prepared to deport – as with Mr Linnas, and as would have been the case with Mr Demjanjuk if you hadn't extradited him to Israel. You have alluded to the constitutional problems in prosecuting. Has the United States government ever contemplated trying to prosecute in the United States and overcoming whatever constitutional difficulties you have in order to have, as Justice Minister Hnatyshyn has said in our House of Commons, a "made-at-home" solution, rather than sending people to a country where, potentially, you have doubts, as Professor Sklar mentioned, about the fairness of their criminal-justice system?

A. ALLAN RYAN, JR: Well, don't hold me responsible for trying to describe everything the United States government has ever contemplated. I suspect it has contemplated quite a lot that I don't know about.

On that particular question, I contemplated it to some extent when I took over at OSI, as I did the other alternative of reconvening the Nuremberg tribunals. My conclusion was that, although those are interesting ideas, politically they would not happen, at least not for many years, and I felt that we had to begin with the tools that we had available. There is now some thought in the United States to looking at amending its Criminal Code and preparing the constitutional arguments. I'm all for that, as long as it doesn't distract from the effective prosecutions that are going on now. I wouldn't want to substitute one for the other.

Q. I am a professor of law at the University of Frankfurt. I have a question for Mr Ryan. This is the second time this morning that I have heard that the West German government is not doing anything about war criminals. Can you substantiate that? The business of prosecuting war criminals in West Germany could start only after West Germany got its sovereignty back, in 1955. Since then, there have been hundreds of prosecutions, some successful ones, some less successful ones. I certainly do not pretend that we got everybody who deserved it. Conveying the idea that nothing has been done about it is, I think, utterly unfair. You might know that there is no discretion for German prosecutors to prosecute or not to prosecute; they are under a legal duty to prosecute if there is a case, if there is sufficient evidence. Now, if you send a suspect to Germany when you can't prosecute yourself, and ask that government to make a case of it, this in my view is not enough. So I would appreciate if you could substantiate something about these cases: were there really cases with sufficient evidence?

A. ALLAN RYAN, JR: Let me substantiate it somewhat anecdotally because the record is a long one, both in its strengths and in its weaknesses. One of the times that I was in Bonn, fairly early on, after I became director of OSI, I met with a senior official in the justice ministry to discuss with him the prospects for Germany accepting back deportees or extraditees from the United States, and I was told quite bluntly, and I quote, "Mr Ryan, why should Germany want to import America's Nazi war criminals?" I met approximately a year or so later with a senior official in the West German Embassy in Washington and raised the question again, in the context of a specific case that was then pending, and I was told in no uncertain terms that West Germany had not the slightest interest and would not accept this person.

In the case of Klaus Barbie – and I think it is not well known, although it ought to be – although the Federal Republic had an arrest warrant out for Klaus Barbie for quite some years, when the Bolivians arrested him and decided to extradite him, they went first to Bonn and were told by Bonn that, despite the extradition warrant, Bonn had no interest and did not want Klaus Barbie. At this point, the Bolivians turned to the French.

I will also point out the case of Arthur Rudolph, where the evidence, I think, is overwhelming as to his guilt. He was not prosecuted in the United States because of the restrictions I've referred to earlier, not because of any lack of evidence.

But having pointed out those four anecdotal instances of documentation, it is only fair to say that the West German government, and particularly its documentation office, has been most professional and most co-operative in assisting us with our investigations, and the government has also been quite co-operative in allowing our investigators access to the archives and the universities and the other documentation centres of that country.

I don't wish to suggest that they are somehow being obstructionist. I was simply stating what I think is the unarguable point that, right now, in the eighties, West Germany is out of the war-crimes business and does not want to get back in.

Q. Well, it is, in a way, distressing to hear. I'm not aware of all the details. The thing is, if these people should ever show up in Germany, they had to be prosecuted.

A. ALLAN RYAN, JR: That is not true, sir. It is demonstrably not true. As a former prosecutor, I am most sympathetic to the question of prosecutorial discretion. You simply cannot prosecute anyone who might possibly be guilty. There are limited resources and all the rest. I don't deny the record, both its strengths and its weaknesses, of the Federal Republic of Germany, but I simply cannot accept, if this is what you're saying, that there are no unprosecuted war criminals in West Germany. I know of at least three that we deported ourselves, and I can speak firsthand as to the strength of the evidence against them in those cases. I would have not the slightest hesitation in prosecuting them criminally if the United States had that jurisdiction, or, conversely, if I were a prosecutor in West Germany. The question of non-prosecution is not because the West German prosecutors have any doubts as to the evidence. A decision simply has been made that these people will not be prosecuted. As long as Arthur Rudolph can sit unprosecuted in Hamburg with the evidence that has been compiled and turned over to the West German justice ministry, I simply cannot take seriously any representations that the West German government is pursuing this matter.

Q. Well, if the evidence is what you say, somebody is breaking the law, that's all.

Q. I am Andrij Hluchowecky, the executive director of the Ukrainian Information Bureau in Ottawa. The Deschênes Commission has precipitated a heated debate, which I believe Mr Justice Deschênes can attest to, between various ethnic communities in Canada and over a whole slew of different topics, from the acceptance of Soviet evidence to the establishment of an OSI in Canada. My question is to the panel, but especially to Mr Svend Robinson: What is your appraisal of the East European contribution to the whole debate on war criminals, and have you noticed a distinct deterioration in the relations between the various communities in Canada, and, if so, what is your remedy?

A. SVEND ROBINSON: There is no doubt that, particularly after the establishment of the commission and then during its hearings, there were tensions, to use that word. Some of those tensions were, I think, most regrettable and unfortunate, and there were very serious efforts made by leaders of the various ethnic communities to ease them. I think that we should pay tribute to the leaders of those organizations in their attempts to do that. Unfortunately, as I say, there were certainly lapses, and I'm not going to name individuals who were responsible; I am referring to the ad in the paper that I mentioned earlier and other things, sweeping allegations that have been made. I think, though, that following the tabling of Bill C-71, there was a genuine sense of coming together. I remember vividly the press conference that was held in the House of Commons, and it was pretty rare to have in that room all of the people who had been involved, coming together basically to say yes. If the government is serious in its commitment to bring these people to justice, then we welcome and support this initiative. So, whatever historical tensions and difficulties there may have been, I would hope that they have been put aside and that now we can move forward collectively, to encourage the government to act with all possible haste, to bring these people to justice.

A. GREVILLE JANNER: This is a very important and very sensitive question in every country, because most of the charges concerned war crimes in the Baltic countries, from where many of us who survived the Holocaust actually came. Indeed, in Lithuania, my own family was locked up in a synagogue to which people set fire – and it was not Germans who did it. So, it's very sensitive. It's also sensitive because a tremendous number of people came into all of our countries as refugees, most of them entirely innocent, but some of them not – certainly in the case of the United Kingdom, where members of Waffen SS battalions came in as refugees. So, we have this problem. At the very start of our effort, we decided how to deal with it. We were very lucky, because there was a man called Stephan Terlesky, a Conservative member of Parliament from the Ukraine who became my Joint Secretary of the war crimes group. His attitude was entirely simple. It was this: If a person is a murderer, it doesn't matter which community that person comes from, that person must be brought to justice. But, equally, there must be no question whatever of any sort of campaign which would seek to impugn the good name of the integrity of a community as such, whether it be Ukrainian or Jewish. This is a viewpoint that the Jewish community takes very seriously, because we have suffered because people attack us as a community and not as individuals. We are as sensitive to this, as you are, sir, and I hope that the situation that Svend Robinson described will prevail here and that it will become the position in the United Kingdom and elsewhere. We are all minorities.

Q. Nous avons beaucoup parlé du passé, vous avez éloquemment discuté des problèmes que pose l'application et la poursuite de ces crimes-là dans différents pays et nous avons bien vu, en en discutant, que ces crimes-là ne peuvent pas être poursuivis de la même façon ni avec la même volonté politique dans tous les pays, ce qui cause des problèmes, évidemment.

Nous connaissons également l'absence de volonté politique dans certains pays d'Amérique Latine où il n'existe même pas de loi pour poursuivre les crimes contre l'humanité. Nous connaissons aussi l'escalade de crimes contre l'humanité qui ne sont pas reliés à la Seconde Guerre Mondiale, mais qui existent tous les jours dans le monde et pour cela je pense qu'il serait utile de penser à l'établissement futur d'un forum international, plutôt que de laisser à certains pays le loisir d'adopter des lois nationales pour prévoir la punition des crimes contre l'humanité commis en temps de guerre ou après-guerre. D'ailleurs, quarante ans après Nuremberg, nous savons que l'on peut compter beaucoup plus de crimes depuis la Seconde Guerre Mondiale – des crimes contre l'humanité – qu'il y en a presque eus pendant la guerre elle-même.

Alors, suite à Nuremberg, je pense que beaucoup de monde s'en souvient, un projet de Cour criminelle internationale a été déposé, proposé, par une Commission internationale de juristes. C'était un projet d'avant-garde; c'était également un projet qui visait à éluder les problèmes que cause la définition justement de "crime contre l'humanité" et l'application différente, de volonté politique à volonté politique, de ces notions-là. Or, est-ce que vous pensez, puisque vous êtes de différents pays, qu'il serait plus facile, plus raisonnable et que cela créerait un forum plus uniforme, de traiter des crimes contre l'humanité à travers un forum international?

Et, deuxième question, ne pensez-vous pas que ça règlerait beaucoup des problèmes d'obtention pratique de preuves, que vous avez justement éclaircis aujourd'hui au cours de la discussion?

A. GREVILLE JANNER: If I may take the first part of the question because it is so important. It would be wonderful, wouldn't it, if we could refer these crimes to an international tribunal. Unfortunately, we can't. I was talking to a professor of international law here last night. I sometimes get the feeling that they invent international law for their own purposes because it doesn't really exist, and this is our problem. I was told that they thought that the British government could find a precedent. This is what I want. I want to be able to show that the British government, which is a party to the Genocide Convention, is in breach of international law in not introducing a law to allow people to be charged with genocide if they live within the United Kingdom. I had a most interesting conversation. I would like to appeal – and I'm dead serious – to anybody here who's an international lawyer, which I'm not, to provide me with some sort of brief on this, showing that it is a breach of international law to do so. Otherwise, what is the point of having an international Genocide Convention if there is no way in which you can require signatories to comply with it?

No, no, nobody's prepared to do it. But you see, that is really the answer. When I ask a perfectly straightforward question of a group of international lawyers of vast distinction, you can't actually get down to brass tacks. And I really am worried. The answer to your question is yes, please, let's have an international forum; yes, please, let's deal with it on an international basis. But, as that is not likely to come in our lifetime, let us, in the meanwhile, deal with it nation by nation.

A. SVEND ROBINSON: Oui, théoriquement je suis tout à fait d'accord avec votre suggestion, mais on doit prendre en compte la réalité. La réalité c'est, maintenant, que les tribunaux qui existent au niveau international ne sont pas respectés. C'est-à-dire, par exemple, la Cour internationale de justice à La Haye a pris une décision vis-à-vis les États-Unis au Nicaragua et les États-Unis refusent d'accepter cette décision. Alors, théoriquement, je suis tout à fait d'accord, mais, franchement, je ne crois pas que maintenant ce soit très réaliste, parce que les pays qui sont les plus graves, qui font les choses les plus terribles dans le domaine des droits de la personne, refuseront certainement d'accepter la juridiction d'un tel tribunal.

A. ALLAN RYAN, JR: Your suggestion has great deal of merit, even though I am not personally ready to accept it as being much of an effective solution. At least it would solve one problem, which came to my attention when I was in Israel this summer at the trial of John Demjanjuk, on which the State of Israel has spent an enormous amount of time and money and effort. I was talking to one of the people who has been very closely involved with the prosecution, and I asked the somewhat indiscreet question as to whether Israel would, after this trial, wish to extradite any further war criminals from other countries, and this fellow to whom I was talking looked at me and said, "From now on, if any country wants to extradite a war criminal to Israel, they've got to extradite the prosecutor and the investigators too." So, perhaps, a common tribunal would avoid that, but I concur with Greville Janner, that let's do it first effectively, nation by nation.

Q. I don't think we are going to see it very soon, but I think it's something that has to be foreseen because the world is becoming a global village and if we have to fix problems in terms of environment and economy, we'll also have to join on certain basic subjects like international crimes against humanity.

Q. I am a student. My question concerns the retroactivity of law and I would like to know: Does it change our decisions from emphasizing legal issues to emphasizing issues of retribution?

A. ALLAN RYAN, JR: I was very intrigued with Minister Hnatyshyn's analysis this morning, which is, as I understand it, that, under the Canadian Charter of Rights and Freedoms, a violation of international law is a violation of Canadian law as well, and therefore there's no retroactivity because these crimes were crimes against international law, the customary law of nations, when they were committed. That sounds fine to me – ignorant as I am of Canadian law, it seems to me a good analysis.

Unfortunately, it is not one that we can use in the United States, as Greville Janner suggests. I think that American judges treat international law somewhat in the way that the rest of us treat unidentified flying objects. They've heard rumours that it exists, but they're not quite sure that such rumours ought to be believed. It is unfortunate, but that is the case and, given that the United States Constitution lacks a provision such as the Charter of Rights and Freedoms has, I do not think that there is much hope. I regret that it's that way but I have to say that I think that the retroactivity problem is insuperable under our Constitution.

A. SVEND ROBINSON: Fortunately, in Canada we have the provision of the Charter. Section 11(g) makes it very clear. But we're not dealing with retroactivity and, quite frankly, I've never understood this argument about retroactivity; I mean, as far as I'm concerned, murder is murder, and let's treat it as such.

Papers

RESPONSE TO THE DESCHÊNES COMMISSION OF INQUIRY ON WAR CRIMINALS: AN EMERGENT MYTHOLOGY AND ITS ANTIDOTE
IRWIN COTLER *

AN EMERGENT MYTHOLOGY. May I begin by addressing the issue of Nazi war criminals and the Canadian conscience, and focusing on the attendant "trivialization of justice." In brief, a number of factors have combined to create a new "mythology" about the mandate and meaning of the Deschênes Commission. This emergent mythology may well have the effect of trivializing, if not distorting, the commission's mandate and thereby, albeit inadvertently, prejudicing the understanding of *why* we must do *what* we must do. Indeed, such a mythology might ultimately prejudice the ability, or undermine the will, to do that which the Deschênes Report has recommended to the government.

Myth number one: The commission was created because of allegations which have now been proven false. Therefore, the commission is unnecessary. We have been told – and, indeed, the final week of the commission's public hearings in December 1985, was clouded, if not confused, by this misinformation – that the commission was created under false pretences; and more, that Prime Minister Mulroney was, as it was put in some representations, duped or misled. And so the media carried, and in some instances curried, a false syllogism, which appeared to have a superficially tidy attraction about it. The

* This paper was prepared as a background paper for the conference.

syllogism goes as follows: The commission was created as a result of
the allegations that Mengele may have attempted to enter Canada;
this allegation has now been proven to be false; ergo, there is no
raison d'être for a commission.

In fact, as I sought to point out then and since – and as I find it
necessary to continue to point out – this false syllogism was turning
the issue, and the commission's mandate, on its head. For the
commission was not set up because of the allegations that Mengele
entered Canada; rather, as the prime minister has put it, the
presence of Nazi war criminals in this country is a "moral outrage."

Mengele, as a suspected Nazi war criminal who may have entered
Canada, was not so much the cause as the legitimate investigative
object of this commission's inquiry. Admittedly, paragraph one of
the preamble of the commission's terms of reference suggest that
the allegation about Mengele may have been a catalyst in prompting
the government to do something that ought to have been done
some forty years ago. But Mengele was not just another Nazi war
criminal. He was a metaphor for evil, for those monstrous crimes
of which the prime minister spoke.

In other words, it was the fact of these monstrous crimes, for
which Mengele was a metaphor, the fact that, as paragraph two of
the preamble points out, concern had been expressed that other
Nazi war criminals may have entered Canada and the fact expressed
in paragraph three that "the Government of Canada wishes to adopt
all appropriate measures necessary to ensure that ... war criminals ...
are brought to justice" that this commission was created. If there is
any embarrassment that attaches itself to this commission, it is that
it is forty years late.

Indeed, even if it had never been alleged that Mengele may have
tried to enter Canada, this commission would still be necessary,
unless one wishes to argue that the passage of time and government
inaction can combine to provide immunity from legal process to
suspected Nazi war criminals in Canada.

Myth number two: The time has come to bury the past. It has been alleged
– and, indeed, this is sometimes the unarticulated major premise of
this confused and confusing mythology – that, as the United Kingdom policy put it as early as 1948 "It is now necessary to dispose of
the past." In brief, the allegation is that the time has come to bury
the past, that these suspected Nazi war criminals have now lived
some forty years as quiet neighbours; that it is best to permit these
old men to live out their remaining years in quiet anonymity; that
the Canadian mosaic into which they have been welded should not

be fractured for the rather insignificant conduct of some old men over forty years ago.

This allegation, increasingly made even by those whose memory of the Holocaust may have faded, let alone by those who were indifferent to the Holocaust to begin with or who have no memory of the Holocaust, also has the effect, like myth one, of turning fact and law on their head. For we are not bringing people to justice for what they did or did not do these past forty years. We are bringing them to justice because, simply put, there can be no statute of limitations for the worst crimes in history.

Myth number three: Bringing war criminals to justice is a Jewish revenge issue. We have been told – and, indeed, this is sometimes a corollary to the "Why now, after forty years?" query – that this is essentially "a Jewish revenge issue"; that we should not – to borrow from the characterization found in Cabinet documents obtained under the Access to Information Act – pander to "Jewish revenge"; that the public policy of this country must be set in terms of what is good for Canada and not in terms of what is demanded by the Jews – a not-so-veiled reference to the ugly canard of double loyalty.

Indeed, this "Jewish revenge" characterization was soon stretched, even in these 1962 Cabinet documents, to a notion of "baiting by Jews," leading to the obscene comparison between this "baiting by Jews" and Nazi racism against the Jews. This comparison is particularly odious when one of the objects of this so-called Jewish revenge, from the perspective of the government of the day in 1962, as set forth in these government documents, may well have been Josef Mengele himself, however mistaken that allegation or speculation turned out to be.

The point is, of course – and one regrets that this point still needs to be made – that the issue then, and now, is not revenge but justice; that what is being sought is not an ethnic need for vengeance but a Canadian need – indeed, a Canadian responsibility – for justice; that Canadian Jews, or any other ethnic group in Canada, must be free to petition governments for redress of grievance without fear of being accused of being vengeful or un-Canadian, or worse. And if any group in Canada – be it Jews or Blacks or Muslims or Ukrainians – is ever told that they can't petition government for redress of grievance because this would encourage anti-Semitic sentiment or anti-Black sentiment or anti-Muslim or anti-Ukrainian sentiment, then this would have a chilling effect on free speech. Indeed, it would impugn the integrity of the democratic process as a whole.

Myth number four: This is a quarrel between ethnic groups. We have been told – in a manner which trivializes, if not distorts, the matter and mandate of the commission – that this is nothing more than a private ethnic quarrel between Jews and Ukrainians; that Canada should not be a battleground for historic animosity that originated in Europe but has no place in Canada.

Again, this is to turn history, as well as morality, on its head. For Canada would have a responsibility to bring Nazi war criminals to justice whether or not the victims petitioned it to do so, and whether or not the victims quarrelled amongst themselves as to how it should be done. The legacy of Nuremberg is a universal and Canadian legacy, not a Jewish one. The International Military Tribunal was an Allied creation and not a Jewish conspiracy. Not to bring suspected Nazi war criminals to justice would be a repudiation of what Canadians fought for and died for; indeed, the injunction of "Never again!" while admittedly the fervent plea of Holocaust survivors, is also a Canadian and universal injunction, one that inspired the United Nations Charter and the Universal Declaration of Human Rights.

Myth number five: The inquiry is a collective indictment of an ethnic group. We have been told that this inquiry is nothing more than, or is mainly, a collective indictment of a particular ethnic group, perhaps amounting to a form of group libel. Admittedly, this allegation may well reflect the anguish of the person making it, but it may regrettably end up trivializing, if not distorting, the underlying justice of the commission's mandate.

What begins as a legitimate concern, that groups not be targeted for their ethnicity or libelled as a group (though for others this may be an exculpatory screen, as it has been acknowledged to be in some war-crimes trials) may end up, however inadvertently, itself labelling, if not libelling, the common commitment we all share: a commitment to bring suspected Nazi war criminals to justice with all deliberate speed.

For if audiences are told, as they have been told, that this is a witch hunt against a particular ethnic group or a witch hunt by Jews against Ukrainians, this will have the effect, albeit unintended, of converting an issue of justice and conscience into a perceived ethnic quarrel between Jews and Ukrainians. This line is one which may encourage the development of an anti-Jewish sentiment against Jews whose concern is *not* Ukrainians or any other ethnic group, but rather whose concern is the bringing of individual Nazi war criminals to justice: who are indifferent to the ethnic origin of the offender but are not indifferent to the crime or the criminal.

At the risk of redundance, but lest there be any mistaken inference or doubt, may I repeat, once again, what has always been not only my position or that of the Canadian Jewish Congress, but has also been the position of the commission itself. We eschew, and utterly reject, any notion of collective or group indictment. We condemn as unacceptable and unworthy of the commission's mandate any suggestion of collective indictment of any group in Canada on ethnic or national lines. Our credo is, and always will be: Criminals, not communities; justice, not revenge; individuals, not nationality.

This does not mean that we can or will shrink from tracking the smoking gun to its source, regardless of the ethnic or national origin of the offender. And neither the commission nor any organization should have its representations chilled or inhibited by an allegation that the pursuit of Nazi war criminals in Canada is somehow the pursuit of a particular ethnic group. As I said, we must be utterly indifferent to the ethnic or national origin of the offender, but we cannot be indifferent to – and are very much concerned with – the crime and the criminal.

Myth number six: The inquiry is an exercise in selective discrimination. It should focus on all war criminals, not on Nazi war criminals. We have been told, and at times as a corollary to the previous point, that the inquiry is an exercise in selective discrimination, that it should be concerned with other war criminals or all war criminals, and not just Nazi war criminals. The short and, indeed, factual answer, is that this is the mandate of the commission. But some will say that this abbreviated response, though factual, begs the question, "Why single out Nazi war criminals?"

The point is that we *should* bring all war criminals to justice. Indeed, that is the universal message and ultimate legacy of Nuremberg. It would, however be wrong to argue that if we do not bring all war criminals to justice, we therefore should not be engaged in bringing Nazi war criminals to justice. Rather, I submit, it should be the other way around: if we don't bring Nazi war criminals to justice, we will have no moral or legal standing to bring any other war criminals to justice, now or in the future. By not bringing Nazi war criminals to justice, we will have created a statute of immunity not only for Nazi war criminals in Canada but for all war criminals generally.

It is also necessary to recall that both the Nuremberg trials and the prosecution of suspected Nazi war criminals in other jurisdictions have identified the distinguishable character of Holocaust crimes and cautioned against the trivialization or distortion of racist mass murder. If everything in this universe is characterized as a "holocaust," then nothing is a Holocaust. This is not intended in any manner to trivialize or otherwise distort other instances of international criminality. Rather, it is to recognize the legacy of the Holocaust and the Nuremberg precedent for what it is: a call to all members of the international community to bring Nazi war criminals to justice, to answer for their crimes. And this is precisely what Canada, in concert with the international community, has done consistently at the United Nations since 1946, that is, joined in United Nations General Assembly resolutions calling on all member states to investigate, apprehend, arrest, and bring to justice suspected Nazi war criminals in our midst.

Myth number seven: The inquiry is part of a Soviet-inspired intrigue. We have been told, in a manner which mistakes, if not masks, the mandate of this commission, that this exercise in Canada may well be part of a Soviet-inspired intrigue and that we may be unwitting dupes of a Soviet-orchestrated initiative which has as its objective, *inter alia*, false accusations against Ukrainians, creating a rift between Jews and Ukrainians, and even destabilizing Canada as a whole. This allegation is more flattering to the Soviets than it is reflective of the facts. Moreover, it has the effect, even if not the intent, of impugning not only the *raison d'être* but the *modus operandi* of the commission and its adherents – let alone all those in government, Parliament, and the people of Canada, who are dedicated as Canadians, and not as unwitting Soviet agents, to bringing suspected Nazi war criminals to justice.

This is not to suggest that Canada and Canadians must not be vigilant against any Soviet policy of misinformation or disinformation. But any practice of Soviet misinformation or disinformation is very different from the suggestion that bringing Nazi war criminals to justice is a product of that misinformation or disinformation.

Myth number eight: Use of Soviet-supplied evidence is unjust and may infringe on the Charter. We are told, as a corollary to this previous point, that the use of any Soviet-supplied evidence should not be permitted. As Mr John Sopinka wrote on page 15 of his submission to the commission of May 5, 1986, "The use of Soviet-supplied evidence in the course of any proceedings against Canadian citizens suspected of being Nazi war criminals, whether under the law as it now stands or under any law which you may be in a position to recommend, would be unjust and should not be permitted."

Indeed, there are times when it appears as if the real or the main issue before the Commission of Inquiry on War Criminals is the use of Soviet-supplied evidence, while the question of bringing suspected Nazi war criminals to justice is a derivative or marginal issue. Moreover, we are told by Mr Sopinka on page 17 of his submission that such use of Soviet-supplied evidence is prohibited by sections 7 and 24(2) of the Charter, so that not only is the core issue of bringing Nazi war criminals to justice seemingly marginalized, but this effort now appears to be anti-Charter as well. Indeed, we are sometimes referred, as Mr Sopinka has done on page 16 of his submission, to my own legal brief on the *Sharansky* case and the comments made therein respecting the character of Soviet-supplied evidence.

Invariably then, the question is put not only to me but to the Canadian Jewish Congress: How can you or the Congress impugn Soviet policy respecting Soviet dissidents like Sharansky, including indicting the evidence – and I acknowledge that my legal brief purports to indict the Soviet evidence against Sharansky – yet be prepared to rely upon Soviet-supplied evidence to be used against suspected Nazi war criminals in Canada?

The contradiction is purportedly apparent on its face; yet, it ignores a crucial distinction. The issue is *not* the taking of Soviet evidence by a Soviet court or other legal process, for use in a Soviet legal process, in accordance with Soviet rules of evidence and procedure, against Soviet dissidents residing in the Soviet Union. Rather, the issue is the taking of Soviet evidence by a *Canadian* court or Canadian commission of inquiry for use, if at all, in a *Canadian* legal process, in accordance with *Canadian* rules of evidence and procedure, against suspected Nazi war criminals residing in Canada, who have been named as suspects by a *Canadian* and not by a Soviet commission of inquiry.

I hold no brief for Soviet-supplied evidence in Soviet courts or for the Soviet legal process involving Soviet dissidents. I believe that my concern here is otherwise a matter of public record. But I do have confidence in the Canadian legal process, and I do have confidence in the ability of Canadian courts or other Canadian legal processes to make appropriate judgments respecting the admissibility of such evidence and the weight to be attached to such evidence if admitted. The point has been made succinctly in the summary on page 2 of the Commission's decision of 14 November 1985 concerning foreign evidence:

The Commission has answered the question about going abroad to take evidence in the affirmative, for, among others, the following reasons:

a. The expedience of hearing foreign evidence was foreseen when the Commission was set up and it was left to the Commission's judgment;
b. The Commission must hear all available evidence;
c. Assessment of evidence is a current judicial exercise;
d. Reasons of policy concerning the Soviet legal and political system do not resist critical examination;
e. Two recent West German judgments have based, in part, the convictions of war criminals on Soviet-supplied evidence;
f. A detailed analysis of eighteen American war criminal cases shows that not once has the admissibility of Soviet-supplied evidence been questioned. Its weight depended on factors which varied, as could be expected, from case to case.

And the commission made its decision subject to some basic precautions. Indeed, the Canadian Jewish Congress proposed a list of suggested safeguards or precautions in this regard.

What must be realized, as the commission's decision states on page 5, is that the crimes that are alleged against certain individuals were committed abroad. Documentation and eyewitnesses are scattered in many countries, and the question of "foreign evidence," as the decision put it, cannot be avoided.

And as for the specific issue of Soviet-supplied evidence within the general context of foreign evidence, this characterization, I suggest, is something of a misnomer, if not entirely misleading. I do not propose to repeat in any detail my submissions concerning Soviet evidence made to the commission in October, 1985. I will, however, review the highlights of that submission.

The considerations warranting the use of Soviet-supplied evidence may be summarized as follows:

1 One must go where the evidence is, and because the battleground was in the Soviet Union and Eastern Europe, the evidence happens to be, in part, in the archives of the Soviet Union and Eastern Europe.
2 "Soviet-supplied evidence" may itself be a misnomer. What we are talking about, in fact, is *Nazi* evidence captured by the Soviets and now available in Soviet archives.
3 Many of the eyewitnesses who can provide testimonial evidence are still in the countries where the crimes were committed, and this includes, in the main, the Soviet Union and Eastern Europe.
4 Many of the witnesses are Holocaust survivors, whose exclusion as witnesses would involve a double victimization, as the commission's own decision put it. On the one hand, they had to endure

the horror of the Holocaust; now, they might be told that they cannot testify against the very perpetrators of that Holocaust to which they fell victim. Indeed, this is a particularly cruel indictment of those who may even be trapped in the Soviet Union, who cannot give evidence for the sole fact that they are living in the Soviet Union, even though many of them might otherwise, if permitted to do so, be prepared to emigrate to Canada, Israel, or elsewhere.

If these Holocaust survivors emigrated to Canada, they would be permitted to give evidence in Canada because they would represent the best available eyewitness testimony that we have. Surely this commission should be able to go abroad and take that same evidence from those same eyewitnesses, the only difference being that their present *locus* – maybe even involuntarily – is in the Soviet Union and not in Canada or elsewhere.

5 Soviet-supplied evidence was used and accepted by the courts of Nuremberg and in the *Rauca* case.

6 There is no known instance in Europe or North America of a Soviet-supplied document having been falsified or an Eastern Bloc witness having perjured himself.

7 The use of such Soviet-supplied evidence does not legitimate the Soviet political and legal system. Mr Botiuk, in his submission, quoted from a rather brilliant piece by Robert Wistrich in *Commentary*, called "The New War Against the Jews." Wistrich appropriately indicted and condemned the kind of falsification that is now gaining currency in the Soviet Union that the Zionists collaborated with the Nazis to bring about the Holocaust – another form of Holocaust revisionism that is not as disturbing as Holocaust denial but nonetheless has a particularly defamatory and group libel aspect to it.

It is worth noting that Mr Wistrich has otherwise stated to me his view that Soviet-supplied evidence in relation to suspected Nazi war criminals may well be admissible, with the weight to be attached to it left to be determined by the court or commission involved in the legal proceedings. Mr Wistrich based his view on some of the very considerations that I discussed above.

Certainly, neither Mr Wistrich nor I hold any brief for the Soviet legal system nor any brief for the manner in which trials and other inquiries have been held with respect to Soviet dissidents. But this is utterly distinguishable from the determination by Canadian courts of admissibility or weight of such evidence.

8 Finally, the opposition to the use of Soviet-supplied evidence is somewhat a declaration, albeit again unintended, of non-confi-

dence in the Canadian administration of justice and the ability of Canadian judges to sort out the good from the bad and to give appropriate considerations to matters of weight and admissibility.

As for the use of Soviet-supplied evidence being, as Mr Sopinka put it on page 17 in his submission to the Deschênes Commission, contrary to sections 7 and 24(2) of the Charter, because it would "bring the administration of justice into disrepute," I adopt here the remarks of Mr Justice Deschênes on this point. On page 875 of the decision concerning foreign evidence, the justice writes, "The whole argument is of course predicated on the existence of the defects which have been alleged. That is the Achilles' heel of the argument: the defects cannot be shown to affect the evidence before the evidence has actually been taken. Assuming respect for the Canadian rules, such defects would *never* arise; assuming their disregard, they *may* arise. Either way the argument is *now* premature."

My final comment on this point refers to the allegation that the commission "may be adopting rules and procedures which are, in effect, contrary to the Charter and section 15 in particular." These appear in the course of the written submission of David Kilgour, MP.

In that regard, I quote now from page 874 of the commission's decision, because I believe it has fallout that is otherwise relevant to some of the other factors or considerations that I referred to earlier:

Let it be made clear: This Commission does not pretend to have the right nor does it have the intention "to opt out of our Charter as the highest law of the land."

Let also an unfortunate and serious misunderstanding be corrected: there has never been any question of this Commission lending an ear to "assertions ... made ... by spokesmen for the Soviet government." What is at issue is simply the hearing of people who are alleged to have been witnesses to crimes perpetrated by suspects now living in Canada.

That much being said, a strong argument could be made under s. 15 if one were considering a trial against a Canadian in the Soviet Union under Soviet rules of evidence: this might indeed be "to adopt rules and procedures which are in effect contrary to our Charter." But such is not the case; such is not the purpose of the procedure which is now being contemplated. One must keep in mind that:

  i) this is an inquiry, not a trial;
 ii) this is a Canadian, not a Soviet, inquiry;
iii) this is an inquiry conducted under Canadian, not Soviet, law;

iv) whatever evidence may be collected shall be tested, accepted or rejected on the strength of the Canadian rules of evidence;

v) should a trial eventually take place on Canadian soil, it shall be governed exclusively by Canadian law.

Myth number nine: The Holocaust is a fraud perpetrated on Germans and others. It has been alleged, though never before any of the proceedings of the Deschênes Commission, that there was in fact no Holocaust, that the issue is indeed an invention of Holocaust survivors, who are perpetrating a fraud upon Germans and others in order to falsely collect certain reparations. It is said – and this is one of the more pernicious aspects of this Holocaust denial that is connected to the Nuremberg judgments – that this fraud began in and through the Nuremberg judgments, that, as Mr Zundel put it in his trial, "the Nuremberg judgments are themselves a Jewish invention."

So, within the Holocaust denial movement, we have the statement that, if there are no crimes, because there was no Holocaust, then there can be no criminals; and then there are no suspected Nazi war criminals to be brought to justice in this country. And while – and I repeat – no allegation of this kind has been made to the commission, and certainly would not be made by any of the parties to this commission, it has been heard in this land; indeed, it is a reminder of the Orwellian world that we live in that, as we commemorated the fortieth anniversary of the Holocaust and the liberation of the death camps in 1985, Canada became the international centrepiece for Holocaust denial litigation. As the order-in-council was issued creating this commission, this country was exposed to newspaper headlines at almost the same time, such as "Women dined and danced at Auschwitz, expert witness says," a report of testimony given by a Holocaust denier admitted as an expert witness in the *Zundel* case.

Auschwitz, in effect, was portrayed not as a death camp but as a recreation centre. I suggest that there may well be a connection between the work of the commission and that of the Holocaust denial movement, a connection that was seized upon by Ernst Zundel in his trial. For as Mr Zundel put it, and I alluded to it earlier, "If there are no crimes, there are no criminals; there are no Nazi war criminals that can be brought to justice for crimes that were never committed."

The implications for the commission, for this country, and for the Canadian conscience, are equally clear. If Nazi war criminals are not brought to justice in Canada, there will be those who will say, "You see, if there are no criminals, it must be because there are no crimes."

Having regard, then, to the new mythology, I suggest that it
thereby becomes important not only to reaffirm what we must do,
but also why we must do it; for if we fail to do this and the *raison
d'être* of the commission is not understood or, worse, is misunderstood, it may prejudice the mandate and, in particular, the appreciation and implementation of any recommendations made pursuant
to the mandate.

Accordingly, the time has come – indeed, it has passed – to
demythologize the issue; to avoid its trivialization or distortion; to
appreciate that it is this sense of moral outrage, of affront to
conscience, that guides us. In other words, it is time to de-ethnicize
and depoliticize the issue. This is not a private ethnic quarrel
between Jews and Ukrainians; rather, this is a common commitment
between Jews and Ukrainians, in concert with all Canadians, to bring
Nazi war criminals to justice. This is not a matter of partisan politics,
where political parties might be able to score points by manipulating
at times the sensibilities of some ethnic groups or others; rather, this
issue is the common cause of the Canadian conscience. Bringing
suspected Nazi war criminals to justice is, to paraphrase the parable
of the Ancient Mariner, a matter of the soul of the Canadian people.

THE EMERGENT MYTHOLOGY: ITS ANTIDOTE. To answer in summary
form the question "Why now, after forty years?," I suggest the
following considerations that ought to inspire us in appreciating the
real reason that we must do what we must do. And I would suggest
that this appreciation is the necessary antidote to the emergent
mythology which I have been discussing.

1 *Fidelity to the rule of law.* The most compelling consideration is
   fidelity to the principle of the rule of law. Simply put, murder
   shall not go unpunished; in particular, the murder of innocents
   shall not go unpunished. In a sense, the term "war criminal,"
   albeit a term of legal art, is somewhat misleading, for we are not
   talking, in the main, about the killing of combatants in the
   prosecution of a war, but about the murder of innocents in the
   course of the persecution of a race.
2 *Respect for Canadian citizenship.* Those who misrepresented
   themselves and acquired Canadian citizenship or landed-entry
   or refugee status under false pretences should not be permitted
   to enjoy that citizenship when, in fact, had we known of their
   criminality, they would not even have been admitted to this
   country, let alone have been granted citizenship.
   And let this point be clear: We are not dealing here with any
   benign or innocent misrepresentation of birthplace and the like

in which an immigrant may have engaged. I am referring to the genre of criminality that is the subject matter of the commission's mandate – namely, war crimes and crimes against humanity.

3 *Fidelity to our international obligations.* Ever since the Second World War ended, we have undertaken, both in the United Nations General Assembly and as a signatory to international treaties, to investigate, apprehend, arrest, and bring to justice suspected Nazi war criminals in this country. If we do not do this, we may well be in breach of our international responsibilities, treaty and otherwise.

The commission, in the decision on foreign evidence, made this same point. After referring to the fact that the question of foreign evidence cannot be avoided, the Deschênes Report at page 870 states,

This is especially true in light of the international obligation which Canada has undertaken in its quality of member of the United Nations Organization.

As early as 1946, the General Assembly of the United Nations devoted its third resolution to "Extradition and Punishment of War Criminals," recommending:

that members of the United Nations forthwith take all the necessary measures to cause the arrest of those war criminals who have been responsible for or have taken a consenting part in the above crimes, and to cause them to be sent back to the countries in which their abominable deeds were done, in order that they may be judged and punished according to the laws of those countries.

In 1947, the General Assembly again recommended that "members of the United Nations continue with unabated energy to carry out their responsibilities as regards the surrender and trial of war criminals."

The Deschênes Report then refers to at least five further resolutions to the same effect that were adopted by the General Assembly from 1969 to 1973. The Deschênes Report also refers to an international convention indicative of the thinking in the international community. That convention is the 1968 Convention on the Non-applicability of Statutory Limitations to War Crimes and Crimes Against Humanity, which provides for the lifting of statutory limitations with respect to war crimes and crimes against humanity.

To this might also be added that, in 1979, during the debate in the West German Bundestag on the issue of the abolition of statutes of limitations in West Germany, Canada recommended through its then-secretary of state for external affairs, Don Jamieson, that the West German government abolish its statute of limitations on the grounds "that there can be no statute of limitations for the worst crimes in our history." Surely, we can do no less here in Canada than that which we have recommended to the West German government in 1979 as part of its international framework of responsibilities.

4 *Fidelity to Holocaust remembrance.* This fourth point, and it is not an unimportant one, is one that I continue to experience whenever I am in the company of Holocaust survivors, Jewish or non-Jewish, and it is fidelity to Holocaust remembrance. We have a responsibility to speak on behalf of those victims who died and of those Canadians who fought the Nazis. At a time when neo-Nazism appears to be rearing its ugly head again, and at a time, as I indicated above, when there are those who are even saying that the Holocaust never occurred, not to bring suspected Nazi war criminals to justice may well have the effect, however inadvertent, of vindicating the old Nazis and encouraging the new ones.

5 *Fidelity to our children.* Finally, the legacy of Nuremberg, of "Never again!," is both an exhortation to justice and, indeed, a warning against injustice.

THE NAZI WAR CRIMINAL AS IMMIGRANT
*DAVID MATAS**

Suppose you wanted to set up a policy to keep war criminals out of Canada. There are any number of different steps you would want to take. I have eleven of them to suggest:

1 Prohibit the admission of war criminals.
2 Set up a screening procedure to determine who is and who is not a war criminal.
3 Put every applicant to Canada through the screening procedure.

* Mr Matas's luncheon talk was an abbreviated version of the paper that he prepared for the conference. The paper is presented here in its original form.

    For more detailed treatment of this subject see S. Charendoff, "Closing Submission to the Deschênes Commisison of Inquiry on Behalf of the League for Human Rights of B'nai Brith Canada," 5 May 1986, and I. Cotler, "Submissions and Recommendations of the Canadian Jewish Congress to the Commission of Inquiry on War Criminals," 10 July 1985.

4 Train screening officials in who is a war criminal and how to detect such a person.
5 Circulate lists of known war criminals to those who do the screening.
6 Have those involved in screening examine all relevant documents and interview all relevant witnesses.
7 Ask applicants if they are war criminals.
8 Do not admit anyone who fails the screening procedure.
9 Keep the admission records.
10 Investigate any admission errors that were made.
11 Correct any errors that were made and expel war criminals wrongly admitted.

That is a pretty common sense list of what to do. There are no doubt other elements that could be added to the list, which is not meant to be comprehensive. What is significant about this list is that, when it came to Canada keeping Nazi war criminals out, the government did none of the above. It did not prohibit their entry. It did not set up a screening procedure, and so on. What I want to do today is go through that list and show, item by item, how Canada failed to meet these requirements.

The first requirement mentioned was prohibiting entry of war criminals. To this day, Canada does not prohibit the admission of war criminals. The Immigration Act contains a number of prohibited classes,[1] but "war criminal" is not one of them. The Refugee Convention excludes war criminals from the refugee definition.[2] When Canada legislated the refugee definition, in the Immigration Act, Parliament did not include the exemption for war criminals.[3] What Canada did do was exclude enemy aliens,[4] Nazis,[5] and members of the German military.[6] If these exclusions had remained in place, it would have been unnecessary to prohibit Nazi war criminals as such, for they would have been caught within the larger group. However, all of these more general restrictions were progressively relaxed.

Nazi war crimes were committed everywhere the Nazis went. There was collaboration of local populations everywhere, except Denmark, in the Holocaust.[7] A nationality exclusion to cover all Nazi war criminals would have had to cover not only every enemy alien, but also nationals of allied countries occupied by the Nazis. There never was such an exclusion. The enemy alien exclusion itself was narrowed over time.

The nationals of Finland, Hungary, Italy, and Rumania were removed from the enemy alien list in 1947.[8] The nationals of Austria were removed in 1948.[9] German nationals who were immediate relatives of Canadians could enter starting in March, 1950.[10] All German nationals could enter starting in November, 1950.[11] The enemy alien exclusion was itself revoked in 1952.[12]

Canada had no criteria for rejecting Nazis or the German military until 1949, four years after the war ended.[13] The Nazi prohibition, prohibiting those who were members of the Nazi party, lasted less than one year from the date of its imposition, to 1950.[14] The 1949 prohibition included the SS, the German Wehrmacht, and collaborators. The first relaxation was in 1951, from non-German Waffen SS conscripted or forced to enlist after 1942.[15] Also excepted in 1953 were Waffen SS German nationals under eighteen at the time of conscription and *Volksdeutsche*, ethnic Germans, conscripted under duress.[16] The general ban for all German military and SS units was lifted in 1956, for cases of "exceptional merit" or where there were close relatives in Canada.[17] Finally, in 1962, the blanket prohibition was withdrawn, even for those without exceptional merit and without close relatives in Canada.[18] There remained in effect an exclusion policy for those "implicated in the taking of life or engaged in activities connected with forced labour and concentration camps."[19] This policy, however, was reflected neither in the statute nor in the regulations.

At no time were police auxiliary units prohibited as such from entry. Aside from the *Einsatzgruppen* and the SS themselves, the units most directly involved in the Holocaust were the police auxiliary of the Nazis.[20] The police auxiliaries were collaborating forces of the local populations. They were not part of the German military. They were actively involved in rounding up Jews for the concentration camps and the death camps. They participated in executions themselves. Yet, as units, Canadian immigration ignored them.

The only statutory prohibition that came close to covering the Nazi war criminal phenomenon was the prohibition against security risks. At least, that was the prohibition that was used.[21] However, it was highly artificial to look at Nazi war criminals as security risks, since the Nazis had already lost the war and, in fact, posed no security threat at all. They could even, indeed, be viewed as security assets, because they were anti-communist and possible sources of information about Eastern Europe.

The next step I suggested for a system to prevent the entry of war criminals was to establish a screening procedure to determine who was and who was not a war criminal. Again, that did not happen for Nazi war criminals. From 1945 to 1948, Canada did no screening at all.[22] Anyone who came to Canada during that period came without a security screening.

From 1948 on, screening was required, but it was a deferential form of screening. Canada did not do its own investigations.[23] Instead, it relied on foreign sources, chiefly the British and the US,[24] and on the International Refugee Organization[25] and the Berlin Documentation Centre.[26]

Both the British[27] and the Americans[28] had amateurish, ineffective screening systems. Those doing the interviewing had no training and were processing large numbers of people. The interviewers were often German nationals themselves. They were told to look for security risks, but not for war criminals. The Americans relied on the Gehlen Organization, run by a former Nazi intelligence chief.

During the Deschênes Commission hearings, a witness testified that a friendly foreign power had knowingly duped Canada into admitting immigrants by providing them with false documents.[29] When Canada was relying on foreigners alone for its own screening, it was easily duped. It had no independent check on those whom the foreigners approved.

The International Refugee Organization (IRO) investigations were superficial and corrupt.[30] Some of those doing screening for the IRO were former collaborators. If a person the IRO was trying to place was rejected by one country because of his record, the IRO would sometimes conceal that fact and attempt to have him accepted by another country.[31]

The Berlin Documentation Centre contained information about German and Austrian war criminals, but not about war crimes from other areas.[32] As well, there was a gap in the Berlin Documentation Centre records, because the Soviets had seized some Nazi records; they did not know what was missing.[33]

The third suggestion I made for an effective system to keep out war criminals was to put every applicant through the screening procedure. Yet again, this did not happen. The Canadian screening procedure, such as it was, was not a procedure to which every applicant to Canada had to submit himself.

From the day the war ended, security screening was waived for women with children, unaccompanied by a male, for men over sixty-five, for women over sixty, for clergy, and for immigrants under eighteen. Screening was not carried out for immigrants who came from countries where visas were not required.[34]

Because of limited facilities, not everyone who was supposed to go through security screening actually went through such screening. The only ones actually subjected to security clearance were Eastern Europeans or those who were suspect for some reason. Others went through the fourteen-day procedure. If a visa officer did not receive an adverse report from the Royal Canadian Mounted Police within fourteen days of having given the application to the RCMP, the officer was free to issue the visa. In some cases, the RCMP did not even have a chance to look at the case for a full fourteen days.[35]

In 1955, screening exemption and waiver categories were expanded to include close relatives of Canadians. That meant spouses, children of any age, and parents. In 1957, the security-screening waiver was broadened; it now covered immigrants from Poland and siblings of Canadians, together with their spouses and children.[36]

Step number four in the system I proposed to keep war criminals out of Canada was to train officials in who is a war criminal and how to detect such a person. That, too, did not happen. The officials who did the security screening had no war-history background. They had no specialized training in Canada before they went to Europe. The officers involved in security screening were RCMP officers with a police background.[37]

Testimony before the Deschênes Commission shows that screening officers were not instructed in what the term "war criminal" signified, and they were uncertain what it meant.[38] One of the striking facets of the testimony about Mengele at the Deschênes Commission was that the Canadian who was the visa officer in West Germany at the time when inquiries were being made, in 1962, did not himself know who Mengele was.[39]

Step number five that I suggested was to circulate lists of known war criminals to those who do the screening. Such lists were compiled, and the government of Canada had them. However, they were never sent to the Canadian visa officers overseas!

Canada had the "Crowcass" list, prepared by the central registry of war crimes and security suspects, as well as the United Nations War Crimes Commission list. These lists just accumulated dust in basements. They were compared with lists of prisoners of war held by Canada, but they were never used for immigration purposes. Nor was an attempt ever made by immigration officials to have them used for screening; those posted abroad did not even know of their existence.[40]

An obvious way to check to see if a person applying to come to Canada was a war criminal was to see if his name was on one of the war-criminal lists. That was never done. To this day, it is still not done for applicants applying to come to Canada. Nor are people who entered previously being checked against these lists. The number of admissions over the last forty years is now too large for retroactive checking to be done easily.

The next suggestion I made was to have those involved in screening check all possible documents and examine all possible witnesses. Canadian security screening, as I said, was deferential, relying on others to do actual investigations. Canada contacted friendly foreign powers. It did not contact hostile foreign powers. Eastern European governments were never contacted. Information about Eastern European war criminals was and is in the hands of Eastern European governments. Yet Canada never asked those governments what information they had.[41]

Soviet forces, when they replaced the Nazi forces retreating from Eastern Europe, came into possession of large volumes of Nazi documents about the Holocaust. All of the Nazi death camps were in Eastern Europe. Surviving witnesses and victims live throughout Eastern Europe. Canada refused, because of cold-war politics, to talk to any of these people and to look at any of these documents.

Instead, Canada developed a "two-year" rule. The RCMP required immigrants from Eastern Europe to reside at least two years in Western Europe before they could come to Canada. In theory, the two years were to allow undesirable tendencies to manifest themselves. However, war criminals did not re-enact their war crimes in the displaced-persons camps. As a screening device, the two-year rule was totally useless. Witnesses at the Deschênes Commission could not think of one case in which the two-year delay led to the turning up of information about an immigrant.[42]

The seventh step I suggested was to ask applicants if they were war criminals. Such a question is unlikely to produce a positive response. A person who has murdered innocents is unlikely to hesitate about lying. However, the questioning does, nonetheless, serve a purpose. If a person is asked the question and lies, he can subsequently be deported for obtaining entry by fraud. If no questions are asked, proving entry by fraud becomes, at best, difficult.

Immigration forms and documents did not ask direct questions about membership in the Nazi Party[43] or actual activities during the war.[44] The application form was changed in 1953 to include military records. Even these forms had no direct questions regarding a person's war duties – what he actually did, as opposed to what his position was.[45] The forms did not ask if the person was a concentration camp guard.[46] Evidence was given at the Deschênes Commission that interviewing officers asked these questions orally, during interviews, even though they were not on the form.[47]

The eighth step I suggested was not to admit anyone who failed the screening process. Yet that happened all the time, and in all sorts of ways. Testimony before the Deschênes Commission showed

that the Minister of Immigration had the power to override a
security rejection – and that power was used. Minister's permits were
granted to overcome security-test failures.[48]

In some cases, an override was not even necessary. Immigration
officials convinced the RCMP, which did the security checks, to
withdraw its security objections, and persons were processed as if
they had passed security. Sometimes the withdrawal occurred
because of the progressive relaxation in the criteria for screening.
People rejected under the old criteria were subsequently admitted
under the new. What that meant was that the earlier, tighter criteria
were not even effective in keeping out the people who had applied
when the criteria were in place. The applicants just re-applied when
the criteria were relaxed, and they were admitted.[49]

The most egregious example of a government override was the
orders-in-council passed for a number of Petainists. Petain was the
head of the French government that had collaborated with the Nazis
during the Second World War. Some of these Nazi collaborators
entered Canada after the war under false names, as visitors, and were
ordered deported. Orders-in-Council were passed allowing them to
stay.[50] Count Jacques de Bernonville, Klaus Barbie's right-hand man,
came to Canada after the war, and remained until 1951.[51]

The ninth suggestion I made was to keep the admission records.
The value of the records is to identify the applicants, to locate them,
and, if fraud was used to obtain entry, to prove fraud. Canada
routinely destroyed completed application forms for immigration.
The typical retention period was two years.[52] Application forms were
destroyed whether the applicant was rejected or accepted.[53] The files
could have been microfilmed. That is what the US did. But the
Canadian files were not.[54]

The most dramatic destruction was that which occurred in headquarters in 1982. A group of files that had been accumulating since
the war was destroyed all at once in 1982, in the midst of the *Rauca*
case, the one Nazi war crimes extradition Canada has seen.[55] This
destruction took place without any attempt to determine whether
the files could be of use in a search for Nazi war criminals.[56] When
the *Toronto Star* asked for the immigration records of the Petainist
collaborators, the files could not be found. They had simply disappeared.[57]

There are some records that remain – landing records, the ships'
manifests. The records that were lost would have added immeasurably to the effort to bring Nazi war criminals to justice.

The tenth suggestion I made was to investigate any admission
errors that were made. Unbelievably, Canada had a policy of non-

investigation. The RCMP, in 1962, articulated what had been, up until then, government policy. Its manual said that unless otherwise indicated, investigations into allegations of war crimes "are not" to be conducted by the force. Officers were told that when a complaint was received, the informant should be told to contact External Affairs. The only concession the manual made was to say that the information might be of interest from the immigration and security and intelligence aspects, and further inquiries might be feasible. The RCMP warned, however, that the inquiry could not be for the purpose of determining whether the person was responsible for a war crime.[58]

This policy was redrafted over the years, but it was not completely reversed until after Robert Kaplan became solicitor general, in 1980. Mr Kaplan rewrote the RCMP manual policy to state, "Upon receipt of information that a suggested war criminal is in Canada, an investigation shall be conducted to substantiate the information."[59]

The final suggestion I had was to correct any errors that were made and to expel war criminals wrongly admitted. The Canadian position has been that that was legally impossible. Once a person was admitted in error, nothing could be done.[60] The RCMP policy of non-investigation I just quoted to you justified itself by stating that Canadian courts have no jurisdiction over war crimes.

In 1983, Mark MacGuigan, the minister of justice, wrote to Robert Kaplan, then solicitor general, that there were a number of serious legal hurdles standing in the way of revocation of citizenship and deportation from Canada of suspected Nazi war criminals. He said that the Crown would have to clear all the hurdles in order to succeed, and that the difficulties of doing so should not be underestimated.[61]

If one thing can be said for the government, it is that it has not underestimated the difficulties of legal success against Nazi war criminals. No revocation of citizenship proceedings has ever been launched. No deportation proceedings have ever been launched. The government's fear of failure has all been hypothetical.

CONCLUSION

I do not believe that the Canadian government purposely devised a scheme to admit Nazi war criminals to Canada and keep them here. However, if the government did, in fact, want to devise a scheme to admit Nazi war criminals to Canada, there is little it would have had to do differently. Virtually every single common-sense precaution one could take to keep Nazi war criminals out was omitted. Virtually every procedure one could think of that would allow them to enter and stay was used.

The slipshod, negligent system does not mean that we indeed have large numbers of Nazi war criminals in Canada. The exact number of Nazi war criminals that entered Canada is something we will never be able to prove with certainty, given the passage of time, the fading of memories, the destruction of records. It would hardly be surprising, in light of Canadian procedures, if the numbers were indeed large.

The *Rauca* case illustrates the failings of the system. Albert Helmut Rauca was a major war criminal; he entered Canada in 1950. He was extradited to West Germany in 1983, thirty-three years after entry, for trial there for his crimes. Yet he had entered Canada under his own name, with a slight variation in the spelling: "Rauka." There was a file against him in the Berlin Document Centre. He lived in Canada, as a citizen, with a driver's licence, a passport, medicare, and eventually an old-age pension, all under his own name. Yet he was not detected until 1982. He was extradited for the murder of eleven thousand five hundred people.[62] If someone like that could enter Canada with ease, how many other war criminals entered, whose murders were perhaps in the hundreds rather than the thousands, and who attempted to disguise their identities?

NOTES

1 1976–77 Statutes of Canada, Section 19.
2 Convention relating to the Status of Refugees, Article 1 F (a).
3 Section 2 (1), "Convention refugee."
4 P.C. 1373, 9 April 1946.
5 O'Leary testimony, Commission of Inquiry on War Criminals (hereinafter referred to as "Commission"), Vol. V, p. 644, line 22; Exhibit P-35, Commission, "Evolution of Policy and Procedures Security Screening 1945–1957" (hereinafter referred to as the "Black Book") Tab 16, memo of 7 February 1949 from Laval Fortier, Assistant Commissioner of Immigration.
6 Ibid.
7 Theodore S. Hamerow, "The Hidden Holocaust," *Commentary*, March 1985, p. 32.
8 P.C. 4850, 26 Nov. 1947.
9 Black Book, Tab 12, Circular No. 42A, 12 Mar. 1948.
10 SOR /50–117, P.C. 1606, Canada Gazette, Part II, p. 518.
11 SOR /50–424, P.C. 4364, Canada Gazette, Part II, p. 1286.
12 SOR /52–341, P.C. 3869, Canada Gazette, Part II, p. 726.

13 See note 5.
14 Black Book, Tab 22, memo entitled "Security," 1 Dec. 1950.
15 Black Book, Tab 25, Immigration memo from Deputy Minister, 9 July 1951.
16 Black Book, Tab 31, letter dated 19 June 1953 to officer in charge at Karlsruhe.
17 Black Book, Tab I, memo from Chief, Operations Division, Immigration Branch to "Posts Abroad," 21 Mar. 1956.
18 Black Book, Tab P, "Criteria for rejection of independent applicants on security grounds."
19 Ibid.
20 See note 7.
21 Kelly testimony, Commission, Vol. VII, pp. 950–1.
22 Robillard testimony, Commission, Vol. XI, p. 1305.
23 Greening testimony, Commission, Vol. VII, p. 1056.
24 Kelly testimony, Commission, Vol. VII, p. 933.
25 Robillard testimony, Commission, Vol. XI, pp. 1346–7.
26 Greening testimony, Commission, Vol. VIII, p. 1012.
27 Tom Bower, *The Pledge Betrayed* (NY: Doubleday, 1981).
28 Allan A. Ryan, Jr., *Quiet Neighbours: Prosecuting Nazi War Criminals in America* (San Diego: Harcourt Brace Jovanovich 1984).
29 Kelly testimony, Commission, Vol. VII, pp. 922–5.
30 Ryan, p. 20.
31 Minutes of Security Panel Meeting, 30 Jan. 1947, Annex "A," p. 6.
32 Ryan, *Quiet Neighbors*, p. 22.
33 See note 26.
34 Black Book, Tab N, "Security Examination of Immigrants," p. 1.
35 Ibid., p. 2.
36 Ibid., p. 3.
37 Black Book, Tab L, memo from Cologne office to Acting Chief of Operations, 24 Sept. 1957.
38 Greening testimony, Commission, Volume VIII, p. 1004, line 29; Kelly testimony, Commission, Vol. VII, p. 913.
39 Bailey testimony, Commission, Vol. XXII, p. 3183.
40 Kelly testimony, Commission, Vol. VII, pp. 913–14; Greening testimony Commission, Vol. VIII, p. 1003.
41 Greening testimony, Commission, Vol. VII, pp. 1064–5.
42 Greening testimony, Commission, Vol. VIII, p. 1065; Kelly testimony, Commission, Vol. VII, p. 934.
43 O'Leary testimony, Commission, Vol. VI, p. 756.
44 O'Leary testimony, Commission, Vol. V, pp. 651–2.
45 O'Leary testimony, Commission, Vol. VI, p. 757.
46 O'Leary testimony, Commission, Vol. VI, p. 769.

47 Robillard testimony, Commission, Vol. XI, p. 1338; Greening testimony, Commission, Vol. VIII, p. 1052; McCordick testimony, Commission, Vol. XX, pp. 2504–5.

48 Greening testimony, Commission, Vol. VIII, pp. 1076–7.

49 Black Book, Tab 24, memo from W. H. Hickman, Security Section, to P.T. Baldwin, Chief Admission Division, 17 May 1951, pp. 1–3.

50 House of Commons Debates, 22 Feb. 1949, pp. 791–7; 9 Dec. 1949, pp. 3033–41.

51 *Globe and Mail,* 11 Feb. 1983.

52 Exhibit P-47, Commission, T.B. minutes 160481 dated 2 June 1936, and T.B. minutes 260530 dated 16 March 1944; Hayward testimony, Vol. X, p. 1184; Exhibit P-48, Administration – Retirement of Records, Appendix A, s 3 (c).

53 O'Leary testimony, Commission, Vol. VI, pp. 743–4.

54 Sabourin testimony, Commission, Vol. X, p. 1229.

55 Kaplan testimony, Commission, Vol. XX, p. 2614.

56 Cook testimony, Commission, Vol. XXII, p. 2986; Bourgault testimony, Commission, Vol. XXII, p. 3015; Mallen testimony, Commission, Vol. XXII, p. 3044; Bertrand testimony, Commission, Vol. XXII, p. 3073; Lebeau testimony, Commission, Vol. XXII, p. 3091; Pommainville testimony, Commission, Vol. XXII, p. 3125.

57 *Winnipeg Free Press,* 26 Dec. 1985.

58 Exhibit P-38, Commission, Brief of RCMP Policy, Appendix A, Sept. 1962.

59 Ibid., Appendix F, 82-04-21, K, 8, 6, p. 1–2.

60 Exhibit P-77, Commission, "Alleged War Criminals in Canada."

61 Letter dated 8 Dec. 1983, p. 11.

62 Sol Littman, *War Criminals on Trial: The Rauca Case* (Toronto: Lester and Orpen Dennys 1983).

Panel Three:
The United Nations and
Human Rights Forty Years Later

Chair

THE HONOURABLE ROSALIE ABELLA

I want to open the session by talking about what an important article of faith the United Nations was to many of us. To try to explain why, I therefore ask you to indulge in a bit of a solipsistic analysis.

Nuremberg and I were born in the same year and in the same country. Both of us came from the experience of the Holocaust and, it can be argued, both of us represent a kind of revenge. Let me try to explain to you what happens to a Jewish sensibility developed in the overwhelming shadow of Nuremberg's morality. You could, as some have, react with a numbing fear and horror and grow protective layers of indifference through which injustices, and the pain they create, cannot penetrate. Or, as most of us did, growing up Jewish and being brought up to avenge the unspeakable, you could develop a searing passion for human rights and the need for outspoken courage in its development and maintenance.

We had learned from spiritual mentors like Wallenberg that individuals can make a difference and from our own histories that they should. My generation boasts many individuals who increasingly left their seats in the audience where, as children, they had been witnessing the universe unfold, not always as it should, and entered the arena to take their place as articulate warriors for fairness in human rights. We knew that individuals mattered.

And we had learned from Nuremberg that a collective international will can be effective in promulgating and enforcing minimum standards below which civilized societies would not be permitted to fall. And so, knowing that one person can make a difference, and

knowing that the international community is capable of being sufficiently outraged to translate political will into political and legal
censure, my generation watched the birth and development of the
United Nations with hyperbolic hope to see if one institution could
make a difference.

Rather than sense, with Hannah Arendt, that the evil of the
Second World War was a progenitor of banality toward gradations
of injustice, my generation became, if anything, overly conscious that
we should never be anaesthetized to human-rights evils and that
each violation called for urgent redress. But we were not unmindful
that behind the Nuremberg curtain were relics of indifference and
insensitivity from the very players who wrote the script, directed the
actors, and produced the morality play that Nuremberg became.
Had they learned, we wondered, aggressive respect for human dignity from Nuremberg, and therefore created a United Nations to
demonstrate the determination never to permit its antecedents to
recur, or was the United Nations created simply as an expedient
repository, to give the appearance of rhetorical democracy, of
international vigilance?

As we grew up, my Nuremberg generation had a tenaciously
exaggerated hope for the United Nations, but it has regrettably been
reduced to a more wistfully realistic one. And we are left to wonder,
frankly, why this one institution, whose historical tutors were
Nuremberg and genocide, has not embraced the lessons from which
it sprang, to make more of a difference.

Perhaps the expectations of my generation were unfairly high, but
childhood, after all, is when nothing appears beyond your grasp and
all good things seem possible. And for a childhood spawned by
Nuremberg, a childhood spawned from times when so little good
seemed possible and the impossible had actually occurred, we needed to feel that our past had conclusively ended and was not part of
an international pattern. And so, we turned to the United Nations,
to human rights advocacy, and to activity as irritants to indifference.

And therein lies the importance of this panel. What can we fairly
expect the United Nations to do, and what is there about its record
that feeds the confidence that it can do it?

In 1945, Professor Ferencz was involved in the liberation of the
concentration camps, and in 1946 he became a prosecutor at
Nuremberg. He was executive general counsel of the Nuremberg
Military Tribunal and chief prosecutor of the SS *Einsatzgruppen* trial.
He developed, first in Germany and then internationally, restitution
centres for those who had been displaced by the Second World War.

He is currently a professor of international law at Pace University School of Law. He has written numerous books on the need to develop mechanisms for the maintenance of peace and the prevention of a Third World War.

Speaker

PROFESSOR BENJAMIN FERENCZ

What I will try to do in the course of the twenty minutes that I am allotted is to solve all the problems in the world – but nothing more. And I will try to put this in the framework of what we have been considering at this very fascinating conference.

Our purpose today is to understand the significance of Nuremberg. I am the only one here, as far as I know, who was at Nuremberg, and so I feel I have some obligation to tell you a little bit about that, and to see how it relates to human rights, to what the United Nations is doing, and also to the concept with which we began: Elie Wiesel's warning to remember the past, lest his past be your future. And, throughout, we must also keep in mind the inspiration of Raoul Wallenberg, one person who dared to do what was right.

Within that framework, let me begin by describing some of my own background and experience. I want to describe what Nuremberg meant to us at the time, what it has meant in the interim, and, as I look back upon it forty years later, what its significance is today.

My involvement began during the war, even a bit before the war. It goes back to my days as a law student. It happened that one of the things I did to work my way through law school was to do research for one of my professors who was writing a book on war crimes. As soon as I got out of the Harvard Law School, I was engaged as a private in the artillery. (The army immediately recognized my talents. I was in the supply room, to be exact – I could not type.) I fought in all the campaigns in Europe. When we landed in Normandy Beach, for everybody else the water was up to the waist – for me the water was up to my neck!

Somehow, I managed to survive. As we began to invade Germany and France, they plucked me out of the artillery and sent me to General Patton's headquarters with the assignment of helping to set up a war crimes division. The Americans had promised that there would be a war crimes program.

So my war-crimes experience began in those early days. Soon, my assignment was to go into the concentration camps as they were being liberated, in order to try to capture the criminals and then to prepare for subsequent trials. I will not go into all of the details of what I saw and experienced in the concentration camps. You have been through quite an emotionally overwhelming experience just listening to Elie Wiesel and watching his suffering.

And I had a similar experience, of course. I was really a witness; the others, like Elie Wiesel, were the victims and the survivors. This experience certainly had an impact upon my subsequent life; in fact, it has had an impact on everything that I have done since then.

When the war was over and the Nuremberg trials began, I was recruited to go back as a civilian with the Department of the Army and to help in the war crimes prosecutions. I became the chief prosecutor of the largest murder trial in history. It was the trial of the *Einsatzgruppen* – we could not translate their name – the special extermination squads that had murdered over one million people. They were two thousand men who, for about two years, did nothing else but march their victims out into the woods and machine-gun them and drop them into a ditch. They did that with the help of the local militia, the Latvians, the Lithuanians, the Ukrainians, and the local police. We captured their daily reports. We picked twenty–two defendants out of the two thousand or so who were engaged in those mass murders and put them on trial.

The question may be asked, Why were only twenty-two men tried? In Canada, forty years later, you are still finding some of these people. We had them! Why did we not try them then? Well, the reason we tried twenty-two and not twenty-three men was the ridiculous reason that there were only twenty-two seats in the dock. Does this sound incredible? It is the truth. We were under the pressure of time to move forward, to get the trials going.

The *Einsatzgruppen* case was one of the subsequent trials. Nuremberg did not consist only of the International Military Tribunal; there were a dozen trials at Nuremberg subsequent to that, at which we tried the next echelon of German government – the SS, the generals and industrialists, the doctors and lawyers – all of whom had perverted their sense of justice.

What were we trying to do? Was it a matter of just punishing the guilty? In that case, to pick out twenty-two would have been rather absurd. We had something more in mind. First, of course, we wanted to establish a historical record. I should say that the very question of whether we should have trials was a big issue. At one time, the British, noted for their fair play, decided that instead of trials it would be better to just take the German leaders out and shoot them. The Russians, of course, would have gone along with that very eagerly, because they never did quite understand why we needed trials. At one time, even Roosevelt had agreed to that. But subsequently, under the influence of some very good lawyers, the United States was persuaded to take the position – and it finally came to be accepted by all the powers – that we should have trials. If you decide to shoot people, the question becomes, Whom are you going to shoot, and when do you stop shooting?

So it was decided that there would be trials. It was decided that we would give them, as Justice Jackson, the chief American prosecutor, said, "the kind of trial which they, in the days of their pomp and power, never gave to any man." And we did. The courtroom was open to the world. Every word that was said in that courtroom was recorded in German and English, and everyone could watch.

My instructions were, and my practice was, to give every single piece of evidence that I had to the defence counsel – and the defence counsel outnumbered us twenty to one – so that they could prepare for trial. It was the fairest possible type of trial. Some of you have raised the question about trying persons for crimes that were legislated *ex post facto*, and some have also noted that this was the first time that there was a trial by the victors over the vanquished. These are fair questions. But if you study the development and evolution of the law of war crimes, you will see that it was not the first time that these issues were faced. These issues were faced after the First World War, and at that time people had the same debate: Will there be an international trial, and who will try them? After the First World War, it was decided not to try the German head of state because aggression had not yet been declared a crime and he had not yet been warned that he might be put on trial for that offence. But, they warned, the next time around it would be different. There were a number of warnings given in the course of the earliest days of the war, when the heads of state of all the Axis powers were warned that they would be brought to justice. So it was not quite as *ex post facto* as it would seem to someone who was not familiar with the history or the evolution of the problem, or with the concept that, at a certain point, mass criminals, no matter what their status, would be brought to trial.

The question remains: Why a trial by the Allies? Well, it is regrettable that there was no real choice. It would have been preferable had there been an international tribunal of persons who were completely neutral. But it was very difficult in those days to find anybody who was completely neutral, and politically it was quite impossible. So we did the best we could, and it was imperfect. It was imperfect, but in many ways it was quite remarkable because these great powers "stayed the hand of vengeance" and put their enemies on trial despite the enormity of the crimes that had been committed. That is perhaps the most important thing that came out of Nuremberg: the recognition that your enemy, no matter what his crimes, is entitled to as fair a trial as you can give him.

But we wanted something more than that. We felt that the time had come "for the law to take a step forward." These are the words of Justice Jackson, who represented the United States. It was declared in the Nuremberg Charter of the International Military Tribunal – which was drawn up by the four victorious powers speaking, in fact, for the so-called civilized world – that there would be a punishable offence known as the "crime against peace." In the future, anyone who started a war of aggression would be guilty of a crime. Why should one murder be considered a crime and one million murders be considered something other than a crime? So, the law took a step forward and declared that aggressive war was a punishable crime. There was another step forward taken, and that was the concept of "crimes against humanity." The concept of "war crimes" was an old, well-established concept under customary law. But the concept of crimes against humanity was something new. In the past it had been the practice, when acts of genocide were committed against minorities, that only diplomatic intervention was permissible. Governments could send a note of protest saying, "You know, we have heard that Armenians are being slaughtered in your country. We would deplore that action should it be true." That was the limited nature of the permissible intervention by the international community. At Nuremberg, we said that that time was past.

When crimes reach such a magnitude that they offend all of humankind, they are crimes not merely against the state but against humanity. And every nation has a right to intervene and insist that those who are responsible, those who have committed these crimes and their accomplices, be held accountable in a court of law. That was another great step forward that we thought we were taking at Nuremberg. We were beginning a process, a legal process, of moving toward a more humane and rational order. That, at least, was our aspiration and our dream at the time. And then I – as a young fellow assigned to prosecute this biggest murder trial in history (it was, incidentally, my first case) – was confronted with the problem of what penalty to ask for. One million people had been murdered in cold blood; clear documentary evidence; no dispute about the facts. I had dug many of the bodies out of the mass graves with my own hands. What punishment should I ask for? How do I balance one million deaths against twenty defendants – should I ask that they be chopped up into pieces? You can never really balance the punishment and a crime of such magnitude. But I wanted the trial to take law and humanity a step forward.

I brought along with me today my opening statement – which was made on 29 September 1947, forty years ago. In the opening paragraph, I said, "We ask this court to affirm by international penal actions man's right" – by that I meant women as well – "to live in peace and dignity regardless of his race or creed. The case we present is a plea of humanity to law."

I think that that reflects what we were trying to do. It was a plea of humanity to allow all people, regardless of their race or creed, to live in peace and dignity. That is what Nuremberg was all about. It was the planting of a seed of what we hoped would be an evolutionary process for a more humane and just society.

What has happened in these last forty years? To what extent has Nuremberg achieved its goals? Let me begin, first, with the negatives, because it is quite obvious that Nuremberg has not put an end to acts of genocide or genocidal-type acts. It is obvious that we do not have any international criminal courts. An important question was raised here this morning: someone asked why Nuremberg was not continued. If this was the beginning, why did we not continue? And we did not. So you might say, Well, Nuremberg has therefore been a failure; it was only "victor's justice." It therefore was unfair; nations engage in wrongful discrimination continually and nobody brings the offenders to trial because there are no victors to try the vanquished. That would be one point of view. I understand that point of view. I have only one thing to say about it: it is wrong. Nuremberg has not achieved all of its goals, but there are certain things it did do, and we must not forget these. We must not forget, because if we forget, we lose hope. We become cynical. In a cynical world, nothing works, everything is seen to be fake. We need hope. We need hope because without hope we will not have the strength to do all the things that we must do if we are going to make a better world. If we believe that everything is hopeless, we are defeated right there. All that is necessary for evil to triumph is for good men and good women to do nothing.

Is there a basis for hope? Let us look at the positive side of what has happened in the forty years since Nuremberg. Let us see what has really happened.

The outrage that was evoked by these trials, which were open to the public, immediately brought forth the Convention on Genocide in the United Nations. The General Assembly unanimously accepted the principles of Nuremberg: that aggressive war is a crime, that there are crimes against humanity, that "superior orders" is not a good defence; and that even the head of a state is responsible under the law. These were the evolving principles we were trying to articulate and confirm at Nuremberg. The United Nations unanimously confirmed these principles and immediately appointed a committee to codify them and to articulate a code of offences against the peace and security of mankind.

And so they began to work on it. Conventions on human rights began to appear. The Universal Declaration of Human Rights was adopted. Many other things happened over the years. Courts of human rights began to appear. We do not have an international criminal court but there is a Court of Human Rights at Strasbourg, which hears complaints of citizens against their own governments. And there are other similar international tribunals – there is one in Costa Rica which is beginning to function. And there is the Court of the European Communities; it functions very well, and it settles disputes which used to lead to war between the nations of Europe. That is a very great and important step forward.

The United Nations has passed many resolutions and conventions advancing international law. For many years, they worked on a definition of aggression. The absence of an agreed definition served to postpone work on an international criminal court. Eventually, the UN did agree upon the consensus definition of aggression. I wrote two volumes on that. It took them about fifty years; it could have been done faster. It was not a very good definition, but there it was.

And the United Nations worked on many other things: it adopted a Convention Against Terrorism; it condemned apartheid as an international crime; it enacted the crime of genocide. The United States has not yet ratified the Convention on Genocide, which is a disgrace because it is symbolically very important. As lawyers, we recognize that the Convention has its defects in substance. But all of these efforts to enact or improve international law have their defects. The definition of aggression was defective. The Convention Against Terrorism was defective – it was more an invitation to terrorism than a prohibition of it, because the definition of terrorism left big loopholes. It said, effectively, that terrorism is very bad; you cannot go around killing diplomats, you cannot go around blowing up buses, except if you are doing it for a noble purpose such as freedom from alien domination or self-determination; in that case, everything is all right. As lawyers, we know that if a contract is written with a big loophole, it is not going to be very effective.

Even though many of the efforts of the United Nations have not been very effective, they nevertheless represent a step forward. They have been accompanied by other, very great developments. There has in fact been an awakening of human conscience. The things that you argue about today are things nobody dreamt of arguing about forty or fifty years ago. In Canada today you are talking about punishing war criminals – looking for some old guy somewhere who may have evaded the net of justice, somebody we threw back into the pond in Nuremberg because we did not want to bother with him – you are now searching him out.

The young generation, the next generation, is recognizing that something is wrong. The world system did not work. You must change the system, and so you are beginning now. It is not late; it is part of the ordinary course of evolutionary events. You are beginning now to try to cope with the problems which arose out of the Nuremberg precedent.

I think that Nuremberg has not been a failure, despite the fact that we have not realized all of our dreams and that I have gotten old in the meantime. It has begun a process and it has a certain significance, which goes even beyond the matter of war crimes. We were trying to create a more orderly and humane world, and the world as I see it now is neither more orderly nor more humane in many ways. The things we tried to stop at Nuremberg – aggression, crimes against humanity – the world is on the verge of committing again.

At Nuremberg, we said that only those suspected of individual crimes shall be tried, and that only those whom the evidence shows to be guilty beyond a reasonable doubt will be condemned. Yet today, as I look around me, I see that the world security system is based on what is called a theory of deterrence. The theory of deterrence in the nuclear age means that if some madman in the Kremlin shoots a missile for some crazy reason, we respond by retaliating with our missiles, which will kill one hundred million or more innocent people who had nothing to do with the problem, who never made the decision to attack, and who may have been opposed to the decision. This is the theory of the "superpowers" on which world security is based. It is a theory which seems to me, after my experience at Nuremberg, to be absolute madness. It is genocidal, suicidal, and ecocidal at the same time. This is the system that we, as lawyers and as human beings, are expected to accept as the basis for our security. It is the basis for my insecurity! I do not know how many of you go to sleep peacefully, quietly, and fearlessly. I faced every German battle without fear. I am now afraid. I am afraid not for myself, but for my children and grandchildren.

So I have come to take Nuremberg a step forward, to talk about alternatives to the mad system of world security that we now have. Discussions of alternatives bring me back again to the United Nations – with all of its defects. We must restructure the world order and we must begin with what we have got: a United Nations, albeit paralyzed by the veto power and crippled by the cold war between the nations, yet we must build it up in a more rational way. Quite obviously, you cannot have a system of security in which those who pose the greatest threat to world security have a veto power over the enforcement of measures to maintain peace. That system must be changed. Various changes have been proposed. I cannot go into all the details because of the time, but we must deal with the armaments problem. There are many proposals: proposals for a system of international control of arms and proposals for the elimination of nuclear weapons – which will largely take care of the economic problems, stock-market plunges, national deficits, and all the rest. We should eliminate this crazy expenditure on useless armaments, which depletes us of the resources we need to eliminate the causes of discontent throughout the world. We should use our assets and our talents for more constructive purposes.

Before we can disarm, we need some acceptable alternative method to settle disputes. Nobody will accept disarmament until something better is put in its place. We have a "wild west" international law system today. We have a system of anarchy. We must replace it with a system of effective sanctions. A question was asked this morning about sanctions again apartheid in South Africa. The system of sanctions does not work because the major powers do not want it to work. After World War I, there was a comprehensive system of sanctions that was ready to be put into effect against Italy if it committed clear-cut aggression against Ethiopia. What happened when Haile Selassie got up before the League of Nations and said, "Look, a clear case of aggression. One member of the League attacks another. What will you do? What message can I take back to my people?" The British and the French double-crossed him. It was said, "England will do her duty," but in the last analysis England and France said, "Why should we risk our assets and antagonize Italy, which we may need against Germany, for the sake of some Africans in Ethiopia?" The League disregarded the ambassador of a small nation who warned, "Whether it is black or white, it should be the same law for all. Someday we may all be somebody else's Ethiopia."

So the world was not ready then, and is not ready now, to apply effective sanctions. The United Nations Charter spoke about an international military force. Where is it? Nobody pays any attention to it. They have even forgotten that it is in the Charter. Perhaps most important of all, we have failed to recognize the need for social justice if we are going to have a peaceful world.

To sum up, Nuremberg was a great step forward. It put in place an evolutionary process which we have since advanced. We planted seeds of hope and seeds of a future legal order based upon a humanitarian consideration of all people as fellow human beings, entitled to equal dignity and to peace.

Raoul Wallenberg was one individual who took it upon himself to do justice where he could. That should be an inspiration for all of you. I have tried to do the same. I have mentioned it only so that you may see that you can do things if you set about to do them.

I have not yet mentioned that I set up a restitution program for Nazi victims. We have an office here in Montreal and one in Toronto, and we have other offices all around the world. This is another example of a program for lawyers to aid the victims. The West German government has been persuaded to enact laws – involving many billions of dollars – to compensate victims of persecution. There are things that the individuals can do and there are things that you, as lawyers, must do. You have a special obligation to try to understand the existing structure and to use your legal skills and talents to try to build a more orderly world. Not only lawyers, but everyone has a role to play. There is a lady here who is "painting for peace," bringing children together to teach them the ways of peace. Everybody must do what he or she can do. I do not ask you to do more than you are able, but if you can do something, do that much.

Elie Wiesel said, "N'oublie pas!" Je ne peux pas oublier. It is a question of remembering, in order that we may use the inspiration of that memory and the light of that memory to guide us to a more peaceful world for all. Thank you very much.

THE HONOURABLE ROSALIE ABELLA Joe Stern graduated in economics from the University of Manitoba and started working for the Manitoba and Nova Scotia governments soon after that. In 1980, he worked for the Office of the Minister of Employment and Immigration and, since May of 1982, he has been chairman of the Refugee Status Advisory Committee. This year, in recognition of his contribution, he was named the first recipient of the Raoul Wallenberg Humanitarian Award.

Speaker

JOE STERN

Despite the fact that we have dwelt on issues of suffering, victimization, and persecution, I am sure that we all share a sense of elation that so many should care so passionately about injustices still present

in the world, and about the moral legacy we will leave behind. I
hope that our example can inspire in our successors a respect for
the dignity of all humankind.

I was pleased to accept the invitation to speak because I believe
that the issue of a new policy toward refugees, which has been a
matter of considerable public discussion in recent months, is a topic
that should concern not only this audience, but all Canadians. This
policy and the attitudes that have shaped it should be evaluated in
the light of the experience of Nuremberg and the lessons that we
have learned from this definitive event in the history of human
ethics.

In order to put the issues confronting us today into a clearer
context, I should like briefly to describe the development of
Canadian refugee policy. It is only comparatively recently that
Canadian public policy has concerned itself with the issue of
refugees. Even though many Canadian settlers clearly thought of
themselves as having fled persecution in their homelands, the first
reference by any public official to "refugees," as distinct from regular
immigrants, came in a 1947 speech by Mackenzie King. When my
father, then fourteen, left Russia and his parents in 1912 to come to
Canada, he was acting out of necessity rather than choice, and he
was in a position similar to that of many refugees. He was welcomed
to Canada not because of his needs, but because of Canada's; he
had the stamina and the will to create a new life for himself in the
Canadian West. My father was one of the many thousands of what
Clifford Sifton, then immigration minister, called "stout-hearted
peasants in sheepskin clothing." Although many of these new arrivals
– Doukhobors, Ukrainians, and Jews – may have been past or potential victims of persecution, this factor did not weigh with the
Canadian authorities, who saw only sturdy and hard-working immigrants, capable of withstanding the rigours of the Prairie climate and
of settling newly developed territory.

The policy of opening our doors to all comers changed in the
thirties, and everyone in this audience will be familiar with the sad
episode in our history, which has been so well chronicled in Irving
Abella's *None is Too Many*. It was a tragedy not only for those who
pleaded so desperately and unsuccessfully for a haven in Canada, but
for Canadians as well. We, as a nation, feel shame, not only because
we were indifferent to the claims of the persecuted for protection,
but also because we were so unpardonably deaf to the urgent
demands of so many of our own citizens to extend help to their
relatives in Europe. Canadian mothers and fathers could not bring
their children to safety; sons and daughters could not bring their

parents. As we later learned, entire branches of families faced extermination while their Canadian relatives were impotent to help. As Mr Wiesel has observed, it is a sobering thought that one man, Raoul Wallenberg, managed to do immeasurably more for the persecuted of Europe than did entire nations. It is a matter for sorrow that Canada's own attitude to this international tragedy was one of indifference.

Canada adopted the position it did because it believed that it was in the national interest to keep the doors closed. It may well have been; the decision not to admit Jews was probably an astute political decision, given the popular attitudes of the day. As public-opinion polling was unsophisticated in the thirties, there were probably no precise figures on just how many Canadians thought we should keep European refugees out of Canada, but Mackenzie King was probably right in assuming that the majority of Canadians agreed that we should. The prime minister of Canada appears to have based his policy decision upon his conviction that his fellow Canadians would favour the furthering of Canada's domestic and foreign-policy interests over the saving of many individual lives.

The attitudes that led to avoidable suffering on this unimaginable scale were not restricted to Canada, but were founded on the concept of sovereignty, which governed relations between countries at that time. In the nineteenth century the concept of individual rights had no meaning in an international context. Rights that an individual might have as an alien arose from the contractual obligations between states. A Canadian travelling to France enjoyed protection not because of his status as a human being, but out of respect for that nation of which he was a citizen; similarly, a Frenchman visiting Canada could expect the same level of consideration.

This appeared a satisfactory way of conducting international relations, and remained the foundation of our policy until the end of the 1939–45 war. Then the liberation of Europe, and the unforgettable and searing horror of the stories and pictures from Auschwitz, Buchenwald, Bergen–Belsen, Dachau, and the other concentration camps, led to a revulsion on the part of all thinking people against this impersonal view of the individual's claim to protection. It was now impossible to go back to a concept of sovereignty that ignored the rights of the individual. It was after the testimony and witness of Nuremberg that the world community felt compelled to change the approach it had traditionally taken to the rights of individuals who faced persecution.

Prior to Nuremberg, the only avenue open to an individual facing persecution was to try to apply for sanctuary abroad. As the fate of millions tells us, this was generally unsuccessful. Many nations, though not all, may have objected to people being stripped of their civil rights, tormented, and killed, but they did not see them as having the right to be protected by countries other than their own.

Nor did such people have the right to take their own salvation into their own hands and to plead spontaneously for protection, since there was nowhere for them to flee. As the infamous case of the *St Louis* reminds us, the few who managed to escape their persecutors were often obliged to return to face death. After the war, it became impossible to ignore the devastating consequences of the argument that it is *states*, and not individuals, that have rights.

The aftermath of Nuremberg manifested itself, first, in the Universal Declaration of Human Rights, which went so far as to set down principles which, while they ennobled the countries that adhered to them, nevertheless stopped short of imposing obligations upon the international community.

It was with the creation of the office of the United Nations High Commission for Refugees in 1950 and the 1951 Refugee Convention that we created an international treaty by which countries surrendered part of their sovereign rights out of respect for the rights of individual human beings. I need hardly say that this was a reversal of the whole concept of international relations as it had existed up to that point. It was no longer the refugee who must ask to be saved, and the individual nation which had the right to refuse. The refugee now had the right to be protected, and the country of refuge was obliged to provide that protection. I cannot stress too strongly that countries which have signed the Refugee Convention have voluntarily placed themselves in a position in which they may no longer offer benefits to, or withhold benefits from, refugees as they see fit. Such discretion continues to have a legitimate role in national immigration policy, which deals with the voluntary movement of people, but it is *not* a legitimate aspect of policy affecting refugees.

Although Canada recognized the tragic consequences of the exclusionary policy of the thirties in the decade that followed the war, it took us eighteen years to sign the Refugee Convention. It is clear from the public debates of the period that we feared that, if we acceded to this instrument, we could be obliged to open our doors to people we would reject as immigrants.

That, after all, is what the Refugee Convention is all about: requiring us to accept people whom we might not otherwise take in. Refugees are not immigrants, despite all this talk that "economic migrants," "abusers," "queue-jumpers," and "refugees" are essentially the same. An immigrant has a choice; he or she can make plans, organize a journey, and come to Canada as he or she chooses. A refugee cannot be so selective.

The United Nations High Commission for Refugees has distributed a poster that shows a refugee looking at a brick wall, on which is scrawled, "Refugee Go Home." Underneath is the caption "He would if he could." Refugees don't choose to be here. I wish Canadians would exercise their imaginations and realize how difficult it is for the young men and women who come here as refugees to abandon their countries, to leave their families, their friends, their whole circle of support, their culture, and their traditions. They are, after all, coming to a new and, very possibly, inhospitable country. They come out of desperation.

When Canada did finally accede to the Refugee Convention, we accepted the obligation to welcome those who were refugees to our shores and to accord them the respect of hearing what they had to say. In the course of our meetings at this conference, we have given much thought to the meaning of the word "dignity." A fundamental human dignity is central to the whole refugee question: the right to be recognized as a human being, with an individual life that is important. We have an obligation to hear the story that these people have to tell.

I have sat in refugee hearings where I was prepared to say in the first five minutes, "Enough, you're a refugee." But I have sat through two, perhaps three days of hearings, because the person had a compulsion to tell his or her story, as part of a necessary and personal healing process. This need, and the mechanisms that we have established to assist such repair of the individual life, ought be regarded as worthy of respect.

The recent debate about refugees in our country has been argued in terms of Canada's sovereign rights and the alleged need to "preserve the integrity of our immigration system" in the face of "abuse" that is taking place. What integrity are we preserving, and what abuse is taking place? To characterize the spontaneous movement of genuine refugees to a country such as Canada as abusive is a total repudiation of the Refugee Convention. It is also a rejection of the lessons of Nuremberg and a turning away from the suffering of all those who have borne personal witness to persecution.

Greville Janner spoke movingly this morning of his experience at Sainte-Agathe, where he was not allowed to ski because the Chalet at that time had a policy that was described as "select clientele." We all understand what "select clientele" meant. That policy did not exist only at ski resorts; it also extended to such reputable institutions as McGill University – thank God, it does so no longer. When we say that it is our right to select refugees abroad and when we say that it is a refugee's responsibility to apply abroad and not have the impertinence to present himself or herself on our doorstep, we are saying that we want Canada to resume the right to have an immigration policy based on the concept of "select clientele." We want to choose who is going to come. It will be argued by some that the people we choose will be the people who deserve to be chosen. However, our record to date gives us no right to assume that our judgment will be infallible. In any case, no state which has signed the Refugee Convention has the moral right to revert to such an exclusionary policy.

Has Canada suffered any losses since its sovereignty has been diminished because of our national obligation under the Refugee Convention? It seems that Canada has managed quite well. Although the media have tried to create the impression that the country is on the verge of collapse because of the inundation of refugees, I don't believe that Canada has been weakened by the hospitality that we have provided. Leaving aside crude considerations of the contributions that motivated, hard-working individuals make to the national economy, the country that welcomes refugees receives intangible rewards of enhanced esteem and a sense of itself as particularly fortunate within the international community. The opportunity to behave justly ought not be rejected as unprofitable or as leading only to the exploitation of the strong by the weak.

In closing, I want to repeat again what has been the theme of this conference: it is important that we should guard against indifference. When Canada received the Nansen Medal for its exemplary treatment of refugees, the grandson of Captain Nansen told his audience that, while no one can do everything, everyone can do something. I hope that all of you, and particularly the young people here, will seize that challenge. Professor Ferencz has reminded us of the meaning of Nuremberg: that all people must be allowed to live in peace and dignity. The achievement of this ideal will require commitment and action from each of us.

Questions from the Floor

Q. I just wanted to add a couple of numbers to the remarks that have been made on refugees. Canada takes roughly one hundred and ten thousand immigrants annually and an additional eleven or twelve hundred refugees. The numbers projected into the future are that by the year 2000 Quebec will begin to lose population in absolute numbers. This is one of the reasons that Meech Lake makes a provision that Quebec will get 5 per cent additional immigrants. The rest of Canada will lose population in absolute numbers in the year 2010.

Those are the background numbers and, just to put Mr Stern's remarks in context, the crisis that we've seen with Tamil refugees and others involve taking one hundred and twenty-seven or one hundred and fifty-two additional people into those numbers and into those totals. And, in each of the cases where this has happened, it's moved the government to think that there is an emergency of crisis proportions, which requires Draconian legislation. I think those numbers are very helpful for understanding exactly what the dimensions of the problem are.

Now, quite beyond that, the way in which Canada selects its immigrants is to go abroad with its immigration officers and to select, basically, the cream of the crop. And there's very little effort on behalf of Canadian officialdom to make dents in the huge populations of people who are not highly educated and who do not have skills. This has to be appreciated against the background of our declining population throughout the next twenty years.

I just wanted to offer those comments because I think it adds some flavour or, at least, I hope it does, to the remarks Joe Stern has made.

Q. My name is Irving Abella. I have two very brief questions – they're really statements. And the first one is to Joe.

It seems to me that this country is a country of immigrants which hates immigration. You know, every single public-opinion survey I've ever seen indicates that a vast majority of Canadians has always been opposed to the idea of more people coming to this country.

The second truism is that the Department of Immigration sees its job as not allowing people in, but as keeping them out. The people in the Department of Immigration like to choose who comes to this country; they don't like Canada to be chosen. They don't like boat people and bus people and plane people arriving here and making us their choice. It seems that what has happened now is an unholy alliance between an unpopular government, which seized a popular issue, and a bureaucracy, which attempted to capitalize on it. What we have done is to produce this monstrous refugee bill that will allow us finally to close our doors.

To Mr Ferencz, just a short comment, if you wouldn't mind. It seems to many of us that the United Nations is not part of the solution, it's really part of the problem. It's endemic racism, it's bloc voting, it's systematic discrimination, it's the equation of racism and

Zionism which makes the victims of the Nazis the heirs to the Nazis; and it makes us wonder whether this organization can possibly deal with such important issues as human rights.

A. PROFESSOR BENJAMIN FERENCZ: I'll be brief. You're quite right. The United Nations consists of appointed delegates who are paid to represent the parochial interests of their government. The moment they take another stand, they would lose their jobs. So it is the worst possible forum to see any progress, and that is why it takes so many years. That is also why my appeal is directed to those outside the United Nations. We have to reform the United Nations. That's as far as we have come. The idea of an independent civil service doesn't really exist. That was the plan. So, it's up to the people themselves to persuade the political leadership of their respective countries to adopt a more reasonable position. Then it will be reflected in the United Nations.

Panel Four:
"Words that Maim"
Freedom of Expression and
Freedom from Expression

Chair

PROFESSOR GISÈLE CÔTÉ-HARPER

C'est un grand plaisir pour moi de présider cette session cet après-midi en compagnie, à ma droite, du professeur Alan Dershowitz des États-Unis; immédiatement à ma gauche, monsieur Ram Jethmalani des Indes et Monsieur le Juge Maxwell Cohen du Canada.

Lorsque nous regardons le thème de cet après-midi, nous pouvons lire: "Words that maim": freedom of expression and freedom from expression.

Et quand nous lisons le texte français, nous y voyons "liberté d'expression," "liberté sans pression." J'aimerais traduire ceci dans les termes suivants: "Protection de la liberté d'expression, protection contre certaines formes d'expression."

And perhaps this is what Irwin Cotler had in mind when he designed this panel. I will quote from a speech that he gave in 1986 at Boston University Law School: "I think that many of us, as we grew up, may remember the refrain, 'Sticks and stones may break my bones but words will never harm me.' I think that we have learned that this may not be the case – that speech can hurt, that words do maim, that many of us have felt the pain in being tarred as a group, vilification either as blacks, Jews, Asians, or the like." And, I think, in this sense the notion of freedom of expression must also connote that which I would call freedom from certain kinds of expression.

Since our speakers this afternoon will be talking about the legislation in Canada, India, and the United States, I will very briefly turn my attention to international instruments, namely the International Covenant on Civil and Political Rights.

Since 1966, over 100 countries have ratified the Covenant, of which article 19 guarantees the right to hold opinions and the right to seek, impart, and receive information. But this right is not absolute. It has limitations: limitations prescribed by law, limitations in the interest of national security, limitations in the interest of public order, and limitations that relate to the right to protection of one's reputation.

I will briefly turn to the European Convention on Human Rights. Article 10 has a similar, though not identical, provision. The European Court has made it clear that the broad public interest in receiving information and in the quality of political and social debate lies at the heart of freedom of expression. The only qualification is that the right to receive information is dependent upon there being a willing speaker. In a decision rendered in March, 1987, in Leander, Sweden, the Court observed, "The right to freedom to receive information basically prohibits a government from restricting a person from receiving information that others wish or may be willing to impart to him."

The essential purpose of articles relating to freedom of expression is to further a democratic society, and I would like to quote Professor Dershowitz, who said, "We have to tolerate a great deal of very annoying, very uncomfortable, very erroneous, very wrong-headed lies. Many of them are, in fact, lies."

How much should one tolerate lies when lies are made out of words that maim? I think this panel will be addressing this question and I do hope that, in the discussion that will follow, you will be raising such questions.

Mr Jethmalani is a lawyer and member and past president of the Indian Bar Association. He is also a former member of the Indian Parliament. He is vice-president of the World Association of Peace through Law.

Speaker

RAM JETHMALANI

I have a very small complaint to make: I have not been adequately introduced. I am the only person present whose credentials would not bear a moment's scrutiny. My only credential is that by some peculiar component in my psyche, I have intensely suffered the agony of the Jewish people. I have shared their experiences, and I am deeply concerned for their future.

I am a small man, but one who looks a little smaller than he is by reason of the cause which he so fervently espouses: the cause of eliminating the incompetence and corruption of governments and the cause of removing the incidence of injustice against those who are victims of that incompetence or insolence. Being a very weak and obedient person, I am perhaps the only one who wrote a paper for this conference because my friend Irwin asked for it. Being, at most, an adjutant at any conference of this kind, I do not particularly admire people who read their papers, nor those who pretend to summarize them. The latter combines boredom with breach of promise.

I propose to do neither but, to put you at ease, let me say this. After careful study of Indian law, as well as of Canadian law, enlightened by American law, I have come to the conclusion that, on the relevant points that arise at this conference, Indian law will yield the same answers to the issues raised as Canadian law would. I am, therefore, relieved from the task of explaining in detail the legal provisions in India. I will however, try to briefly summarize the pertinent legal provisions in my own context, making comparisons to the Canadian situation where appropriate.

The advocacy of, or incitement to, hatred against ethnic, religious, communal and caste-based groups is of longstanding concern in India and has been increasing in recent years. Indeed, the growing incitement to hatred – and explosion of violence – tend to challenge India's claim to be a liberal, pluralistic democracy that has succeeded in respecting the diverse mix of ethnic, religious, cultural, and linguistic groupings – a population of some 860 million, consisting of at least six major religious groups, many of which are further divided into dozens of sub-groups, with fifteen officially recognized languages and over 1,500 dialects.

These tensions, compounded by a set of historical dynamics too numerous to mention, has given rise to attempts to balance individual and group rights, commitments to democratic pluralism with the needs of public order, and freedom of expression and reasonable restrictions upon it. This has resulted in a unique set of "balancing" principles, both in the Indian Constitution and in Indian Criminal Law, with some of them even resembling the Canadian experience.

For example, India's Bill of Rights contains a clause, Article 19 (1)(a), which is somewhat similar to Section 1 of the Canadian Charter, and which says: "All citizens shall have the right to freedom of expression." This clause is then followed or limited by Article 19(2) which reads as follows: "Nothing in this right (Article 19(1)(a)) shall affect the operation of any existing law, insofar as such law imposes reasonable restrictions on the exercise of the right in the interest of foreign states, public order, decency, morality, or in relation to contempt of court, defamation, or incitement to an offence."

As with Canada, this basic constitutional balancing principle has served as a testing ground for anti-hate legislation. As examples I will single out the three major provisions of the Indian Penal Code which address freedom of expression and incitement to hatred against targeted groups on grounds of their religion, race, language, region, caste or community.

The first of these, Section 153A of the Penal Code, makes it an offence, *inter alia,* for any person to promote or attempt to promote, whether by the use of words (spoken or written) or by signs or other visible representations, "disharmony or feelings of enmity, hatred or il-will between different religious, racial, language or regional groups or castes or communities." The offence is punishable with imprisonment for up to three years or with a fine or with both.

A related provision, Section 153B, prohibits the making or publishing of imputations or assertions which:

a. imply that "any class of persons cannot, by reason of their being members of any religious, racial, language or regional group or caste or community, bear true faith and allegiance to the Constitution of India as by law established or uphold the sovereignty and integrity of India"; or
b. suggest that "any class of persons shall, by reason of their being members of any religious, racial, language, or regional group or caste or community, be denied or deprived of their rights as citizens of India"; or
c. cause or are likely to cause "disharmony or feelings of enmity or hatred or ill-will between such members and other persons."

These offenses are also punishable with imprisonment for up to three years or with a fine or both.

As for the judicial interpretation of these provisions, the courts have held that the essence of the offence is the "malicious intention" of the inciter, which can be determined either from the offending words themselves or extraneous evidence; also, and of particular relevance to Canadian jurisprudence, the offending words must be directed at a well-defined group having a degree of permanence or stability, and sufficiently numerous and widespread to be designated a class.

A second provision which criminalizes incitement can be found in Section 295A of the Penal Code. This section makes it an offence for anyone "with deliberate and malicious intention of outraging the religious feelings of any class of citizens of India" to insult or attempt to insult the religion or religious beliefs of that class whether by words (written or spoken) or by signs or by other visible representations.

The Indian Supreme Court, in a challenge to the constitutional validity of this provision, upheld it on the grounds that it constituted a "reasonable restriction" in the interest of public order; as well, it held that malicious intent, which like Section 153A, could be inferred from surrounding circumstances, was the requisite element of the offence. As with the Canadian jurisprudence, the context in which the incitement takes place is no less crucial than the content of the offending words.

A third provision, more akin to Canada's anti-hate legislation but broader in its language and conception, is Section 505(2) of the Penal Code, which reads as follows:

Whoever makes, publishes or circulates any statement or report containing rumour or alarming news with intent to create or promote, or which is likely to create or promote, on grounds of religion, race, place of birth, residence, language, caste or community or any other ground whatsoever, feelings of enmity, hatred or ill-will between different religious, racial, language or regional groups or castes or communities, shall be punished with imprisonment which may extend to three years, or with fine, or with both.

This section was also the subject of constitutional challenge, and again the legislation was upheld as being a "legitimate restriction" within Section 19(2) of the Indian Bill of Rights. It should be noted that, unlike Canada's anti-hate legislation, truth may not serve as a defence to a charge under these provisions.

Accordingly, you may see that I understand, ladies and gentlemen, the nature of the poison and the purpose of the propaganda that have given rise to this panel. I have carefully studied the judgment of the Court of Appeal in the *Zundel* case. The actual decision in the case – the fact that the conviction was upset and a retrial ordered – causes me no perturbation of any kind. The court rises to its fullest stature when it ensures a fair trial to the despicable and the despised. In general, however, as the *Keegstra* case demonstrates, I must compliment the Supreme Court for having correctly understood your recently acquired Charter of Rights and Freedoms, and refusing to extend constitutional protection to those who wilfully promote hatred or contempt against vulnerable minorities.

I am conscious, then, of the propensity and power of the written word to insult and to annoy, to pour salt over wounds not yet healed, to rip open scars not yet raised. But what disturbs me more than anything else, and should disturb everyone, is the racist mentality that prompts the hurtful words – the dark and devious motivation that inspired them, and above all, the enormity of the numbers of people who share both the motivation and the mentality.

To me, these numbers represent the total failure of the Nuremberg experiment, the total frustration of the purposes for which those trials were held. I wish that I could share the optimism of Greville Janner, who said that these trials generate hope. They do nothing of the kind – though the punishment meted out to the wicked defendants at these trials satisfies the retributive instinct of human beings. I think that if the purpose of these trials was deterrence – to prevent like-minded people from indulging in conduct of the same kind that is alleged in these cases – then the trials have totally failed their purpose.

Let us contemplate the scene as it existed then and let us contemplate the scene today. I believe that the scene today is more dangerous than it was when the Nuremberg trials were held. When those trials were held, there were a bunch of sycophants and psychopaths, insane criminals who had managed to take control of the German state. Today it is not merely wicked governments, but entire populations of countries that share the mentality and motivation of Zundel.

I suggest, ladies and gentlemen, that today enormous elements of humanity are trapped in a literal hell on earth. What saddens me beyond measure – and this is something that torments my soul – is that some of the very states that prosecuted war criminals at Nuremberg are the ones that today are encouraging, befriending, financing, and sometimes even arming states whose racist and violent leadership is capable of committing the same Nuremberg crimes.

In the terms of an Indian proverb, we are supplying milk to venomous vipers, and they are not as harmless as the proverbial serpent who hissed strong advice in the ear of Mother Eve. These are genuine snakes, and I am surprised that democracies – educated democracies, democracies which could do without expedient alliances and treaties – are parties to what is, but does not appear to them to be, intended genocide. The international community must soon learn to reckon with this sad fact.

We did not have a United Nations then; today, we do. It is unfortunate that those very states which today would like to destroy an existing state on the basis of the religion of the inhabitants of that state are practically dominating the floor of the United Nations. The United Nations has given them an additional platform on which to practice their duplicity and preach their doctrines and make nonsense of the provisions of the United Nations Charter. Something is wrong somewhere.

This is not an occasion for jest, but it reminds me of a short anecdote of dubious authenticity, which, nevertheless, effectively makes the point. It is said that Justice Holmes, while travelling in a suburban train one morning, was asked by the train inspector for his ticket. The judge fumbled in his pockets, but could not find either the ticket or any evidence that he had bought one. The train inspector said to him, "Judge, I know you. Don't try to find the ticket, I don't need it." The judge turned to him and said, "Young man, it's not for you that I am looking for the ticket. I have to find it because I've forgotten where I'm going."

So, it seems to me, that the ticket that we bought at Nuremberg has been lost has somewhere along the way. Unless humanity learns to recover that ticket and find where it was supposed to be going, I think we are on the wrong track and we are on the wrong road.

The depressing features of the present situation are twofold: first, we have a proliferation of criminals, so that the purpose of punishment, and particularly the Nuremberg punishment, appears to have failed; second, we have the depressing fact that sometimes the victims themselves, actual and potential, are divided – ignorant of the menace – and guilty of quiescence, if not of aiding and abetting the activities of their potential tormentors.

I think that states which respect the human rights of citizens and practice democracy must now decide to join their destinies together. Together we will have to suffer, and together we will have to march forward. We must urgently pool all of our material, moral, and spiritual resources. The first step, which we must quickly take – and there is no other way of grappling with the sword of reality of today – is to sanction those states that make the human rights of their citizens dependent on the religion they practice, or the colour that their skin bears, or the economic or political beliefs that they hold.

If, in the process, a parallel United Nations organization may have to be created, then it is worth the price. Not that we should stop all communication with these nations, but it is not necessary to combine Hell and Heaven in the same place. We do keep our rest rooms separate from our bedrooms, and that is precisely what must be done with some of the governments and nations that make a mockery of human dignity and freedom.

I am a student of religion and, in my opinion, there never lived a wiser man than Lord Buddha. I do not intend to tread on anybody's toes – I am not a Buddhist; I am a Hindu. After painful years of meditation, Lord Buddha concluded that human suffering is part of life and it can never be relegated. Finally, he advised that the whole of human endeavour is deliverance from the bondage of rebirth. I fully accept that philosophy, but with a slight amendment. While we are on this planet, we have to remain perpetually on the treadmill on which we must rise and fall. The moment we stop the process of rise and fall, we extinguish life, because it is no longer life when devoid of a noble purpose. Elie Wiesel talked about memory yesterday. I think that we have already arrived at the stage when the memory is betrayed. In man, mind and purpose are all undone. Let noble purpose go and set the mind. We must try – that is all that is left to individuals – we must try to make the world better than it was when we were born. Maybe Buddha was right and we shall never succeed, but let me close with his words: "We, of the wise and of the wondering mind, that moan for the rest we will find ... So is mortal life: a sigh, a sob, a storm, a strike."

Let us not run away from a strike. Thank you.

PROFESSOR GISÈLE CÔTÉ-HARPER Professor Maxwell Cohen is formerly judge (*ad hoc*) of the International Court of Justice and scholar-in-residence at the Faculty of Law at the University of Ottawa. He is professor emeritus and former dean of the Faculty of Law at McGill University. He was the chairman of the Special Committee on Hate Propaganda, 1965–66; chairman of the Canadian Section of the International Joint Commission, 1974–79; and he received the President's Award from the Canadian Bar Association in 1986, and the John Read Gold Medal of the Canadian Council of International Law in 1983.

Speaker

JUDGE MAXWELL COHEN

I must say, I cannot be in this room without memories, many memories. The building we are in was built during the time I had the pleasure and the honour of being dean. This room was used for a variety of purposes. We once had a royal commission sit here. We had two live trials that the late Chief Justice Challies brought down here, one with a jury and one without a jury. The pioneering spirit of the law school is to be seen in a variety of ways, and especially in the National Program. Irwin Cotler's meeting today is part of that ongoing tradition of experimental work done here and done, I think, with good results. Tonight the room is full of former students at whom I am able to look with a friendly eye. Indeed, the test, ultimately, to the teacher who returns rarely to his home base may be how many "enemies" lie in wait for him. Since I find that very few give me what is often called the "evil eye," but instead a friendly hand, I assume that courtesy has triumphed over memory.

This issue of hate propaganda is particularly close to me. My wife and I were watching television one night, the eleven o'clock news, after having seen blood on the floor in some good classic movie. Suddenly it was announced on the news that the minister of justice was appointing a special committee to study the issue of hate propaganda. The names of the members of the committee were listed, and suddenly I heard my name announced as chairman of the committee. Nobody had asked me. Nobody had warned me. I thought the appointment was an excellent one. Even so, I had little or no notice. Immortality arrives so unexpectedly.

It was a remarkable collection of men that the late Guy Favreau put together: Pierre Trudeau was then a young associate professor of constitutional law at the University of Montreal; Mark Mac-Guigan, then an associate professor of law at the University of Toronto; Dr Alec Corry, principal of Queen's University; L'Abbé Dion, one of the pioneering minds of the "quiet revolution" and an unusual person in every way; Saul Hayes, the executive vice-president of the Canadian Jewish Congress and perhaps the most effective public servant that any minority community ever had serving it; Shane MacKay, the executive editor of the *Winnipeg Free Press*; and a young man and former student, now with white hair, who served as the secretary of the Committee, namely, Mr Harvey Yarosky – today a distinguished criminal-law practitioner at the Montreal Bar.

We were not given any terms of reference; we were simply told that there was a problem. The problem was put this way by Mr Favreau. He said that they had been under pressure in the House of Commons by the Tories and by the NDP – he said that we have to do something and we need to have a good inquiry. I asked him what our budget was; he told me that we did not have one. I asked him what we could pay the members of the committee; he said he was not sure. I asked him who the secretariat was; he said that he would see what he could do. To make a long story short, we had no budget, we were virtually unpaid except for a very modest per diem, and at the end of seven months we had a unanimous report fully printed, at a total cost to the Canadian people of $35,000. Today, that might get you one lawyer part-time for half a year ...

The Report on Hate Propaganda was published in November of 1965 – twenty-two years ago. It dealt with the classic dilemmas in this field. "Sticks and stones may break my bones but names will never hurt me" had become, in the light of the increasing sensibilities of people everywhere, an impossible cliché with which to live. It may have suited an older, fairy-tale time; it was impossible in the post-Nuremberg generation in which we lived. So, we faced the classic philosophical dilemma of determining the limits on free speech, when speech is not directed to a serious political debate as such, but is directed to race or to religion in some unpleasant, intentionally hurtful way.

I had had some experience with that kind of thing myself. At the height of the "new left" campus troubles of the late sixties, one of their leaders came up to my daughter, who was a student then, and said, We are going to destroy your father, we are going to destroy Dean Woods – who was then the dean of the Faculty of Arts and Science – and we are going to destroy Mr Robertson – who was then the principal. My daughter, who was an innocent second- or third-year arts student and thought that this young man was a friend of hers, naturally reported this happy news to me and wanted an explanation. I did not really have one. But I found out what they meant about a year later, when the *McGill Daily* carried a scathing editorial about me, all sorts of words, some almost four-letter words, others not quite reaching those heights, the thrust of which was that I was a man of very low character, that I should not be holding any public office, and so on.

That editorial came out at about ten o'clock in the morning. At about eleven o'clock, I had a call from a very able and distinguished psychiatrist/lawyer who ran the Montreal Institute for Mental Health, a very good friend of mine, a Dr Alastair MacLeod. He asked if he could come over and see me at once. He came over and he asked me if I had read that morning's *McGill Daily*; I replied that I had not. He told me not to read it. When I asked him why, he said that it was meant to be *lethal.* It was meant to hurt me in such a way that I might have a dangerous problem of recovery. I thought it was a very strange kind of statement to make. I could not believe in its validity. I did not see what it had to do with ordinary life – but there it was. When I did read it, I knew exactly what the intent of the persons who wrote that article had been. They meant to say words in such a way as to affect that modicum of self-image with which all of us must wrestle in order to survive the slings and arrows of life as it is lived every day. Now, I survived that attack, and I was only a single individual. I was a person with a family, but not a member of a group that had to worry about its collective position.

What happens, however, when words of that character are directed to an otherwise "identifiable group"? What happens when words are intended to affect the self-image, the reputation, the social viability, and the very existence of a minority which feels itself vulnerable? That was at the heart of this particular exercise. So, we decided that the essence of the terms of reference was how to do a study, at the least possible cost, which would do justice to the contemporary problems presented by the hate-literature campaign then being conducted in Canada and elsewhere.

May I say that the literature, at that time, was coming in primarily from three or four places: Sweden, Virginia, Georgia, and Ontario. We never found out, even with the co-operation of the Royal Canadian Mounted Police, why those were the four central sources of anti-Black, anti-Catholic, and anti-Semitic literature. But they were the prime source of it, often in very large amounts.

The committee sat for seven months, and eventually, as I have mentioned, we issued a unanimous report. The government sent it to the Senate – not to the House of Commons – and for three years running it failed in the Senate, on the argument that this was an infringement of the whole theory and practice of Anglo-Canadian, Anglo-American, and Commonwealth concepts of free speech in a democratic society.

On the fourth try, in 1969, the bill was introduced in the House of Commons by the Honourable John Turner, then minister of justice. Mr Trudeau, who had participated in the committee and who was prime minister at the time of the bill's introduction, could have backed off in the face of a very severe debate in the House and in Canada among some civil libertarians who, from coast to coast, argued that we did not need this legislation. They argued that an experienced democratic society with a high level of education can tolerate the marginal insult that touches a particular group and, therefore, that we did not need these restrictions. Mr Turner, as minister of justice, led the debate over the bill. Mr Trudeau could have stood aside, but he did not flinch, and the bill passed. To his credit and to the credit of John Turner, this difficult, controversial piece of legislation became, with all of its weaknesses and all of its strengths, the law of Canada.

I have given you the story because you should have some understanding of the difficulties that were faced in this debate. A very responsible organization, the Canadian Civil Liberties Association, led by Alan Borovoy, is, to this day, dead set against it. Borovoy believed that sections 281.1 and 281.2 of the Criminal Code [editor's note: now sections 318 and 319] were unnecessary. That entire section, as you recall, had three main purposes: first, to prohibit the advocacy or promotion of genocide; second, to prohibit any word, spoken or written, against an identifiable group, that was intended to incite to hatred and was likely to lead to violence in a public place; and third, the controversial "group libel" provision, which states that wilfully promoting hatred – the word "wilfully" was deliberately put in there – was something which the criminal law of Canada should not tolerate. Here, a series of defences – truth, belief in truth, and good faith – were put in to assist the accused and to safeguard the classic position of the civil libertarians.

One of the effects of the legislation has been to keep the whole debate alive for the last twenty years, to the point where today, I believe, there is still a divided public opinion. Despite the few cases tried by the courts in Canada, in my view, the Supreme Court is likely to sustain the legislation under the Charter. [editor's note: The Supreme Court of Canada did, in fact, uphold the constitutionality of the section in its decision in the *Keegstra* case, December 1990.] Free speech under section 2 of the Charter and the power of Parliament to set reasonable limits under section 1 will not lead to an overturning of these particular provisions.

I am going to keep my remarks short, because I think that this question deserves a very large amount of debate today. I want to say simply that the cases which we have had so far tend to sustain the constitutionality of section 281 of the Criminal Code under the Charter. I leave it for my colleagues and the rest of you to open this important discussion before us today. I think that the hate-propaganda issue is the cutting edge of the whole of the Elie Wiesel "memory" discussion, so eloquently put before us last night.

One way to look at it is to accept the classic theory that really everything *spoken* goes, because our society is tolerant enough and resilient enough to allow it. Others will say that there are limits because we do not deserve to be faced with the dilemmas of hurtful phrases thrown against vulnerable, visible minorities. It seems to me that this side of the debate is also worth remembering. Now, with the Charter, with the new Meech Lake Amendments, with only five or six cases, and with the *Keegstra* case yet to come down from the Alberta Court of Appeal, we are in the midst of a serious ongoing debate on this issue, multiplied in terms of significance by the presence of the Charter and its role in Canadian life.

I would say, finally, that although you may argue that a well-integrated society can tolerate this amount of speech abuse and, indeed, that the strength of a democracy is its ability to withstand that abuse, let me ask you whether, on balance, you think that we should allow the advocacy or promotion of genocide. The answer, of course, is no. The report is unanimous and firm on that. On the next level, do you think that we should allow the incitement to violence against an "identifiable group" in a public place? A little more difficult, but the answer is still no. Finally, do you think that we should prohibit the wilful promotion of hatred against a particular group, for which several defences are available and for which the permission of the attorney general of the province is necessary before a prosecution may take place? For the committee, this was the most difficult of all of the offences to formulate and to agree upon.

Where does Canada of 1987 stand with its Charter in the face of the 1965 Report? What role does the memory of Nuremberg play? If, as appeared today and last night in some of the discussion, our problem has sometimes been indifference, sometimes loss of memory, sometimes a blind rejection of the past and its pain, is it wise to be so uncaring, so indifferent? Is it wise to reject this protective regime? Or shall we face up to it in a continuous debate that takes these issues for re-examination, in a public forum or in Parliament or in meetings like this conference or in the courts? Must we not constantly examine these basic values and the uses of language? Language must become part of the cement of social order, not a divider. That, it seems to me, is the issue we must face – language as a cement or language as a divider for a people that seeks to live in harmony in a multicultural mosaic, such as we already have in Canada. Thank you.

PROFESSOR GISÈLE CÔTÉ-HARPER Professor Dershowitz is a professor of law at Harvard Law School. He is a leading American civil-liberties lawyer and a former director of the American Civil Liberties Union. He is author of *The Best Defense*.

Speaker

PROFESSOR ALAN DERSHOWITZ

I have already learned a great deal from my distinguished and wise co-panellists, but I have not, at least not yet, changed my mind about my conclusion that the content-neutral approach to free speech in which the government never asks the question "Is the speech true?" may be the worst of all approaches to free speech – except for all the others.

I am hoping today that I will come away from this discussion and the questions that follow with a neutral rule of free speech which allows me to suppress Holocaust denial, racist speech, propaganda, and hate propaganda, without also permitting other governments to censor speech that we would all find highly desirable. I am not optimistic. I have been looking for that rule for twenty-five years, and I haven't found it. There may be more wisdom in this room than there has been in the rooms that I have sat in and debated this issue for all those years, but I am pessimistic that any such rule will evolve.

Therefore, I suspect that we will be relegated to a discussion about whether we, who are in power today, whether it be in this country or in your neighbour to the south or in some other democracy in the world, shall have the power to determine what is true and what is false, what is hateful and what is not hateful, and what is the stream of truth that somebody might be accused of muddying and poisoning. Without defining that stream of truth, one cannot distinguish the mud from the water. And that has been the problem.

Let there be no mistake that what is being proposed here today is censorship. It is benevolent censorship, it is censorship in the interest of good, but it is censorship. Let me tell two stories to illustrate what I think are the evils of even the best forms of censorship. One took place when Irwin and I were in Madrid several years ago at a Helsinki meeting, and at the time I was debating a Soviet lawyer on the question of anti-Semitism in the Soviet Union. I got up and produced a great deal of anti-Semitic material that was being published in the Soviet Union at the time, and I turned to him and said, "Comrade, in the name of Lenin, who opposed anti-Semitism, how can you justify your government's action in publishing this terrible hateful material?" And he turned to me and said, "I am prepared for you, Comrade Professor," and he took out of his briefcase even worse, more virulently anti-Semitic, Nazi hate propaganda published in the United States. And he said to me, "Is this not worse?" And I looked at the material and substantively it was much worse. But then I looked at his material and my material and I held them both up to the audience and I said, "Don't you see the difference?" The audience saw the difference and he saw the difference. In the lower lefthand corner of the Soviet material was a stamp which said, "Approved by Glavlit, the Soviet Censorship Agency." There was no such stamp on the American material. It had been printed by the Nazi Party, Hoboken, New Jersey. There had been no government imprimatur because there had been no government censorship. When a government censors, it must also approve, and when the government gets into the business of determining what is true and what is false, there is a demand for what I call "ism equity." If you allow one "ism," then you must allow another "ism." If you censor in the interests of one "ism," then you must censor in the interests of another "ism." I used to think a few years ago that, at least on the issue of pornography, perhaps we could agree. That was no political speech, it wasn't speech that was central to any point of view, it wasn't propaganda. But now the feminist censors in my country have talked me out of that position. They have persuaded me that pornography is genocidal propaganda, that it sends a sexist message. Now I spend a great deal of my time defending pornography, and the right of pornographers, whom I now see as even more evil than I used to see them.

I used to think that pornography was like a vibrator, that it was a sex aid, and if the government can ban vibrators or limit the use of sex aids, then it could ban pornography. But now that I have been advised that pornography really hurts because it sends a message, a negative message about women, I have to be doubly careful to make sure that that form of disgusting speech is protected as well.

I want to give you another vignette from my own life, just a very recent one. I went with my son to Auschwitz to see for ourselves what the Martyrology Museum is teaching the Polish students and young people; I came away appalled. We didn't go to any museum to actually learn about the Holocaust. I had been at Yad Vashem, I had been to other places; I think I know a bit about the Holocaust. I had gone to see what the Polish government was teaching their young people about the Holocaust.

So when we went there, we didn't join into any Jewish tour or American tour, we followed around a tour of young Polish students, who are compelled by their school rules to attend Auschwitz, and what we saw was appalling – a complete denial of the uniquely Jewish nature of the Holocaust; names of victims singled out for their Polish surname, with no mention of Jewish victims; when it came to pictures of children, there were no names, only numbers under them, because there were no Polish children murdered at Auschwitz because they were Polish. A sign that appeared on one of the pavilions says that the theme of the exposition is not the fate of the Jewish people, but that what it wants to narrate is Hungarian history. This was on the Hungarian pavilion. On the Czechoslovakian pavilion, there was a memorial to all the concentration camps, Treblinka, Mathausen, Auschwitz, Bergen–Belsen, Dachau; and surrounding these names were hundreds of Christian crosses – not a single Star of David. And on and on and on. And so I came back and I wrote a syndicated column in this country. It was shortly after Vice-President Bush had been to Auschwitz and the column was entitled, "What Bush and Others Missed at Auschwitz." The point to this story I am telling you today is that Polish-American leaders throughout the United States, as well as some of the newspapers that they publish, thought that I had libelled the Polish people in the column that I wrote. They wrote a letter to the president of Harvard University, Derek Bok, urging that I be fired because I was fomenting racial hatred and I was denying the central truth that it was Poles and not Jews who were killed at Auschwitz; that Auschwitz was a political concentration camp and not a genocidal or religious concentration camp. Fortunately, Derek Bok wrote his usual Dershowitz letter – he has a thick file of such letters – simply saying that I am a professor and, as such, can say whatever I please, and that he doesn't take positions on free speech, and, finally, that if they wanted to oppose me, they could oppose me. That was the right thing. I would have been very upset if the president of Harvard University had written a letter defending me. I don't want to be defended on the merits by my president. I simply want him to permit me to speak and others to criticize and attack me, because I don't want there ever to come a day when the president of Harvard says, "Well, now you've made a speech that I can't defend and so I will not defend you, nor your right to say it."

The key to me is neutrality. Can you come up with a rule that does not today give the Canadian government the power to determine that the Holocaust did occur, whether through judicial notice or appellate opinion or jury verdict, and to deny another government some time, somewhere in the world, the power to say that the Holocaust did not occur? How can you give this government the power to determine truth of that kind, without giving another government the power to say that Zionism does in fact equal racism? As you all know, I'm sure, universities in England and in Sweden and surely in the Soviet Union have denied Zionist speakers the right to speak from their platform, because in those countries Zionism is a lie. It tells a false story.

In my country, I was challenged to a debate on Zionism versus Palestinian rights by Terzy, the Palestine Liberation Organization representative to the United Nations. I accepted the debate. I wanted to debate him on the merits. The American State Department denied him the right to debate me and denied me the right to debate him, for fear that he would beat me in the debate, that his lies would prevail over my truth. I did not thank our State Department for that paternalistic intervention. Let the people judge. Let people sit in judgment over what is truth and what is falsity.

I think there are limits to free speech. I think one can set up a hierarchy of speech and one can begin to ask questions about when certain kinds of speech may go too far. The paradigm of free speech that I think is censorable are military secrets, the names of spies, the movement of troops, the location of weapons, and the codes of weapons.

I regret to say this, but I think that Holocaust denial speech is not even a close question. There is no persuasive argument that I can think of in logic, in law, in constitutionality, in policy, or in education, which should deny Zundel, Keegstra, or anybody who chooses to the right to take whatever position he wants on the Holocaust. The existence of the Holocaust, its extent, its fault, its ramifications, its political use are fair subjects for debate. I think it is despicable for anybody to deny the existence of the Holocaust. But I cannot sit in judgment over the level of despicability of anybody's exercise of freedom of speech.

To compare the *Zundel* case to the *Nuremberg* cases is to fail, I think, with all due respect, to understand the central core of democracy, which is the difference between words and acts. Of course I agree that sticks and stones can break your bones, and words can harm you and maim you. That's the price we pay for living in a democracy. It's not that speech doesn't matter. If speech didn't matter, I wouldn't devote my life to defending it. Speech matters. Speech can hurt. That's not why those of us who defend free speech, particularly free speech of this kind, do it. We do it because we don't trust government. Because we know that if today's censors are the benevolent people who would like to do it in the interests of Jewish sensitivities or black sensitivities, tomorrow's censor will be an evangelical president of the United States, a Pat Robertson, a Phyllis Schlafly, a Ronald Reagan, or a William Rehnquist. Those are the people who will be determining what is censorable speech and what is acceptable speech.

So, I would urge you in this discussion to please give me guidance. Please give me a rule. Please suggest to me a way in which I can justify the *Zundel* case, which I find as dangerous as any higher-court decision I have read in recent years, primarily because it is so benevolent and done in the interests of so worthy a cause.

Our last speaker quoted Holmes; I will paraphrase Brandeis, who said, "We need not be concerned about the dangers of evil tyrants because we are prepared to defend against tyranny. We must be most concerned about people of goodwill and good intention who would take away our liberties in the interests of benevolence." And that's what I believe happens when free speech of this kind is censored. Thank you.

Questions from the Floor

Q. My name is Ron Sklar. I agree with much of what Professor
Dershowitz has said, and yet I'm disappointed by the way he said it.
I am very troubled by some arguments that were made by the panel
today, arguments I heard yesterday from Elie Wiesel, and arguments
I heard in a private heated debate with Mr Jethmalani. Words can be
like knives, they can hurt like knives. They can cause great anguish,
not only among Holocaust survivors in a case of Holocaust denial,
but among good-thinking people everywhere. They can cause
sleepless nights, they can cause great pain. Yet all I heard from you,
Professor Dershowitz, in defence of the speech involved, was
something that sounded like a "slippery slope" argument. I expected
more. I want to hear a justification according to the great values of
the American First Amendment, which I believe in.

My second question is a shorter one. Are American values exportable to volatile societies like Jethmalani's society, where words
can cause violence? There are societies that do respond violently to
libel. The American and Canadian societies tend to answer libels
with truth, but there are societies that respond to hateful language
with violence. So, my second question is whether the panel thinks
that free-speech values of the American and Canadian constitutions
are exportable to more volatile societies.

A. PROFESSOR ALAN DERSHOWITZ: I'm very sorry to have disappointed
you, and I think I will continue to disappoint you. I don't have very
much more. I am not a believer in the American First Amendment
or in the American Supreme Court. I don't speak about the First
Amendment because I don't believe in any originalist view of the
Constitution, I don't think that the framers of the First Amendment
were very wise. They were bigoted white, male, Protestants who had
a narrow view of American society. Thurgood Marshall was right
when he said, "The original amendments to the United States Constitution were meaningless." The First Amendment was not intended
to give power to people. Robert Bork was right about that and it
takes me a lot to say that. The First Amendment was intended to give
power to the states and to take it away from the people. We have had
five constitutions in the United States, and the only two that make
me happy at all are the ones that occurred with *Marbury* v. *Madison*
and after the Civil War, when the Civil War amendments – for the
first time – took power from government, rather than transferring
it among governments, and truly gave it to the people. It has taken
a fifth constitution over the past fifty or so years to give any meaning

to that. I do not believe in Brandeis's "market-place of ideas." I'm sorry to tell you that. I am a cynic. I do not believe that truth rises and falsity falls. I do not believe that if free speech is allowed the best ideas will prevail. Brandeis did not live through Nazism. Brandeis did not live through other forms of tyranny of the majority that worked as the result of the "market-place of ideas." I'm sorry that I can't sell you a theory of the First Amendment which is a positive, productive theory. My theory of the First Amendment is a negative theory – it's a distrust of government. It says that the least worst alternative is to allow people freedom because the government is the only alternative to the people to decide what to say and how to regulate it. If we indeed had a bevy of Platonic guardians – you and I and the members of this panel who could forever sit in judgment over what speech was free and what speech was not, what speech was offensive and what was not – I'd probably vote for it. I might not be sure of all the members of the panel but I think I could probably come to an agreement. I would be the one I'd have the most doubt about. And yet I'm serious when I say that the question is never one of substance, it's always one of process. I have a profound distrust of government. I have a profound distrust of the judiciary. I have a profound distrust of the press. I have a profound distrust of people. I have a profound trust of chaos and of the chaos that is caused by the separation of powers. I love the fact that when Bryce came to America in search of sovereignty, which was what the great nineteenth-century Europeans always were looking for, he went back saying that he couldn't find sovereignty. To me that's the magic of America. You can't find sovereignty. We do not allow the establishment of religion, and we should not allow the establishment of truth. That's why the Holocaust-denial cases are so testing, because we all know the Holocaust occurred. Elie Wiesel is testament, if testament be needed, and yet I would allow somebody to stand up, look Elie Wiesel in the face, and say to him, "Sorry, you're wrong. It didn't happen." That would be a knife, I would agree with you, and yet I have no way of saying to people, You are right and you are wrong. I can't say that. I wouldn't allow a Holocaust denier into my living room. I wouldn't allow a pornographer into my living room. On the other hand, I would defend the right of both of them to speak.

Can you export that out of the United States? I think so, but with limits. Nothing is totally exportable. But most of the excuses I hear from other governments, I hear in the United States as well. I distrust other governments as much as I distrust my own. I guess I distrust my own a little bit more because I'm closer to it. But I also distrust the arguments that are made by other governments, and therefore I do think that, presumptively, ideas of free speech are exportable, subject to being persuaded otherwise in any particular case.

Q. Professor Dershowitz, I respect your intellect, your passion, and your humour, and yet, to very core of my being, I fundamentally disagree with pretty well everything you've said. I would say that I believe in government, I believe in the Department of Justice, and I thank God for a country that allowed somebody like Maxwell Cohen to define the beginnings of our hate propaganda laws. I thank God for a country that allows us to re-examine that and determine how we will redefine, refine, and make an even better law to protect ourselves.

When someone denies the Holocaust, they deny my very existence here. To those who are Jews, who had family who were victims in the Second World War, to deny the Holocaust is to deny their existence. I will not allow that to happen.

A. PROFESSOR DERSHOWITZ: What do you mean, you will not allow it to happen? What are you going to do? You're going to beat somebody up? Or you will try to get a law passed, right?

Q. Right. And that's what we have in this country.

A. PROFESSOR DERSHOWITZ: What if somebody else says, I will not allow you to say the Holocaust occurred. He may be bigger than you. Then you have to go to government and then you count noses and, if you have more people saying the Holocaust occurred than he has saying it didn't occur, you win. Is that what you're saying?

Q. I will not allow you to walk up to me in the street and hit me in the nose. I will not allow you to hurt me to the core of my being, my dignity, my self-respect, as witnessed in the preamble to the Universal Declaration of Human Rights – everyone shall have the dignity of a human being. And in this country we have the Canadian Charter of Rights and Freedoms, which establishes a fundamental freedom of expression that can be limited through section 1. We have a Criminal Code hate propaganda provision, and we will continue to redefine it. The Law Reform Commission of Canada is examining it now, and the Department of Justice is examining it now.

One could say that you have total, absolute freedom of thought. You may think to yourself how much you hate somebody around you. I will say, however, that when that thought becomes verbal expression which may lead even to physical expression, that is where we draw the line. I think if anybody had had the courage and the guts – if there had been an international community that had been willing to deny Hitler the platform he had in 1931 and 1932 and 1933 and so on – perhaps the Holocaust might not have occurred. It is because he had the platform and people were unwilling to challenge what he said.

A. PROFESSOR DERSHOWITZ: No, there weren't enough people who were big enough and physical enough. You're making it ultimately into a power struggle. You're saying, if you have the power to suppress the speech, you will. You're not going to try to tell me I'm wrong, you're going just to beat me down, either by the laws or physically beat me down. I just don't understand that argument. We do not live in an ideal world. It would be wonderful if everybody could live in dignity. But dignities clash. What you're eventually moving toward is a power resolution. You're saying we must resolve these disputes and I'm saying that the cost of not resolving these disputes is to live in a society where you have to tolerate not punches in the mouth, not knives in the chest, but words that hurt.

Q. I believe in freedom of speech. I don't believe in violence. I don't believe in licence. I think where Professor Dershowitz goes wrong is that he does not distinguish between the right to say what he thinks and to deny what he may want to deny, and speech which provokes violence by those who hear it or against those to whom or about whom you are saying it. There is a fundamental difference between the *Zundel* and *Keegstra* cases. Keegstra was not merely indulging in free speech or even in the right to deny the Holocaust. Keegstra was teaching children. The problem that we are faced with, with hate propaganda, is the issue of: I hate the Jew, I hate the Black, I deny his humanity. That is not free speech, nor even licence; it is provocation to violence. Anybody who is a human being and lives in society must oppose the provocation to violence. The question is not whether I happen to like or dislike your speech, but that you will not be allowed to abuse the right of free speech.

Q. Part of the common law, part of our tradition, part of our understanding is that one of the limits to our speech is that we cannot make libellous statements about people. Assuming that we can accept that, is it not also true that perhaps we have to understand the ramifications of libel against *groups* who are libelled not because of their opinions, but simply because of their identity, their race, colour, or religion? Is this not a means of moving forward in terms of an evolution of human rights; libelling groups is an extension of our understanding of the danger of libelling individuals.

A. JUDGE MAXWELL COHEN: I certainly would accept that position. What puzzles me about Mr Dershowitz's general position is to grasp whether he is speaking as a student of the nature of government or whether he's speaking on some other plane. If he's speaking as the former, surely he has a concept of what makes a society work, what are all the areas of intervention that are legitimate and what are those that are illegitimate. In every society, we have institutions and principles that make a society operationally possible in a very complex order. Certain values and certain freedoms are given status in the hierarchy of values. So the basic question to ask Professor Dershowitz, it seems to me, is what is his view of the nature of a modern society, given all the complexities of communication, given all the knowledge we have through psychology of the impressions of the psychic consequences of certain behaviour and verbal patterns. How would he see a modern order operating with the least harm to the most people? Once you express that in some kind of terms, then we can discuss the technique of furthering your ambition. But let's deal with the fundamentals first. Where do you stand on the nature of society and the legitimate means for the maintaining of order in that society?

A. PROFESSOR DERSHOWITZ: I think that that is a fair question. To me, the hallmark of a modern society is heterogeneity. We are a country, as is Canada, that is experimenting with being the most diverse, heterogeneous, multi-ethnic, multi-religious, multi-cultural, multi-belief group of societies in the history of the world. I think we need rules. My suggestion is very simple: that the rules of free speech be content-free. On this I completely agree with the previous speaker – I abhor violence. That is one of the reasons that I want more free speech. It is my experience that free speech is an antidote to violence, and in fact I would be very, very rigid about any situation where somebody provoked somebody else to fight back. I would arrest the person who fought back and I would protect, if it took all the police in the city, the right of those persons who wanted to speak, even if they provoked others. In my country, violence is not caused by speech. The government says violence is caused by speech. There are many Supreme Court decisions under the "clear and present danger" rule that stop speech because of the fear of violence. But if you study, as some people have done, the number of actual incidents of violence that are provoked by this kind of speech, what you find is that, if violence is allowed as a veto, then violence will follow speech. But if the government sets up a rule saying you cannot stop that speech by violence, there will be no violence.

People like to debate, people like to argue back and forth, people may even shake their fist, but violence is largely a function in my country, at least, and I suspect in this country, of what violence will get you. If it will get you censorship, then people will be violent. I suspect that even in a discussion like this, which is very civilized, in a university, I can get provocative enough so that if, in fact, the rule were that if one person were to try to stop me from speaking I would have to stop, that would probably happen. It happened at Harvard two weeks ago, when the head of the Contras came to speak at Harvard and a young man from Tufts, who belongs to a Marxist organization, in a very well-prepared violent outburst, jumped up on the stage because he knew in advance that, by doing that, the man would not be allowed to continue his speech. That was the violence veto. That must be stopped. I am appalled by and opposed to violence.

I have a theory of government, but my theory of government and my theory of speech is that the government shall not determine truth. Zundel was a pamphleteer in the great tradition of Thomas Paine. Everything he did was wonderful, he obeyed every rule. I hate the fact that I have to come to Zundel's defence. It's your fault that I have to come to Zundel's defence. In my country, I don't have to defend scum like Zundel, I can spend all my time attacking him, and thank God we've never brought Zundel to trial in my country. It is because you brought Zundel to trial in this country that I get letters asking me to join the Zundel Civil Liberties Defence Fund. Shame on you!

A. RAM JETHMALANI: Now, Professor Dershowitz has favoured us with a long list of things which he distrusts, without telling us a single thing which he trusts. I really don't know whether he does believe in the existence of an ordered society, because society must have the powers necessary to exclude those actors who disturb its stability.

It all depends upon the advanced state of the society, its stability, its tranquillity, the character of its people, and the nature of the activities which are thought to be for its protection.

Alan says, "I don't trust this, I don't trust that." But ultimately, in every ordered society, we trust at least the judiciary. Every day, the judges, who are independent of the government, decide issues of fact. Every day, we try actions of truth and falsehood in the law courts. Why can't society have the right to punish and prevent the kind of falsehood that shakes the very foundations of ordered society? It's wholly untrue to say that words do not cause provocation, that words do not produce violence. You have to come to my country to realize how words do produce the most acute kind of violence and the disturbance of the very stability and the foundations of our society.

Nobody suggests that the government has a right to declare what the truth is, in the absolute sense. It is left to the independent judiciary to decide what is true and what is false on the facts of a particular case. I believe, and my Constitution provides, that the use of free speech shall be subject to reasonable restrictions in the interests of the law of libel. We have preserved the law of libel by an express provision in the Constitution, and so have the Americans. The Americans committed the first mistake of drafting their articles in undiluted terms and then, by judicial decision, creating restrictions. We have written these restrictions into the text of our Constitution, and I'm glad that the Canadian Charter also writes these restrictions in express terms. The law of libel has got to be preserved, because reputation is the most important asset of an individual, and – except in the case of public servants, whose reputation must be susceptible of public scrutiny and investigation – everybody is entitled to preserve his reputation unsullied from attacks of any kind. If an individual has the right to complain of libel, there should be no reason that groups as such should not be able to complain of libel.

Q. I was a little nervous coming up, given the ability and background most of the speakers. And it occurred to me that that might be part of the problem here. I don't think that speech is as much of a problem when there is real equality among people, because then everyone can go home and no one's hurt by it. You can throw out an idea and everyone can share it.

Part of this whole freedom-of-discussion debate concerns pornography, which concerns women. It is violence against women, direct violence. It is not an intellectual debate. You are all men here talking about this issue. I know I can't speak for all the women here, but I certainly know a number of women who feel out of place talking in a forum like this because the discussion never gets around to the violence they feel. It's a power issue.

A. PROFESSOR DERSHOWITZ: It's precisely because I don't want to say that society upholds pornography that I don't want it to be censored. I don't want my society to say: *Hustler*, no, *Penthouse*, yes. I don't want the government to get into the business of deciding what's offensive and what's not offensive. In some parts of the United States, legislation is still on the books, which legislation, right along with banning pornography, bans material on birth control and abortion. There is no way you can limit the power of the government to prevent what you think some woman will find offensive, without also giving that same "ism-equity" to other groups, whether it be Blacks who are offended by showing pictures of lynching or Jews who are offended by the use of certain words. What I can't agree with is the limited question about pornography. How can one claim some special right to censor one genre of speech that offends one group of people in our society without also censoring that which offends another group?

VOICE IN AUDIENCE: Pornography is not speech.

PROFESSOR DERSHOWITZ: That's what you say.

VOICE IN AUDIENCE: Ask a woman who has been raped.

PROFESSOR DERSHOWITZ: Well, ask a Jew who has been discriminated against. Ask a Black whose grandfather was lynched. I mean, that's an argument that gets you nowhere, saying that it's not speech. That was Justice Black's stupid argument about the First Amendment. Justice Black said, "Congress shall pass no law abridging freedom of speech." And then somebody walked into a courthouse wearing a jacket that said "F— the draft." And Justice Black said, "That's not speech." Well, he didn't like it, so it wasn't speech. I don't want to sit in judgment about what's speech.

JUDGE COHEN: Yes, but then you ought not to be a law teacher. The life of a self-conscious lawyer is a life of drawing acceptable and intelligent lines in a society which cannot draw the lines automatically by itself without some institutional basis for it.

PROFESSOR DERSHOWITZ: I've drawn a line. You just don't like where I've drawn it.

JUDGE COHEN: You're refusing to accept the primary role of the law maker and the law giver and the law teacher, which is to say: How do I find a rational line which is defensible in a democratic, free society? You're not prepared to face up to that. Yours is a *laissez-faire* view, "Let the chips fall where they may, I'm willing to risk that because I know society democratically is, *per se*, strong." You don't know that. We are all vulnerable entities living together, hoping that we will survive in a society with many pressures; we need some basic guidelines, some minimal intervention that respects the vulnerability of people and societies and does something rational about it.

PROFESSOR DERSHOWITZ: You need a kind of elitist judiciary, somebody above and beyond democracy, to draw lines. My answer is, I'd rather have no lines drawn at all on the issue of offensiveness.

I'm prepared to see some lines drawn on other grounds, so long as
they are neutral lines, but I am not prepared to give to a judge or to
democracy the power to define what offensive speech shall be
permitted and what shall not. And I still think I can teach law with
that point of view.

Q. I am a history professor at the University of Quebec in Montreal.
As a Professor of Russian and Soviet history, I am very leery of
accepting government-imposed and law-imposed historical truths.
On the other hand, I'm also not ready to accept that freedom of
speech should go so far as to allow the advocacy of violence in the
name of a fact that was denied. I have a question concerning
another genocide which perhaps is less known, I'm sure it's much
less known here, and perhaps we can tackle this dispassionately. I'm
talking about the two famines in Ukraine; Ukraine, under Soviet
rule, has suffered two famines. The first, in 1921–23, had about a
million and a half to two million victims. If there were no more than
that, it's to a large extent due to the fact that the Jewish community
in North America and in Europe came to the aid, first of the Jewish
community in Ukraine, which was suffering from this famine, and,
in doing this, they brought aid to the whole country.

The second famine was much worse. No aid was allowed to come
in from outside at all. This was in the thirties, and it left about six
million dead.

Now, the Ukrainians have lived with genocide denial ever since.
It was denied by the *New York Times*. It was denied by scholars. If you
take a textbook of Russian history written any time before the sixties,
there is no mention of this famine.

Now, it is finally coming to be known and it's even getting into
some of the curricula, together with other types of genocide – the
Armenian, the Jewish, and so on. In Canada, it has been announced
recently that a book will be published that will not only deny the
famine but will also try to discredit the people who talk about the
famine.

And in the same way as the Jewish question was not just a Jewish
question, this is a world question. Famine is still being used by
governments as one very effective means of dealing with opposition,
much more effective than bullets. What is the attitude that the
Canadian society should take toward this book that is supposed to
be coming out in December?

A. JUDGE COHEN: Well, first of all, let me say something I should
have said in describing the Report on Hate Literature. I should have
explained that in the Report it was thought that section 177 of the

Criminal Code [editor's note: now section 181] on spreading false news was not very sound policy. The report recommends repeal of section 177. Therefore, I don't think that it's really going to be helpful to examine in depth the use of section 177 when we have the very specific provisions in the Code of section 281 dealing with hate propaganda *per se*. I don't know if that will be helpful to dealing with your problem.

But let me turn to the broad issue you've raised. What should be the public reaction? Having rejected Zundel's right to publish pamphlets that deny the existence of the Holocaust, what do we say about people who want to publish a book denying the existence of the tremendous famine in the Ukraine which killed six million people in the thirties? By the way, the famine was also dealt with in a series of articles by the *Christian Science Monitor* in the thirties, and a very important series of articles it was.

I'll give you my own reaction on short notice. I won't prejudge. I'll simply prejudge the process. We have a democratic process. We have a jury system. On the whole, the jury system works in a variety of situations pretty much to the satisfaction of democratic orders in the Anglo-Canadian, Anglo-American world. Should we trust them in the illustration you give? My answer is yes.

A. PROFESSOR DERSHOWITZ: I don't usually give free legal advice but I'm going to give it to you. Please do not bring a lawsuit. Do not allow the history of your people to be determined by twelve mediocrities in chairs, who are called a jury. You are taking an enormous risk. What if they rule that the famine didn't occur? What if there is a hung jury? What if they do what they did in the *Zundel* case and parade every Holocaust-denier kook from around the country, which resulted in headlines all through Canada, saying "'Auschwitz a Recreational Facility,' says expert. 'Auschwitz didn't kill Jews,' say experts." Spend your time answering the book on the merits. Do the research, discredit the writer, beat him to a pulp in the market-place of ideas, but do not bring that lawsuit or you will regret it, I believe, even if you win a very shortsighted victory.

JUDGE COHEN: I'm not supporting section 177. I want to see 177 left out of the Criminal Code. But there must be a judicial answer if there can't be an immediate popular answer. I think Professor Dershowitz's theory of doing the research is a sound one, and I support it. It does not mean, however, that you must distrust the entire judicial process for the administration of this thing.

Q. I was going to suggest a hypothesis as to why Professor Dershowitz is never convinced that he's wrong and why so few people are ever convinced that he's right. And my hypothesis is that what Professor Dershowitz is doing is expressing an axiom, something that is true because it's true, because it's true. Speech must be absolutely free under all circumstances because it must be absolutely free under all circumstances. If, for instance, there was scientific proof that there is a word that I could pronounce that would kill half the people in this room, and another word that I could pronounce which would make everybody in this room happy for the rest of their lives, Professor Dershowitz would say that you cannot forbid the word that kills half the people because, if you can do that, you can forbid the other word.

My suggestion is that Judge Cohen is right, that there are rational distinctions to be made and that stopping a Zundel before he becomes a Hitler is worthwhile; that one can stop what is not just despicable but harmful, criminal, and inciteful. This can be done without introducing tyranny into our country.

Q. My name is Morris Manning. I'd like to ask Professor Dershowitz to comment on speech which gives rise to direct action, such as the shouting of "Fire" in a crowded theatre.

I also want to direct a scenario to Judge Cohen, arising out of the hate-propaganda section of the Criminal Code. I acted in the Ontario Court of Appeal in the case of *R. v. Buzzanga and Durocher*. That case involved two individuals who were sympathetic to the Acadians' plight and the history of their people. These individuals, part of the Acadian community, were well-meaning; they felt that their community was being torn apart from within and found a solution, they thought, in distributing hate literature which appeared to come from without in order to bond their people together in a cohesive unit – a misguided decision, we might think, in hindsight. The Ontario Court of Appeal set aside the conviction. The Ontario Court of Appeal recognized the folly of that prosecution and interpreted the section in such a way as to make it more difficult to apply this section in the future, thereby giving all the attorneys general of this country an opportunity not to use the section. I'd like you to comment on that situation because it seemed to me, when I argued the case, that that was one of the best cases against drawing the line anywhere when it comes to free speech.

A. JUDGE COHEN: Well, I may say that that case has always bothered me too. I think that it's an unfortunate scenario. These two young men thought they were going to mobilize opinion by committing this particular social prank – it was a social prank with a particular objective. What was the *mens rea* here? Was there an evil intent?

There certainly was an object of intent to foment a particular reaction, a lot of reaction if they could. But they had as their ultimate intention something else.

The task of the reasonable man, whether a law teacher, an editor, a judge, or a parliamentarian, is to help society collectively to draw reasonable lines. In the *Durocher* case it may be that reasonable lines were not adequately discovered in the doctrine of *mens rea* by the courts and by the attorney general.

A. PROFESSOR DERSHOWITZ: No discussion is ever complete on free speech without invoking Holmes's example of shouting "Fire" in the theatre. It was one of the most dishonest analogies ever used by a judge. He didn't mean shouting "Fire" in the theatre, he meant setting off an alarm bell in the theatre. He used the word "fire" in a sneaky effort to try to expand from a clang sound, which is not an idea, but, in fact, is exactly the opposite of an idea. When you set off an alarm bell in the theatre, the very concept is not to think about it with your mind. And he used "fire" because that is a word. I don't believe all words should be protected. The previous gentlemen said, what if a word could be uttered which would save lives. Of course, I would make that word be uttered. Or a word that would be uttered which would take lives? We're not talking about ideas there. I agree with you that words with no social utility, that are not intended to communicate ideas, don't come within my principle. I have a list at home, I could bore you with it, of every time anybody invoked the concept of shouting "Fire" – everything you want to ban is like shouting "Fire" in the theatre. In fact, nothing is like shouting "Fire" in a theatre, except setting off an alarm bell. I think we can come up with objective, neutral, content-free rules that do say you cannot say things the intended immediate impact of which is not to allow a response but an immediate violent confrontation. But that's not what we're talking about. We're talking about ideas which are false.

A. JUDGE COHEN: Just one moment. It seems to me a mistake to allow Professor Dershowitz to get away permanently with his vacuum theory. His neutrality theory is a vacuum theory. We don't live in a vacuum, we live in a constant state of tension in which values are constantly in conflict. The idea of lawyers, law schools, or the courts trying to formulate so-called neutral principles seems to me to be a fiction, not even fit for a first-year seminar, to say nothing of this room.

Q. PROFESSOR IRWIN COTLER: I must say that I was reluctant to get up and say anything at all, but I felt that my silence in the face of your remarks, Alan, might be construed as consent, and so I feel obliged to speak. And there is another reason.

I have a sense – and I don't impugn this to anything you intended or even said, but rather to a kind of psychological fall-out – I have a sense that there is a subtle labelling going on in the name of content neutrality – that somehow those who would permit racist hate propaganda are the only good civil libertarians and those who would prohibit hate propaganda are somehow anti-civil libertarians; not that you intended or suggested it.

A. PROFESSOR DERSHOWITZ: Not anti-civil libertarians, just anti-free speech.

PROFESSOR COTLER: Oh, anti-free speech. I happen to think that that kind of configurative analysis really begs the question and indeed presupposes the outcome. In a word, there are good free-speech people on both sides of the question. We should not determine the outcome by the nature of the labelling as to who is for or against free speech.

PROFESSOR DERSHOWITZ: I agree.

PROFESSOR COTLER: Indeed, I think one can take judicial notice that the very fact that I would invite you here to speak the way you have is a testimony to my belief in free and offensive speech.

PROFESSOR DERSHOWITZ: I've never doubted that, Irwin.

PROFESSOR COTLER: But let me take you up and conclude on your challenge. I think that you have posed us with a serious challenge. You have said that there is nothing, nothing in reason, law, policy, press, or anything that you have seen that would justify limitations of the kind in the *Zundel* and *Keegstra* cases. I think, however, that you would agree, as I've heard you say elsewhere, that freedom of speech is not an absolute right.

PROFESSOR DERSHOWITZ: That's true.

PROFESSOR COTLER: It's clear also in our Charter that we have laid down a certain balancing principle; there can be limitations if they are reasonable, prescribed by law, and demonstrably justifiable in a free and democratic society. I would like to suggest some concluding conceptual guidelines respecting that kind of speech and whether it should be limited. I suggest to you that one has to take all of these guidelines together, not any one of them.

Number one, does this "Zundel-type" speech constitute an assault on the inherent dignity and worth of the human person?

PROFESSOR DERSHOWITZ: Yes.

PROFESSOR COTLER: Second, does this constitute not only an assault on the human person but on the equal dignity and worth of all human persons?

PROFESSOR DERSHOWITZ: Yes.

PROFESSOR COTLER: Then equality rights are at issue and not just free speech ...

PROFESSOR DERSHOWITZ: Right.

PROFESSOR COTLER: Number three. Does that derogate from the principles of multi-culturalism by which we are to interpret the rights and freedoms in our Charter?

PROFESSOR DERSHOWITZ: Yes.

PROFESSOR COTLER: Four. Does it breach our international obligation to prohibit the dissemination of this kind of hate propaganda?

PROFESSOR DERSHOWITZ: The same international obligations that require you to ban Zionism as racism. If you think you're going to get me to make anything turn on what the United Nations decides is truth, forget it.

PROFESSOR COTLER: One should not compare a General Assembly resolution of substantial dubious value ...

PROFESSOR DERSHOWITZ: No, there is more good will and intelligence in this room than in the General Assembly. I would much rather leave it to a vote here as to whether or not we should allow Zundel to speak than to leave it to those racist-bigots at the General Assembly. Forget it. That's worse than one government. That's three hundred governments. We're agreeing. We're really getting somewhere when we're agreeing on almost everything. Let's just leave out the United Nations, okay?

PROFESSOR COTLER: I can understand why an American would not want to worry about those international obligations. The United States remains unique in not having been a signatory to those international convenants requiring ...

PROFESSOR DERSHOWITZ: Over my strong objection. I want to sign on to those but I don't want them to restrict my free speech. In fact, if you continue to make this argument ...

PROFESSOR COTLER: Then you had better read what you are signing on to because it will restrict this kind of speech.

PROFESSOR DERSHOWITZ: Well, if you continue to make this argument, you're going to persuade me to support, which I don't want to do, the United States' refusal to sign on to international declarations that the Soviet Union signs on to and the United States doesn't – and compare the free speech allowed in those two countries!

What I'm saying is that the United States can teach the world something about free speech and not learn anything from almost anybody in the world about free speech. It is one of the few things that we can teach you something about.

PROFESSOR COTLER: I think that our speech is abusing the sensibilities of others at this point, so let me just continue on the other point. I think that there is one other sort of subtle and misleading issue. We're not talking about political speech against governmental authorities that can withstand the worst kind of offensive speech imaginable. We're not talking, in a word, about political speech against "the establishment." We are talking about the kind of hateful speech against vulnerable minorities which, if repeated over time, will have the effect of reducing the status, the standing, the appreciation, et cetera, of that minority in society over time – in a word, ultimately reducing their right to have their speech protected. I suggest to you that that's what the real issue is – the assault on vulnerable minorities, not free speech against political establishments.

PROFESSOR DERSHOWITZ: I agree with that. I think that's an important distinction, but it's a distinction that is often abused by government. One of the great clichés being used by my government today to suppress individual rights is called "victim's rights." The government never says any more that we're doing it on behalf of the government; we're doing it on behalf of particular victims; I think what you've done is you've created, brilliantly, a concept by which the government can take notions of individual victimization and turn it into a governmental power. To me, the most fundamental right is the right to be wrong, not the right to be right. Nobody has the right to be right. It's the right to be wrong and not to have the government ultimately sit in judgment as to whether you're right or wrong.

Q. Jack London, University of Manitoba. I share your view on the *Zundel* case in terms of the unhappiness of the prosecution, not because I care about Zundel, and not because I think that he ought to be allowed to say what he did, but because of the inability of the press to properly and comprehensively cover a trial of that kind.

One of the great restrictions on speech in that kind of context is the contempt of court power, which prevents the newspapers from reporting critically the absurd evidence that is given at the time when the defence is calling its case.

But I have a question for you that was skipped over long ago. I want to take you back to *Keegstra*. Governments act through different forms of instrumentality. In the *Keegstra* case, what would you do if you found Keegstra teaching Holocaust denial in a classroom? Would you prosecute him? Second part of the question: If you wouldn't prosecute him and you were an elected school board, that is another form of government instrumentality. Would you remove him from the classroom and penalize him in that way?

A. PROFESSOR DERSHOWITZ: Absolutely, I'd fire him without a moment's hesitation because the classroom is a closed situation; it's not a market-place situation. Because students have no choice but to go to school, we have to censor what goes on in the classroom. That's where lines have to be drawn. A child is not in a position to fully understand, comprehend, and refute. I think the state did absolutely the right thing in firing Keegstra. I would even have no hesitation about a properly drawn statute prosecuting him, that's really a detail. Because once I'm prepared to censor ...

JACK LONDON: Draw the statute for me.

PROFESSOR DERSHOWITZ: The statute that would prosecute or fire him?

JACK LONDON: The properly drawn statute that would prosecute him.

PROFESSOR DERSHOWITZ: I would say that school boards in general have to be given great latitude and the power to determine within a lot of rules. Let me tell you why I have to do this, and it's very painful for me, because here there really is no alternative. There is no free market in a classroom, there is no unlimited and unrestricted space. Frankly, I'd much rather have a paradigmatic situation in school where Holocaust deniers could come, where they could be answered, where everything was created in a free market. That's not the way it happens. In school there's one teacher, who will take one class in one subject, and therefore we have to pick and choose. That's a tragedy. That is a denial of the paradigm of democracy. That is a compromise we have to make. So I would allow censorship of what Zundel says to children, but I would not allow censorship of the very same ideas in the free market-place, where people could turn off the television set, boo him, answer him, respond to him, and engage in a debate. Not because I think he's wrong, not because I think we're right, not because I don't think his ideas will prevail, but because there's no other alternative.

Q. Richard Janda of McGill University. Perhaps things are different at Harvard, Professor Dershowitz, but I've yet to encounter an objective, neutral, value-free rule of any kind.

A. PROFESSOR DERSHOWITZ: I'll give you one: decibels. You can't have speech above a certain decibel. Or you can't have speech at certain times of night or day. You can't have over a certain number of words; there are millions of neutral and objective content-free rules; we live with them all the time. That's the rule primarily today in the United States. We have case law this thick on that.

Q. But let me get to the question, and it really goes back to something that was asked earlier. In one domain, we've already tried – I might agree, with difficulty – to establish rules that work in the area of libel and slander. I want to know why the questions that are being raised today are of any different character, and if they're not, why isn't it simply that in this area of the law, like in so many areas of the common law, judges, juries, and the institutional system as a whole must grapple with difficult moral questions and try to come to some arbitrary line. The fact that there's a difficult line to be drawn doesn't seem to me to say that we shouldn't draw a line, it simply says that it's difficult and we have to face it. So, I don't really understand this business of objective, neutral, and value-free.

A. PROFESSOR DERSHOWITZ: But would you agree that neutral rules exist? Let me give you another one that suggests itself. In the law of libel, there is a rule that, if you know you are lying, you are not protected. So that the jury never need ask the question, Is it the truth or isn't it the truth? If you can prove that the person – this is kind of the *mens rea* suggestion that was made before – if you can prove that the person said it, knowing it was a lie, it's like the reckless disregard or falsehood notion of libel in the United States against a public official. I have less trouble with that, because that's the jury's traditional role. It asks the question whether or not this person is defrauding another by claiming a belief which he doesn't himself have. Even in the United States under the First Amendment, we can prosecute that. I am willing to accept that kind of rule, but it is different when you put the jury in a libel or slander case – or the government, worst of all – in the position of judging whether a person who believes something to be the truth is right or wrong ... I don't think the government or a jury or a judge should make that decision.

Q. I am a student in this faculty. My question is for Professor Dershowitz. It seems to me that you're either advocating an anarchist-
like position, where no lines can be drawn, or you're saying that
lines can be drawn only if they're content-neutral, and you're replacing the government with yourself and saying that you can draw
the line, as opposed to the government. I wonder what gives *you* the
right to decide whether they are content-neutral, as opposed to the
government.

A. PROFESSOR DERSHOWITZ: You have to give somebody the power to
determine whether it's within or outside the rule; I'm just advocating
a rule that basically says, let's try to be as content-neutral as we can.
The rule will fail sometimes. The United States Supreme Court
imposed zoning laws last year on pornographic theatres, saying it was
content-neutral. Nonsense – it was not. I'm not saying it will always
work. My basic point is that, deep down, everybody wants to censor
something. Your very reaction to my talk, I think, demonstrates that.
Censorship, ability to control, is the norm in human behaviour. Let
us try our human best to make it hard to do.

Q. My name is Kathleen Mahoney. I'm a professor at the University
of Calgary, in the law faculty. I have a question as well for Professor
Dershowitz, and it's in the context of pornography.

First of all, I'd like to say it doesn't surprise me that there hasn't
been any woman other than myself making a comment, because I
find your argument, which is the classic liberal argument, basically
anti-female and hostile to women in its origins and fundamental
assumptions.

A. PROFESSOR DERSHOWITZ: That is an absurd, insulting, degrading
question, which I think is sexist, and I'd like you to defend it.

PROFESSOR KATHLEEN MAHONEY: Before you draw that conclusion,
perhaps you could hear me out.

PROFESSOR DERSHOWITZ: You have made a comment, now defend it.
Why is traditional liberalism, content-free liberalism, when advocated
by a man who has spent a great deal of his life in the interest of
feminism, why is that a sexist argument?

PROFESSOR MAHONEY: Well, first of all, you suggested that the proper
approach to deciding these questions is an approach based on
"equal-ism," if I ...

PROFESSOR DERSHOWITZ: "Ism-equity."

PROFESSOR MAHONEY: "Ism-equity." Fundamentally, I think, this is based on the assumption that all people have equal access to the market-place of truth. And clearly that's not the case.

PROFESSOR DERSHOWITZ: I agree.

PROFESSOR MAHONEY: We hear certain forms of speech in which the content of the very speech itself denies access to that market-place.

PROFESSOR DERSHOWITZ: Like?

PROFESSOR MAHONEY: Well, if you'd just let me finish, please, I'd appreciate it very much.

PROFESSOR DERSHOWITZ: Go ahead.

PROFESSOR MAHONEY: When the very form of speech denies the actual access to the market-place of ideas, that basic concept is fundamentally flawed.
    Second, you made the assertion ...

PROFESSOR DERSHOWITZ: You say "second," but how about explaining what you've just said. I don't understand a word you've just said. What denies you access to speech?

PROFESSOR MAHONEY: The fact that women do not have access to the money, the media ...

PROFESSOR DERSHOWITZ: And that's all my fault? That's the fault of us liberals who want to have free speech?

PROFESSOR MAHONEY: It's a fundamental assertion underlying your argument that the only ...

PROFESSOR DERSHOWITZ: No, it's not.

PROFESSOR MAHONEY: ... proper way to approach this issue is through equality of "isms" and what I'm saying to you, sir, is that we can't approach any equality problem assuming that all plaintiffs seeking equality begin from the same place as those with whom they're seeking equality. It is a truism, I think, in human-rights law that if you treat equals the same, you will, without question, end up with an equal result. We have, in this country at least, established the principle that, when members of different groups are different in terms of their power and their access to power, that we treat them differently because we look to equality of *results*. It's my view, and I'd be interested to hear you comment upon this, that this basic principle applies to the concept of freedom of speech, because in our country, as well as having section 2, which protects free expression, in our Charter of Rights and Freedoms, we also have sections

15 and 28, which affirm the notion of equality and therefore require the balance between these two concepts.

Second, you've made the point that violence is not caused by speech, and when I said that your comments are hostile to women's reality, it was more directed at this particular point that you're making, because even though it may be true that we cannot prove, beyond a reasonable doubt, any connection between, for example, violent pornography and violence against women, it doesn't take any great genius to realize that in our society today, there's incredible violence against women in every way, shape, and form of their existence – in their own homes, on the streets, in their places of work, and so on – and that pornography celebrates that kind of violence and eroticizes it.

You've also made the assertion that judges and governments cannot be trusted. Now, there is some veracity to that comment. I think history tells us that, but I would much rather have judges decide these issues, keeping in mind the Charter of Rights and Freedoms that binds them, than the Jerry Falwells or the Larry Flints of this world.

Finally, you've said that no one knows the truth; therefore, anyone wishing to restrict speech is imposing his or her version of the truth on others. What I would say to that is that, when we come to an issue like pornography, and I think we could extend this as well to hate propaganda against a definable group, we are not imposing our truth upon others when we rail against that kind of speech. What we are saying is that we want to impose the qualities of equality and dignity and respect for all humankind on the liar and on the malingerer as well as on the person who wishes to defend humanity.

PROFESSOR DERSHOWITZ: I think that your comments were excellent and probing, other than the sexist beginning. I certainly would never prevent you from railing against anything. That's part of my philosophy. You can rail, you can argue, you can protest, you can boycott; just don't censor.

It would take a long time for me to prove to you that there is no relationship whatsoever between the sexual explicitness of material and violence. There is a direct relation, I believe, between the violent nature of sexually explicit material and violence, but every single experimenter, even the Meese Commission, concluded that there was nothing to support, and everything to contradict, the fact that the level of sexual explicitness of material has no relationship whatsoever to the level of violence. To the extent that pornography has a meaning that has to do with sexual explicitness, there is no relationship. There is a great deal of violence against women in our society, and it is clearly on the increase, as is pornography clearly on the increase. There is a tremendous amount of violence against women in the Soviet Union, where there is no pornography, and very little violence against women in some Scandinavian countries, where there is total permissiveness about pornography. But that's not the point, because I agree with you. I said it right from the beginning, speech hurts, pornography hurts, especially if it causes violence. I will defend, equally, all kinds of speech, no matter whom it hurts. I haven't singled out women in any way.

I also agree with you about equality. I am prepared, in the interest of my concerns for equality and speech, to have an affirmative action program for disadvantaged people in the area of speech so that those people who have least access to the media will have most access. I agree with decisions in the United States which are moving a little bit in that direction in terms of electoral reform laws. Those are totally separate issues. I think you make a lot of sense in much of what you're saying, but to argue that the traditional liberal position is anti-feminist is just simply and categorically wrong. It may have some anti-feminist impact, but no greater than it has anti-Jewish impact, anti-Black impact, anti-gay impact, anti the impact of every single group in society that feels aggrieved. Women have no special claim over any other aggrieved or disadvantaged group to a special argument in favour of censorship. I think the argument is offensive.

PROFESSOR MAHONEY: That wasn't my point.

Closing Plenary:
Against Injustice

Chair

PROFESSOR ANDRÉ TREMBLAY

Mesdames et Messieurs, les organisateurs de ce congrès ont eu l'amabilité d'inviter un de leurs collègues de l'Université de Montréal pour présider cette dernière séance. Ma présence ici veut être un témoignage d'estime et d'amitié de mon Université et de ma faculté de droit à l'endroit de la Faculté de droit de l'Université McGill. Ma présence se veut aussi être un appui empressé et authentique à l'initiative généreuse pour les droits fondamentaux que représente cette conférence.

Quarante ans après Nuremberg, il reste encore tellement à faire et tellement d'injustices à corriger, de torts à redresser et de discrimination à juguler, dont l'apartheid. Dans le domaine des droits de l'homme, on ne peut jamais s'arrêter. Il faut défendre les droits et les faire progresser et quand nous cessons la lutte, c'est la régression.

Bravo à Irwin Cotler! Bravo aussi à ses collègues pour avoir organisé ce congrès éminemment réussi. La tenue de ce congrès fait honneur à ses organisateurs, elle fait honneur aussi à ses contributeurs et à ceux qui assistent à ce congrès.

Il permet l'espoir. Il stimule la réflexion et favorise des développements juridiques susceptibles de mettre un terme aux injustices de notre temps.

Professor Chaskalson is the founder-director of the Legal Resources Centre in South Africa. He has litigated some of the major cases involving apartheid law and was former defence counsel to Nelson Mandela. In 1987–88, he was visiting professor at Columbia University Law School.

Speaker

PROFESSOR ARTHUR CHASKALSON

I suppose that it is impossible to talk about injustice in our times without talking about apartheid. If I were asked for a "neutral" definition of apartheid, I think that I would say that it is the ideological formalization of policies of segregation and discrimination that has been pursued for centuries by white governments in South Africa. It was institutionalized and enmeshed in the laws of the country during the fifties and the sixties through statutes and regulations which sought to classify, define, control, and regulate the lives of all South Africans; it advanced the interests of the already powerful and dominant white community and excluded from the mainstream of society persons who were not white.

Apartheid has undergone changes in recent years, but its underlying structures, which are designed to ensure white supremacy, are still in place. At the centre is the Population Registration Act, which classifies each person according to his or her race. Once that classification has been made, that person's place in society has been determined. Political power is held by the white community, which accounts for approximately 15 per cent of the total population. Whites have the ultimate power of deciding what the laws should be and how the resources of the country should be distributed. The Indians and the so-called coloured people, who together represent a little more than 10 per cent of the total population of the country, have some say in the legislative process, but no power to promote or prevent the passage of legislation contrary to the will of the government. Africans, who account for over 70 per cent of the total population, have no say in the central government, no say in the passage of legislation, and no say in the allocation of resources.

The primacy of the whites in the political process is reflected in the way in which the resources of the country have been allocated. Whites have the exclusive right to the ownership and occupation of over 80 per cent of the land. Black, coloured, and Indian people, who may once have owned land in areas which were designated as being for whites only, were forcibly removed from such land. Blacks are required to live in segregated, underdeveloped, and overcrowded ghettos in urban areas, or in single-sex hostels at the places where they work, or, precariously, as labour tenants on white-owned farms, or in overpopulated and impoverished homelands.

Living conditions for coloured and Indian people are somewhat better, but they too have been forced into segregated, overcrowded townships. Conditions there have become so bad that many people have moved out of the ghettos into vacant accommodation in the so-called white areas, where they risk prosecution if they are reported to the police.

Whites have access to skills which are the direct or indirect result of their political and cultural dominance. They have had the benefit of an education system designed to prepare them for a superior status in society and to prepare Blacks for an inferior status in society. This was the shameless principle of Bantu education, which was engineered under the direction of Dr Verwoerd in the fifties. Under this system of segregated and differential education, ten times as much money was spent on a white child as on a Black child. As it was intended to do, this placed Blacks at a considerable disadvantage in the labour market.

Access to skills by Blacks was further impeded by labour policies which reserved the best jobs for whites and denied Blacks the right to be apprenticed in white areas or to be employed there in managerial or skilled positions. Those Blacks who were able to find employment in the limited fields open to them were not allowed to strike, and their unions were not recognized – that was a privilege reserved for white workers only. These policies effectively excluded Blacks from acquiring the skills that are needed to succeed in a modern technological society and reinforced their inferior status within South African society.

Labour policy went hand in hand with the influx-control system and the homeland policy. Influx control, epitomized in the pass laws, prevented Black women born in rural areas from going to live or work in the city. Approximately half the black population was confined to rural homelands through this legislation. Black men born in rural areas were not allowed to leave their homelands to look for work without permission from government-controlled labour bureaus. Such permission was given only for work as a migrant labourer, and then only to persons who could satisfy a labour bureau that they were needed to fill vacancies in the white areas.

This policy had a devastating impact on family life – separating husbands, wives, and children and forcing married men into single-sex hostels while they worked in the white areas. It made criminals out of men and women who sought employment in towns or sought to live together as families in circumstances in which the law denied them the right to do so.

This was all part and parcel of the government's homeland policy, which contemplated that blacks would become citizens of homelands and would be aliens in South Africa. Thus, when homelands were offered independence and, in some cases, through unrepresentative legislatures accepted it, part of the deal was that Blacks associated with that homeland would become citizens of the newly "independent" homeland and would lose their South African citizenship. Citizenship went with ethnic origin; irrespective of their own wishes, or where they were living or working, millions of Blacks were denationalized through this process and became citizens of states which many of them wished to have no part of.

These apartheid laws created an environment in which it was difficult for Black persons to develop self-esteem and a sense of worth. They were forced into inferior positions in society and made to live in degrading and humiliating conditions in which self-fulfilment was impossible.

There has been resistance to these policies. But resistance has been contained by a network of security laws. These security laws are built around the provisions of the Internal Security Act which, in its present form, is a consolidation of legislation dating back to 1950. Under this act and its predecessors, major political organizations representing the interests of the black population have been banned. These include the African National Congress, of which Mr Mandela is the president, the Pan-African Congress, the Black People's Convention, and a large number of other organizations. It is an offence to belong to or to further the objects of any of these organizations, or to further objects similar to their aims.

In 1963, provision was made for detention without trial in security cases. This has since become a permanent feature of South African law and the cornerstone of its security legislation. The Internal Security Act makes provision for preventive detention of persons believed to be security risks, the detention of suspects without trial for an indefinite period for the purpose of interrogation, the detention without bail of prisoners awaiting trial on the order of the attorney general, and the detention of potential state witnesses.

Detainees can be, and most often are, denied access to their legal representatives. They are usually not permitted to see their families or to receive other visits whilst they are in detention. They are usually held in conditions approximating solitary confinement, receiving occasional visits from a magistrate and otherwise having contact only with their jailers and their interrogators. Reports of torture in detention are frequently made by former detainees, and over sixty deaths in detention have been recorded. Their experience symbolizes, in a very stark form, the solitude and the isolation of which Elie Wiesel spoke last night.

The state has a vast array of discretionary powers under the Internal Security Act and other legislation, exercisable by ministers and officials. These include the power to place persons under house arrest; the power to restrict particular persons from belonging to any organization or taking part in any activity, or making or receiving any financial contribution, or making speeches or publishing any material; the power to cause suspect organizations to be investigated and, to that end, to have premises entered, documents seized, and any person interrogated; the power to prohibit gatherings, generally or specifically, and to cause places in which gatherings take place to be closed; and the power to disperse gatherings that have assembled and to prohibit or restrict processions. For several years now, there has been a general ban on all outdoor gatherings and processions, which are unlawful unless permission has been obtained from the authorities to hold them. The state also has powers, which are frequently used, to intercept mail, to tap telephones, and to deny passports to opponents of the government. Terrorism, subversion, and intimidation have been made statutory offences – defined in wide terms and attracting severe penalties – and the rules of procedure and evidence have been changed to facilitate prosecutions.

A security trial today has a familiar pattern. The accused persons will be denied bail. They will have been arrested and held for interrogation in conditions which are substantially equivalent to solitary confinement. They may be, and often are, tried at places distant from their homes. Witnesses against them are likely to have been held by the police in similar conditions and to be brought from solitary confinement to court to give their evidence in the knowledge that, when they are finished with their evidence, they will be returned to the custody of the police. Often, witnesses give their evidence in courts that are closed to the public, with a prohibition against publication of their names.

The freedom of newspapers to publish has been eroded. Restrictions exist regarding the publication of information relating to the activities of the military, the police, and prison officials. Political censorship is exercised through the Publications Appeal Board as well as through provisions of the Internal Security Act.

Fundraising may not be carried out without the permission of the state.

These are some of the laws that exist in South Africa today as part of the permanent law of the country. In effect, they have permitted the state to control the flow of information; to proscribe political opposition; to break up organizations that may be seen to be gaining support, particularly within the black community; to cut off an organization's source of funds; to pick off leaders of particular organizations and render them impotent by detention, house arrest, banning, or other restrictions; to extract information from detainees, which enables the security police to bring to trial persons charged with having committed offences under the security legislation; and to instil fear. Long-standing resistance to its policies has been kept down by the government through the application of these laws, through the use of its police, its army, and through other means.

It has become apparent, however, that apartheid as originally conceived cannot succeed. Bantu education failed to produce a subservient and compliant Black community. Today, young Blacks are the most radical sector of the society, and are at the forefront of the resistance to the government's policies. Bantu education also failed in another respect. The growing and modernizing economy needed a skilled labour force. Most Blacks had not received the education and training to equip them for such work, and there were not enough whites to fill all the positions that were required. White immigrants were brought into the country at great cost to take positions which could have been filled by properly trained Black people, and, in order to preserve white hegemony, the economy was not permitted to grow at the rate it was capable of doing. At the same time, grievances against the apartheid policies that were being pursued began to express themselves in forcible dissent. All this led to pressing economic and political pressures, and as a result of this the government has been obliged to reformulate its policies.

In the late seventies, following the youth uprisings in Soweto, the government set in process a series of labour reforms through which the principle of job reservation was abandoned, Black trade unions were legitimated, and Black workers were permitted to take advantage of labour legislation which had previously been there for the exclusive benefit of white workers. It became legal for Blacks to strike.

The government also made a commitment to improve the system of education for Blacks. Segregation remained, but there was an undertaking, which has not yet been met, to equalize the per capita expenditure on education across racial lines.

In the eighties, the tricameral Parliament, giving limited representation to the so-called coloured and Indian communities, was set up and certain apartheid laws were repealed. The most important of these reforms are probably the repeal of the pass laws, the abandonment of the policy that prohibited Blacks from owning their own houses in urban townships – though the Group Areas Act still prohibited their ownership of land in white areas outside of the townships – and the passing of the Restoration of South African Citizenship

Act, under which some of the people who had lost their South African citizenship as a result of the homeland policy were given the opportunity of reclaiming their citizenship. These changes marked a fundamental shift in government policy. They acknowledged the permanence of Blacks as citizens of South Africa and an abandonment of policies based on the assumption that Blacks were temporary sojourners in the "white cities" and had their homes elsewhere.

The fundamental apartheid structures have, however, been retained. These are race classification, white political control, reservation of most of the land for ownership by whites, segregated residential areas, segregated and differentially state-controlled education, and the homelands policy. What is happening is that apartheid is being modernized, and, in certain aspects of society, divisions of race are being replaced by divisions of class.

These developments have not reduced dissent within the country. On the contrary, the tricameral Parliament proved to be divisive and to be a catalyst for political mobilization against the government on a scale that had not been seen for over twenty-five years. Resistance was widespread and was associated with violence. By 1985, violence had reached a level that the government was not willing to accept; it responded by declaring a state of emergency.

We have now lived through over two years of emergency rule, during which the state president and cabinet ministers have made laws by decree. On occasion, laws have even been made by policemen acting under powers delegated to them by the state president. During this period, the security forces have been vested with arbitrary powers of arrest, detention, and censorship, which they have used rigorously. Fundamental freedoms have been put under even greater constraints than previously.

One of the main targets of the security clamp has been the young people of the Black community. They have been at the centre of the resistance to apartheid, and they have been subjected to the full force of the action taken by the state in its attempts to put down dissent. They have borne the brunt of emergency rule. They have been shot at with live ammunition, they have been tear-gassed, and many of them have been subjected to detention without trial and all that goes with that.

They have shown great bravery in these circumstances, gathering the band in the knowledge that the police may intervene and in the knowledge that if the police do intervene, events may take a course which leads to confrontations with the police and to their being shot at, and they may die. And when someone dies, there is a funeral, at which attendance of more than twenty-five people is banned. But they go in thousands to the funeral, again risking the same process, knowing that the police will be there, knowing that at the funeral they may experience tear gas and bullets and knowing that some of them may die.

Another target of the emergency has been the media. Audiovisual recordings of the security forces in action have been prohibited, and reporting of their behaviour has been placed under strict censorship. This has resulted in the disappearance from the television screens of the world of any scenes of the South African forces in action; the reporting of events in South Africa has been muted.

I think that one of the ironies of this conference has been that it has shown us that we are probably better at dealing with the past than with the present. Despite worldwide protest, apartheid is still firmly in place. The country is still ruled by white South Africans, who continue to organize it to ensure that wealth and privilege vest in them. All attempts to mobilize the population against white domination have been broken up, and civil liberties and peaceful protests have been curtailed. This has led to violent resistance, and the Black population, excluded from political power in South Africa, has sought allies outside the country. Today, the justness of their cause is recognized by practically the whole world. The South African government stands isolated, defending itself behind a screen of security legislation and military power. There is deep-seated anger within the black community caused by the laws of the state and the methods that are being used to put down dissent. The view that conflict can be resolved only by force is being acted out in day-to-day life in South Africa, and, in the process, young people are dying and a society is being brutalized.

This will inevitably continue until there is a shared commitment to creating a non-racial and democratic society. The Black political leaders have made that commitment. Unless and until the political leadership of the white community is willing to make the same commitment, degradation, destruction, and death will continue.

The victims of this evil policy deserve the support of the world. And I think that it is up to all of us to see that they get it.

PROFESSOR ANDRÉ TREMBLAY Mr Boateng is a lawyer and member of Parliament in the United Kingdom for the Labour Party. In 1987, he became the first Black elected to the UK Parliament. He was a member of the Greater London Council from 1981 to 1986, and executive of the National Council on Civil Liberties from 1980 to 1986. He is a member of the Labour Party Sub-Committee on

Human Rights and a member of the Home Secretary's Advisory Council on Race Relations.

Speaker

PAUL BOATENG, MP (UNITED KINGDOM)

I want to thank and pay tribute to my hosts' hosts. I want to pay tribute to the old Canadians, the native peoples of Canada, those who never asked the guests into their homes, those who never lived to enjoy the feast. We need to have a thought for the old Canadians when we talk about genocide. We need to remember what Elie Wiesel taught us and showed us so clearly and so movingly last night: the importance of memory. And we ought to remember them when we meet here, in Canada, to discuss this subject.

As Elie Wiesel taught us, and as Greville Janner showed us with his use of the Yiddish and Hebrew languages and his drawing on the folk culture, wisdom, and humour of the Jewish people, one of the best depositories of memory, one of the best ways to keeping memory alive, is with a story. And I can do no better, in paying tribute to the old Canadians, than to share with you a story that I learned from a Native American person. It is the story of a shaman, a holy man, a medicine man sitting on the banks of a creek after a flood, with the creek swollen and the sides of the creek caving in. A little Native American boy observed him, picking up a scorpion, and then another scorpion, and then another scorpion from the swollen creek. Each time the shaman picked up a scorpion, it stung him, but he still went on picking up the scorpions. And the little boy asked the shaman, "Why is it, Medicine Man, why is it that you keep on being stung and yet you keep on picking up those scorpions?" The shaman looked at him and said, "Boy, it is in the nature of a scorpion to sting. What else would you have it do?"

I am a member of humankind. It is in my nature to care for all of God's creation. What else would you have me do? What else can we do but be true to our nature as human beings and have respect for all of God's creation?

And when I look at the Nuremberg Charter I am reminded of that story. Because when you look at that Charter, it is as if you were looking into a pool. And that is how we, as lawyers, should see the Nuremberg Charter – as the pool of principles from which we draw.

When we look into that pool, we see reflected, with all its flaws – and it has its flaws, some of which we have dwelt on in the course of these hours – what we want as human beings. We see in the Charter the duties we have as human beings, one to the other, and the sanction that must surely follow if we fail in those duties. We also must see the Nuremberg Principles and the Charter that enshrines them as something we draw upon to refresh international law; something we draw upon as a source of inspiration; something that can address some of the urgent questions and issues of our times.

We need to be quite clear about the context of that Charter if we are to see its value and its applicability now. We must not see the Holocaust as some sort of monstrous aberration in European history and culture. Certainly, it was monstrous, most monstrous. But when you examine European history and culture, you see how the Holocaust developed. You see where its origins lie. The Holocaust is the most extreme manifestation of racism. European culture is shot through with racism. Racism and religion have been Europe's two main exports over the years.

When you look at the history of Canada, when you look at that genocide I referred to earlier, where do you find its roots? Where do its roots lie? Its roots lie in Europe.

This morning we heard Svend Robinson talk about the memorandum that came from Britain in 1948, which contained the directive that it would be best to "dispose of the past as soon as possible." To dispose of the past – that was the message from London.

You can see why they would want to dispose of the past. But the past cannot be so easily disposed of. We, who are part of the imperial legacy – each and every one of us in our different ways, whether we are white or black, whether we are Native American, Afro-Caribbean or Asian – we are each a part of the imperial legacy and cannot dispose of the past. The past shapes the present and the future. We have to confront it, and we have to cope, and we have to determine what our own future is to be and the principles upon which it is to be based. We must say that there is no room for racism, not in our present nor in our future. This means that the climate that produced the genocide must be changed, must be eradicated. That is the imperative.

For no one should believe, for one moment, that the roots of the Holocaust have been eradicated in Europe and that therefore we can dismiss it as something that happened in the past and will not happen again – not if we take the Nuremberg Charter seriously. There are even those today who seek to deny the Holocaust. Those who deny the Holocaust cannot lightly be dismissed.

Two days before I came here, I received an attractively packaged glossy publication on my desk in Westminster. I receive lots of attractively packaged glossy publications on my desk in Westminster. Most of them are consigned to the garbage bin. This one was different. It was entitled *Holocaust News*. That, in itself, caught my attention. I read it. It consisted of an obscene denial of the very existence of the Holocaust, spuriously presented with a gloss of academic research. I do not know how many other members of Parliament received that publication. I did not consign it to the garbage bin; I sent it to the attorney general. Let me tell you, however we may debate the issue here, if that publication were distributed outside a synagogue or outside a rum shop or outside a church or in a shopping arcade in Brent or in Brixton, I know how my community, the people I represent, would deal with those seeking to distribute that document. They would be physically dissuaded from continuing to do so. Because no one is coming into our community – a community of Blacks, Afro-Caribbeans, Asians and Jews, whites and Irish, all living side by side – and distributing that sort of racist hate propaganda. No one!

No one is going to be allowed, as those who are behind that publication would like to do, to divide Jew and Black. They do not like Jews, they do not like Blacks. They hate our guts. The only thing they hate more than the Black, Paul Boateng, the only thing they hate more than the Jew, Greville Janner, is the Jew and the Black standing together.

Now, I should hasten to add that as a member of Parliament, and as a lawyer, I do not want scenes of physical dissuasion taking place on the streets. So, I sent the document to the attorney general. I only regret that in Britain we do not have a law as tough as that which exists in Canada. Because if we did, then I could be more confident that the attorney general was going to be able to do something about it. As it is, I fear that the material, having been passed over to him, will in fact, at the end of the day, be consigned to a garbage bin – his. Therefore, the question of what will happen when and if this document hits the streets of Brent or Brixton still remains.

That is why we need tough laws. That is why such laws are in complete accord with the Nuremberg Principles. That is why I stand firmly behind them. Neither the American Civil Liberties Union nor any other civil liberties union or school of thought is going to persuade me otherwise. The imperative to act is there in the pool of principles that is the Nuremberg Charter.

Those people who are behind that publication have not given up on the unfinished agenda of the Second World War. The "new right," who are linked with those who are behind that particular publication, and the anti-Semitic extreme left, who are linked up with those who are behind that publication, have an unfinished agenda, and we must make sure that it stays that way. We must make sure that they never have the opportunity to revive the spirit, the attitude, and the mentality that made Nuremberg necessary.

The political imperative then, it seems to me, is to combat racism in all its forms. Today, in 1987, in Europe we are faced, day in and day out – not in an academic sense but in a very real sense – with what racism means. I can share with you some of what it means, by taking up and reading to you a copy of a publication produced by the European churches, called *Migration Newsheet*. I am a sponsor of this publication and I recommend it to the library of McGill University.

Let us see what it has to say. It is dated 2 October 1987. We can begin with the situation in Switzerland. The government plans to introduce changes in the naturalization law which will eliminate the right to automatic acquisition of Swiss citizenship by foreign women married to Swiss nationals.

We go on. We look at the situation in the United Kingdom, where a woman has been forced to take refuge, to take sanctuary in a Hindu temple, because of the state of our own immigration and nationality laws. She is married to a British citizen, but she may not remain with her husband in the United Kingdom.

We go on. We look at the situation in France. An increase in racial attacks is reported in France. A policeman responsible for the death of a North African youth receives a very light sentence.

We look at the situation in the Federal Republic of Germany. We find there that the maximum age of children for family reunion is to be lowered from eighteen to sixteen and both parents have to be residents in the Federal Republic of Germany. It goes on to report new visa restrictions for Turkish nationals and increased attacks on Turks in Germany.

In Scandinavia, home of liberalism and tolerance, we hear of the increased popularity of the extreme right in Sweden, successes for the extreme right in Denmark and Norway, a resurgence of populist movements in Scandinavia against state intervention and taxes, and growing hostility to the presence of immigrants and asylum seekers.

Spain. No legal proceedings to be taken following complaints of racism by temporary black workers.

And so it goes, on and on. Everywhere in Europe, a resurgence of racism. Everywhere in Europe, the day-to-day manifestations of the ugliness that characterizes racial oppression: the cruelty and the suffering, the divided families, the exploitation of migrant workers, the blackmail by their landlords of private migrant tenants whose papers are not in order, and increased exploitation by employers of workers who will do anything in order to be allowed to remain. That is the reality of life in Europe for those who are migrants.

Now, when we look at the reality, what response are we to have? On what are we to draw in order to give those individuals redress? We have to draw on something. When we look at state law, we find, all too often, very real inadequacies in the remedies that individual states offer to those who live within their borders. Increasingly, those remedies and rights of appeal that do exist are being curtailed, or "streamlined," as the saying goes. Whenever I hear that rights are about to be streamlined, then it seems to me we have to look out, because in the "streamlining," all too often, rights disappear by the wayside. That is what happened in Europe. Where are we to have a remedy? Because a remedy we must have.

Why is it that the Nuremberg Charter was a declaration and not a statute? It is because individual states, even in the aftermath of the Holocaust, were hostile to the idea of calling the Charter a statute, because they feared an attack, an assault on their sovereignty, because they understood the implication of the spirit and intention of the Charter.

So it seems to me that we have to be very clear about the nature of politics and the nature of political parties. We must not see the political process as something over which we have no control and something which we can afford to wipe our hands of, as being the concern only of politicians. Each and every one of us has responsibility for the political content of our states. Each and every one of us has responsibility for the process by which laws are made. It is not good enough to say, "Oh well, that is the nature of states. States and sovereign powers are just like that." We cannot afford to have that attitude if, in fact, we are to protect our own rights and preserve and extend the rights of minorities – such an attitude is a luxury that we cannot afford.

Yet we have to be honest about the nature of politics. I am reminded of the story of Socrates. You know, after he had been convicted, some friends came to him and said, "Socrates, you are in dead trouble! Socrates, what do you think is the likely result of the fact that you have been found guilty of what amounts to an organized conspiracy against the public; what do you think the result of that is going to be?" "Well," Socrates said, "it ought to be the usual result of an organized conspiracy against the public, high political office!"

When we think on that, we might be tempted to dismiss the political process. I think, instead, that we must have on each of our agendas the extension of the rights of individuals in relation to international treaty obligations. We ought to look at the right of referral to the European Court of Human Rights, with all its limitations – and there are limitations. We ought to look at the example that is provided within the Council of Europe. We ought to look at those international conventions and protocols, such as the International Convention on the Elimination of All Forms of Racial Discrimination, which would in fact, if ratified, have the potential of giving to individuals the right of individual petition. Article 14 of the International Convention on Racial Discrimination, and the various optional protocols that attach to it, contain a right of individual petition. We have to make sure that, when people come around at election time, we ask them "What is your attitude?" Not simply their attitude toward the fall in the stock exchange or the price of wheat, nor simply toward welfare benefits or the state of the nation's health, but also, their attitude toward the individual right of petition under that particular convention.

Many of the politicians will not have heard of it. But at least you are asking a question which will oblige someone, somewhere, to look for an answer. These questions ought to be asked. The issue of the individual right of petition ought to be a matter for complaining within our communities.

There are other matters of priority. We should also say to our governments, like the United States government, which has not ratified the Convention on Genocide, "Why have you not ratified the Convention of Genocide?" It ought to be on the political agenda for the citizens of the United States to ask this question of their leaders and to require of their leaders that the Convention be ratified.

One can see why they have not ratified this Convention. The fact of the matter is that if you look at the southern part of this continent, the southern part of America, genocide is taking place as we speak. That is the reality of the experience of native Americans in Latin America, and the complicity of each and every one of our countries in that process is very real. The multinationals are responsible for the elimination of tribe after tribe and nation after nation of American Indians. We must think of them; we must let them speak.

In closing, I want to give one native American woman the opportunity to do just that. We need to listen to her words and the words of countless other women and men who understand, as the Jewish people have come to understand, the meaning of genocide.

Her name is Eliane Dos Santos. How right Elie Wiesel is when he says that they must be named. The mere act of naming – I should carry that away with me for as long as I live – the mere act of naming, if it were to take up the rest of one's life, as Elie Wiesel said, would be worth it.

Eliane Dos Santos says this:

Today, we are hardly a hundred and eighty of the original nine hundred. A scattered two hundred thousand out of the original five million Indians. Why is it that European populations can survive? Why is it indigenous populations cannot? Is it because they are blond with blue eyes? Does our fault lie with our dark skin and eyes? With our traditional culture? With our history? ... The multinationals already destroyed our green Brazil. The ashes of misery, of abandonment, of battles and of diseases, are permanent pictures in the shacks of the large urban centers, Rio, Saõ Paulo, Salvador, Porto Allegre. In the Palacipi houses, on the narrow river bank in the Amazon region, along the northeast. The indigenous people not only speak our history, we speak your history.

She says to us, The indigenous people not only speak our history, we speak *your* history. We cannot dispose of the past. It can never be necessary, it can never be right to dispose of that history. We must treasure it. We must extract and guard the lessons of that history. We must make it a living and constantly refreshing and developing aspect of our lives so that it permeates our lives and our societies.

There is, at this moment, in France, a response to the racism and the xenophobia in Europe. A response to the failure to deal justly with the issue of refugees. People whose problem is not that they are having to seek refuge in a foreign land, but whose problem is seen as being the fact that they are refugees. The response in France at this time is that of an organization called SOS Racisme. They have a saying that bears repeating: *"Ne touche pas mon pote!,"* which, loosely translated, means, "Don't touch my mate!" A white French person says of a Black neighbour: "Don't touch my mate!"

When we look at the Nuremberg Principles, when we dip into that pool, we see the same message, it seems to me. We see it there with a sanction. The message of the Nuremberg Charter can be translated as *"Ne touche pas mon pote!"* Don't touch my mate, because if you do, however long it takes, and no matter where you hide, we will come after you. "Don't touch my mate!" *Merci.*

PROFESSOR ANDRÉ TREMBLAY Mr Justice Kirby is the chief justice of the Court of Appeal of New South Wales. He is a former judge of the Federal Court of Australia and for nine years served as chairman of the Australia Law Reform Commission. Mr Justice Kirby is also a member of the International Commission of Jurists in Geneva.

Speaker

CHIEF JUSTICE MICHAEL KIRBY (AUSTRALIA)

A few weeks ago, there was an excellent program on the radio in Australia. It was about "workaholism." Sadly, I did not have time to listen to it. I was too busy working. So it was that the organizers of this conference caught me at my desk, fighting off those waves of reserved judgments which always threaten to swamp appellate judges. It was seven o'clock in the morning on a Sunday, in faraway Sydney, where summer marches in. Learning of my visit to Montreal for the Atwater Institute on Informatics, the organizers invited me to participate in this closing plenary. It was a privilege which, of course, I immediately seized. I did so for three reasons. First, out of respect for the important topic of this conference, upon which there have been recent developments in Australia, as I will tell you. Second, out of respect for this famous law school and two of its deans, whom I have been privileged to know, Maxwell Cohen and John Humphrey. And, third, because, as it happened, the judgments on which I was working when the call came through indirectly touched upon the issue of justice and injustice, which is the theme of this closing plenary.

Let me say something first about the background to the Menzies Report in Australia. Our situations in Australia and Canada are sufficiently similar to make it important that we be aware of the developments in our two countries. Our legal traditions are close, and our position as recipients of large numbers of postwar refugees confronts our governments and people with like dilemmas. We were both combatants in the Second World War against fascist dictatorship. In 1948, we were both the recipients of the suggestion of the United Kingdom authorities that Commonwealth countries should switch the focus of their concern from the pursuit of war criminals to surveillance of the communist threat. Each of us has large ethnic populations that are nervous about the reopening of old controversies. Until lately, each of us had tended to treat the prosecution of war criminals and others accused of crimes against humanity as a closed chapter. Indeed, in Australia, this was the expressed official position of the government, so declared in 1961 by the then attorney general, Sir Garfield Barwick, who later became the chief justice of Australia.

So the Menzies Report was commissioned. It was prepared by a distinguished retired public servant, Mr Andrew Menzies. He prepared it with commendable speed in six months; it was delivered at the close of 1986, and it is now a published document.

Mr Menzies's report contains a great deal of detail, much of which I will spare you. The details are known to some of you, and they are available to those of you who are interested. In essence, the recommendations involved the reversal of the Barwick statement of 1961 that war crime was a closed chapter. They suggested the establishment of a very small unit to work with the director of public prosecutions in Australia to review the cases of all suspects, past and future.

They proposed some reforms of federal statutes and procedures for extradition, local prosecution, and, in some cases, the closure of the file. Cases could be put aside on various grounds, including the offence not being sufficiently serious, or insufficiency of evidence now available or likely to be available. The Australian government, with some specified reservations, has accepted and endorsed the Menzies Report. Although politically sensitive, the issue has been dealt with in Australia with a much higher degree of bipartisanship than is usual for my country. The federal opposition specifically endorsed the retreat from the Barwick statement, which had been made during a period of Conservative government. Generally, conservative journals have commended this decision to move to a "firm framework" of laws and policies to guide future investigations and, specifically, to bring Nazis to justice.

There are commendable developments. They may serve as a stimulus, perhaps even a model, for other countries with like problems and circumstances. It remains to be seen whether they lead to more cases of actual extradition and prosecution.

These are not issues which I wish to address in these closing moments of this important symposium. Instead, I choose my theme from the judgments over which I was labouring when the invitation to participate came through and from the topic that has been assigned to these closing moments: "Against Injustice."

Does this mean injustice for all? Are we so dedicated to justice and to the rule of law that we will extend even these precious features of our societies to those suspected and proved guilty of war crimes and crimes against humanity? These are the questions that I choose to address.

The Menzies Report rightly points out that the common law of England, whose traditions have so profoundly affected the law in Canada, Australia, and the United States, did not contain a general limitation on the prosecution of serious criminal offences. Thus the report says, "In the Australian system of justice, lapse of time has never been regarded as justification for withholding prosecution action for the most serious crimes, such as murder." So it has also been in England. So it has also been in Canada. This is not, however, a universal rule. It was not so by Roman law. The introduction into Prussian law of statutory limitation periods for criminal prosecutions was praised at the time it happened as being the hallmark of the liberal legal tradition. The idea spread to most European legal systems and to every state of the United States of America, except in cases of prosecution for murder. However, English law and its derivatives have provided relief from stale prosecutions in a quite different way. In my own court, this has lately led to a reflowering of this jurisprudence and it was upon this subject that I was working when the telephone call came through from Montreal.

With the Magna Carta, King John of England promised that he would not deny or delay justice. I am not going to tarry to explore the scholarly debates as to whether this promise extended to ordinary subjects or was confined only to those of higher station, or whether it was confined to the civil and did not apply to the criminal process. The right to a fair trial on criminal charges is now a fundamental constitutional right, which the courts of both our countries will enforce. In some countries, the right to a speedy trial as an attribute of a fair trial is enshrined in a written constitution. So it is in the United States of America, as the Supreme Court decision in *Barker* v. *Wingo* makes clear. In many of the post-independence constitutions of the Commonwealth of Nations, the idea is captured in the promise of a right to be tried on criminal charges "within a reasonable time."

In Jamaica, the Privy Council adapted and applied the United States jurisprudence from *Barker* v. *Wingo* in the decision of *Bell* v. *The Director of Public Prosecutions.* And this is the way that the powerful idea has spread into the common law of countries such as my own, which do not have a written guarantee of this kind. Courts were told to consider the length of the delay in the prosecution, the reasons given to explain the prosecution delay, the prejudice caused by the delay to the trial of the accused, the seriousness of the crime, the complexity and difficulty of prosecuting that might explain the delay, and the obligation of the accused to act for his or her own part with due speed. Lately, as my own court and the Court of Appeal of Ontario have emphasized, there is to be added a further criterion; namely, the public interest in the prosecution and trial of serious criminal offences, which must be weighed against the public interest in the fair and speedy trial of accused persons.

In Canada, the advent of the Charter of Rights and Freedoms is a notable chapter in the struggle for the preservation of human rights. It is an example to other countries of the same tradition, including my own. The idea that accused persons should be tried within a reasonable time is enshrined in section 11(b) of your Charter. A series of very important cases, which we have been studying in Australia, have lately come from your Supreme Court dealing with the provision in its present form. The court's instructions – including those given in *Mills* v. *The Queen* and in *Rahey* v. *The Queen* – the latter as recently as 17 June 1987 – show the difficulty, the controversy, and the division of the judges in balancing, in ordinary criminal cases, the public interests that are in competition here.

I emphasize the public interests. The tensions are not between the public interest in prosecution and trial and the private interest or individual interest in a speedy trial. In conflict are two *public* interests. For in our just societies we declare that the whole community has a public interest in the prompt trial of accused persons. It is an attribute of our respect for human rights and for the justice of our societies that we guarantee these rights.

In Australia we have no charter, but we do have the common law. We have used common law techniques to fashion powerful instruments to terminate old prosecutions of old crimes or even of old disciplinary offences as an abuse of the court's process. In the case of crimes, the Crown recently challenged the right of the courts to terminate a prosecution which the Crown chose to bring. It invoked the common-law tradition, referred to in the Menzies Report, that there is no arbitrary limitation period in the prosecution of crime. However, this argument was rejected in my own court in June, and in the High Court of Australia as recently as 23 October 1987 in the case of *Watson*. It is a reserve power to be used sparingly – but to be used where perceptions of justice require it.

Now I will come back to war criminals and the principal subject of this conference. I am not interested in considering here the arguments – other than delay – that have been advanced to justify the closing of the chapter on the prosecution. You all know the excuses and the reasons that have been advanced: that the acts alleged were performed under duress in obedience to superior orders or in the performance of an "act of state"; that the only persons usually prosecuted were minor functionaries and that the holders of high offices generally escaped detention and prosecution; that the crimes were political or have been retrospectively declared; that they are not subject, in most countries, to lawful extradition procedures; and that they are disproportionately concerned with the past, whilst modern crimes against humanity, such as apartheid, go unredressed. Nor am I concerned to debate whether an exception has been established now in international law for war crimes and crimes against humanity. Upon this subject, there has been a great deal of academic writing.

Instead, against the background of the provisions of your Charter, and the recent common law developments in Australia, I want to pose a much narrower and more practical and pressing question. What will our municipal courts do? What should they do, if a prosecution were launched now for acts of such enormity, done so long ago, by people apparently living peacefully in our midst?

For some, of course, the answer to this question is quite simple. The crimes are of such a magnitude, and it is so important that they not be repeated, that the chapter must never be regarded as closed. The crimes shocked the human community. The offenders often escaped punishment by hiding, evading detection, or unlawfully securing succour and asylum from countries such as Canada and Australia, which opened their doors to thousands of refugees. These offenders cannot escape prosecution by the shield of their own unlawfulness perpetrated during the reign of tyranny. During such time, the clock of human rights stopped for them, as it did for their victims. Unless the rule of law can be brought to bear peacefully against them in courtrooms, the only remedy of the outraged conscience would be violence and lawlessness, which a peaceful society will seek to avoid.

But there is a legal and a moral dilemma here which we cannot, out of self-respect, ignore. It is posed not by our respect for war criminals, for they have forfeited the right to claim such respect, but by our respect for ourselves and for the high value we place on the attainment of justice in our courts. This may be a discordant note in this conference. But it must be struck – at least, it must be struck in my own country by its law, and possibly in Canada as well. If we are truly defenders of human rights, we do not advance the attainment of justice by wishing away hard problems, by silence about difficult questions, or by contenting ourselves with ringing phrases. In Australia, Chief Justice Latham once said that the test for our adherence to the respect for religious freedom was not whether such freedom was accorded to members of majority religions. That was simple. It was whether such respect would be extended to small minorities – possibly unpopular, possibly unorthodox minorities. The test of freedom and of human rights generally is how we act when dealing with the unpopular, with the contemptible, with the probably guilty, when they invoke the rule of law and assert their human rights in our courts. It is when it is hardest to accord rights that they matter most.

If it be the case that Australia and Canada, through their governments, consciously and deliberately delayed, for whatever cause, the prosecution or extradition of war criminals who were known to be in their midst, would their trial now be just? Would a prosecution now be an offence to the human rights of our communities? Would our courts – and this is the central question – step in to protect the right to be tried fairly and within a reasonable time? Would our courts now stop such prosecutions, or at least some of them, as an abuse of the legal process?

There are some who could appeal to practical considerations in answering these questions. Crime is a disturbance of public order; old crimes cause no disturbance, so let them alone. War crimes are political in character and their prosecution may upset sensitive ethnic groups, may even engender anti-Semitism. Memories fade; a fair prosecution and trial at this remove from events cannot justly be had. Still others would appeal to high principle, invoking mercy for those who gave none; invoking redemption and the possibility of reform, even for those who showed breathless cruelty. But the gnawing argument comes back to our conception of justice and to our insistence that, even for such offenders, the rule of law must be observed. Even their human rights must be respected, lest our temples of justice be debased by an abuse of process. We pride ourselves on acting on higher principles than those who are guilty of war crimes and the greatest crimes against humanity ever conceived. We must not, of course, let our insistence on such principles divert us from exposure, even today, of the horrendous crimes of such offenders. But, equally, we must not allow that insistence to deflect us from our own observance of the rule of law and of the protection of human rights. Our seriousness about justice and human rights is tested by our resolution of this dilemma in some cases. These rights are fragile and precious features of humanity's struggle toward civilization. As this century, which has seen so many horrors, draws to its close, we shall turn unequalled calamity into good fortune if we derive from our bitter experience this simple instruction: that the best guarantee against repetition of such wickedness is the exposure of how it happened and the reinforcement of the institutions, including the institutions of the law, that will help to prevent and redress its moderns manifestations, some of which we have heard vividly described in this closing session of this important conference.

Presentation:
The Robert S. Litvack Memorial Award
in Human Rights

Introduction of Recipient

SYLVIA LITVACK

I am here to present an unusual award to a very unusual young woman. This award is the Robert S. Litvack Memorial Award, established by McGill's Faculty of Law and InterAmicus in memory of my husband, who died this year in March. The young woman is Carmen Gloria Quintana, who, at the ripe old age of twenty, has become a legend in her native Chile.

The award was created to honour, every year, a person who, through his or her own efforts and initiative, has contributed to the defence of the rule of law – that is, the defence of the individual against arbitrary power. It is an unusual award, because Robert, though known to many of you here tonight, was not a public figure. He was a practising attorney who would take time out from his ordinary law practice to do battle with injustice when he encountered it. He did so without waiting for a constituency, a power base, or, very often, even an actual client. It was his conviction that rights can exist only where ordinary citizens are prepared to defend them and that he did, very well.

Carmen was a young engineering student who, like thousands of other students, was taking part in a nationwide day of protest against her government. That is what she was doing in Santiago, with her friend, Rodriguo, when they were cornered by military police, who beat them, covered them with gasoline, and set them on fire. Their bodies were then dumped in a ditch out of town. Her friend died. Carmen lived and was flown to Montreal for treatment, which she is still undergoing.

Although she continues to live with pain, her spirit was not scarred. The first thing she did, when she had the strength, was return to Chile to confront and testify against her attackers. She did so at great risk to her own safety and in the face of a hostile and jeering military tribunal. I was just talking a little while ago with Maître Denis Racicot, her Montreal attorney. Maître Racicot was telling me of a continuing campaign of terrorism and intimidation going on in Chile right now against the very people who witnessed what happened to Carmen and Rodriguo. This is happening in spite of the glare of international attention! Carmen is not being honoured tonight only because she was a victim of brutal repression; she is being honoured for her incredible courage and her belief that justice should prevail, even when the odds are not good, and that bullies should be shamed, even when they are the government.

I think that Carmen and Bob would have liked each other. It gives me great pleasure to present her with the Robert S. Litvack Memorial Award. I already know that we will have great difficulty in the future in coming up with a recipient of her calibre.

J'ai appris également ce soir que le nom de Carmen sera perpétué au Chili et au Canada par la création toute récente d'un prix en son nom qui a été établi par les efforts de son médecin, le docteur Jacques Papillon, qui est ici avec nous ce soir, qui est le médecin qui l'a traitée à l'Hôtel-Dieu de Montréal. C'est un prix qui a déjà été décerné cette année à son médecin, au Chili, le docteur Ilogur Ileas, et sera décerné chaque année pour récompenser la recherche dans le domaine des grands brûlés.

Et maintenant, sans vous faire attendre davantage, je voudrais vous présenter quand même Carmen qui va nous dire quelques mots en français, qui n'est pas sa langue maternelle mais qu'elle parle avec beaucoup de charme.

Inaugural Recipient

CARMEN GLORIA QUINTANA

Bonsoir, mesdames, messieurs. Je désire remercier la Faculté de droit de l'Université McGill pour l'honneur qu'elle me fait de me décerner le prix "Robert S. Litvack Memorial Award," prix à la mémoire de monsieur Robert Litvack, avocat et infatigable défenseur de droits de la personne.

Je suis citoyenne chilienne et je vis maintenant ici au Canada avec ma famille, tous en exil forcé pour notre sécurité. Le 12 juillet 1986 est une journée qui a bouleversé ma vie. Ce jour-là, avec Rodriguo Rojas, jeune citoyen chilien et photographe, jeune exilé chilien qui était retourné à sa patrie pour retrouver ses racines, je participais à une grève nationale comme l'ensemble de la population chilienne. Tous les deux, nous fûmes arrêtés, sauvagement battus et brûlés vivants par des militaires chiliens. J'ai survécu, mais Rodriguo est mort de ses blessures. Permettez-moi de dédier le prix que je reçois ce soir à la mémoire de ce jeune homme comme un modeste hommage à sa vie qu'il a perdue dans sa patrie.

Ce que j'ai vécu le 12 juillet 1986 avec Rodriguo est similaire, dans sa signification finale, à de nombreux autres cas de violation de nos droits fondamentaux qui se produisent continuellement au Chili et affectent la vie, la sécurité et l'intégrité physique et morale des personnes.

Je crois que mon cas n'est pas isolé. Je dois être considérée comme une survivante d'une grave attaque au droit à la vie comme de nombreux autres cas au Chili qui se maintiennent dans l'anonymat et qui méritent aussi notre attention.

On doit également prendre en compte le cadre généralisé et institutionnalisé des violations de droits fondamentaux qui peuvent être observés au Chili et qui a son origine dans une dictature militaire et fasciste qui s'impose de manière sanglante et qui livre une véritable guerre à sa population civile. Dans ce cadre généralisé, les violations se perpétuent aujourd'hui grâce à une constitution politique anti-démocratique.

Et enfin, mon cas illustre les défauts du pouvoir judiciaire, en particulier, de son indépendance, et l'expansion de la justice militaire. Défauts qui se doivent d'être corrigés afin de garantir minimalement la protection des personnes.

Mon pays vit les mêmes problèmes que les autres pays de l'Amérique Latine qui ont tous tant souffert pour le respect du droit à la vie, le droit le plus fondamental, mais aussi pour le respect du droit à la sécurité de sa personne, c'est-à-dire pour le droit de ne plus être victime de la torture généralisée sous toutes ses formes, pour le droit de ne plus être victime de la terreur d'État au nom de la doctrine de sécurité.

Je veux oeuvrer à la promotion de la paix et la justice sociale, au respect du droit à l'éducation et la santé pour tous et au respect du droit à l'autodétermination pour tous les peuples.

En terminant, je souhaite que la remise annuelle du prix "Robert S. Litvack Memorial Award" consacré aux droits fondamentaux aide les Canadiens à sensibiliser à la promotion et à la défense de ces droits si fragiles. Je souhaite également, surtout cette année, qu'elle soit l'occasion d'un rapprochement des jeunes d'ici à la cause du peuple chilien aux prises avec l'interminable dictature de Pinochet et toujours en quête de liberté, de paix et de justice.

Merci beaucoup à tous les Québécois et à tous les Canadiens. Bonsoir. Merci.

Translation of Carmen Gloria Quintana's Speech

Good evening, ladies and gentlemen. I would like to thank the Faculty of Law of McGill University for the honour of being awarded the Robert S. Litvack Memorial Award, a prize in memory of Mr Robert Litvack, lawyer and untiring defender of human rights.

I am a Chilean citizen now living in Canada with my family, in forced exile for our safety. The 12th of July, 1986, was a day that turned my life upside down. On that day, with Rodriguo Rohas, a young Chilean citizen and photographer, a young Chilean exile who had returned to his homeland to rediscover his roots, I participated in a national strike along with the rest of the Chilean population. The two of us were arrested, savagely beaten, and burned alive by Chilean soldiers. I survived, but Rodriguo died from his wounds. Permit me to dedicate the prize that I am receiving this evening to the memory of this young man, as a modest homage to the life that he lost in his homeland.

What I lived through on 12 July 1986 with Rodriguo is similar, in its final meaning, to numerous other cases of violations of human rights, which continuously occur in Chile, affecting life, safety, and the physical and moral integrity of human beings. I believe that my case is not isolated. I must be considered a survivor of a serious attack on the right to life, like numerous other cases in Chile that are kept anonymous but that also merit our attention.

Also deserving of attention are the generalized and institutionalized violations of human rights that can be observed in Chile today. They have their origin in a military and fascist dictatorship that rules with bloodshed and is waging a veritable war against its civilian population. The violations continue today, thanks to an anti-democratic political constitution. My case also illustrates the failings of judicial power – in particular, its lack of independence and the growth of military justice; these failings must be corrected in order to guarantee the minimal protection of people.

My country lives with the same problems as do other Latin American countries, which have all suffered so much for respect of the right to life, the most fundamental right, but also for respect of the right to security of one's person – that is, the right to no longer be victim to generalized torture in all of its forms and the right to be no longer the victim of state terror in the name of state security.

I want to work toward the promotion of peace and social justice, respect for the right to education and health for all, and respect for the right to self-determination for all peoples.

In closing, I hope that the annual awarding of the Robert S. Litvak Memorial Award consecrated to human rights will help sensitize Canadians to the promotion and defence of these human rights, which are so fragile. Above all, I hope that this year will be an occasion to bring some young people from here closer to the cause of the people of Chile, Chileans burdened with the unending Pinochet dictatorship, yet still seeking liberty, peace and justice.

Thank you very much to all Québécers and all Canadians. Good evening. Thank you.

Appreciation

GORDON ECHENBERG

Ladies and gentlemen, I rise on a point of personal privilege to address a few remarks to the convenor of this conference: Irwin Cotler. I address them as a participant who has sat through the last twenty-four hours of this conference.

My relationship with Irwin spans twenty-five years and has taken such forms as student, debating partner, roommate, friend, and soulmate. Over the years and through these various levels of relationship, I have listened to his pleas for justice. I was witness to his effort to speak for those who had no counsel. I participated, in a very limited way, in a few of these efforts to defend human rights. In effect, over these last twenty-five years, I have borne witness to Irwin's work which has, in turn, led to his conceptualizing and defining the need for an independent, activist, international advocacy centre. Only in the last twenty-four hours have the four corners of Irwin's reasoning and vision come together for me. To have InterAmicus formally launched at this conference gives additional meaning to the conference and to the institution that he wishes to create.

Allow me to speak in personal terms. Last night, Elie Wiesel spoke as a witness to the Holocaust. But it was equally evident that he spoke as one of its victims. Yet, even though a witness, he brought a message: to learn from history and then to reach out to the future with hope.

Today, I heard members and former members of the elected bodies of Britain, Canada and United States, in effect, complain of their own government's actions, inactions and inabilities to act. Today, I heard how – in both Canada and the United States – action, albeit late, is being taken in respect of Nazi war criminals. But as I listened, I became aware that these efforts were the result of private, individual initiative.

Today, I listened to how the United Nations has tried and failed as an international forum in the field of human rights, but still represents our best hope.

And today, I listened to how words maim and still maim. I listened to how injustice still persists. For me, it was this assemblage of facts, and my personal exposure to the people and to their eloquence, profundity, and conviction, that has made me startlingly aware of Irwin's vision for InterAmicus. It is your willingness to participate and support such an organization that ensures its success.

The world has changed and evolved since Nuremberg, as have the issues. Today the injustices include apartheid, Chile, Ethiopia, different "killing fields." The institutions have also changed since Nuremberg, as have the rights and the obligations of individuals.

In the past twenty-four hours, we have heard a witness to the Holocaust, we have had our memories jarred, and we have been rocked out of our solitudes. If that is to have any meaning for the future, it must mobilize us to act. We must, as individuals, have vehicles to influence our people, our governments, and our international institutions.

The world has need for such vehicles. InterAmicus can serve that role in part, since it is provided with the benefit of being associated with this law school, albeit independent from it.

This conference, and your participation, are active proof that a concept like InterAmicus can work. It will help us to better deal with today's problems and tomorrow's problems and, hopefully, to never again face yesterday's tragedies.

Closing

PROFESSOR IRWIN COTLER

When I went over the program with André Tremblay earlier this evening, the one thing that I had no notice of and therefore could not control was the intervention of my very good friend, Gordon Echenberg. I take it that we have learned one more thing during these last twenty-four hours: that a friend has unbounded freedom of expression!

In introducing Elie Wiesel yesterday evening, Principal Johnston said that if Raoul Wallenberg were here he might well have invited Elie Wiesel to bear witness. I suspect too that if Elie Wiesel were asked, and indeed he shared this with me this morning before he left, he would have pointed to Carmen Quintana to bear witness at this closing, as one who has shattered the silence, as one who has broken the wall of indifference, as one who has demonstrated *"que dans la lutte contre l'injustice à notre époque; qui s'excuse, s'accuse"* – that whoever remains indifferent indicts himself or herself.

And so in this closing, one comes back, in a sense, to the beginning. Carmen Quintana joins up with Elie Wiesel, and both tell us that this end is really only the beginning: the beginning of what we say and, more importantly, of what we do, in our good deeds, in our struggle against apartheid, against racism, in our struggle for aboriginal rights, for the integrity of the rights of women, for the rights of the poor and the rights of minorities; in our concern – and anguish – with respect to disappearances, and in our concern – torment – regarding the torture that Carmen Quintana just spoke of. It is in that struggle that we will define ourselves as people.

And yet in listening these last twenty-four hours, I suspect that, therein, in some existential way, lies the problem. Where and how do we begin? In a world with so much injustice – and yet with so few who struggle against that injustice – where and how does one begin? For we live in a world where the *cri du coeur* of each victim is so powerful that it competes, if not cancels out, the *cri du coeur* of the other victim whom we must also hear; in a world where, if everything is labelled as a holocaust, nothing really is a Holocaust; in a world where there are still those who, in a kind of Orwellian inversion of everything that we have sought to remember, deny even that the Holocaust ever occurred at all. It is a world where there are those who would invite us – as Paul Boateng and Elie Wiesel said yesterday, and the rest of the speakers have said in their own way – to kill the victims a second time, whether it be native Americans in Central America, or whether it be the victims of the Holocaust. It is a world where there are those who would invite us in their own way, in their own Orwellian way, to turn a blind eye to injustice, to remain indifferent, to engage in a conspiracy of silence rather than a conspiracy of hope.

And yet if we are to begin, how then to begin? On behalf of what cause? Against what injustice? On behalf of which victim? How does one choose the victim? How does one rank human suffering? How does one say we will speak on behalf of this victim, if it means not being able to speak, or speak as powerfully, or in as sustained a way, on behalf of another victim?

But if I have learned anything from this conference, from Nuremberg, and from the struggle for human rights in our time, it is that the problem is not which cause shall be served, but are we really serving the cause of human rights at all? Not which victim shall be helped, but are we not too indifferent to the cry of the victim, whoever he or she may be? Not whether a tribal claim may have to be asserted by blacks, by women, by aboriginal people, or wherever a tribal claim may have to be asserted, but why must the victim always have to stand alone? Why can we not make common cause with the Carmen Quintanas of our time so that they do not have to stand alone, even if they have to begin alone in the assertion of their cause?

The lesson I have learned has found common expression in everything I have ever been involved in, whether it be with "refuseniks" or dissidents in the Soviet Union; whether it be with blacks, including the struggle against apartheid in South Africa; whether it be with the victims in Central America. Everywhere, I can tell you, no matter who the victim may be, the code words – *le cri du coeur*, the angst – is always the same: that we are each, wherever we are, the guarantors of each others' destiny.

Each one of us here in this room is an indispensable part of an indivisible struggle for human rights. Each one of us can and does make a difference. And if we ever feel tired, fatigued, overwhelmed by it all, "burnt out," as the popular metaphor goes, by trying to stay involved in this struggle, let us remember – and from this, let us take hope – that it was *one* person, one Swedish non-Jew, Raoul Wallenberg, who saved more Jews in the Second World War than any single government – that it was one person, one courageous woman, Carmen Quintana, who stood up against the whole of Chilean oppression and prevailed.

As Edmund Burke put it so well, the surest way to ensure that evil will triumph in the world is for enough good people to do nothing, to be indifferent, to be silent. But I happen to believe, with everything in my being, that there are good people who are prepared to do something, to speak out, to shatter the silence, to break the indifference. And so, inspired by those who have come before us in this conference – in their word and in their deed – let this be our task: to speak on behalf of those who cannot be heard; to bear witness on behalf of those who cannot testify; to act on behalf of those who have put not only their livelihood but, indeed, their lives on the line. To remember, to bear witness, to act. And may I close as I began yesterday – may this conference, and this theme, serve not only as an act of remembrance, as it will, but as a remembrance to act, as it must be.

CITATIONS FOR CASES REFERRED TO IN PART I

Barker v. *Wingo* (1972) 407 US 514.

Bell v. *The Director of Public Prosecutions* [1985] 3 WLR 73.

Marbury v. *Madison* (1803) 5 US (1 Cranch) 137.

Mills v. *The Queen* [1986] 2 SCR 683.

R. v. *Buzzanga and Durocher* (1979), 49 CCC (2) 369.

R. v. Keegstra (1984) 19 CCC (3d) 254, [1988] 5 WWR 211.

R. v. *Rauca* 34 CR (3d) 97.

R. v. *Zundel* (1987) 31 CCC (3d) 97.

Rahey v. *The Queen* [1981] 1 SCR 588.

The Raoul Wallenberg Forum
on Human Rights

HUMAN RIGHTS, ANTI-SEMITISM, AND
THE WALLENBERG LEGACY
THE HONOURABLE PER AHLMARK

In June 1984, I listened to one of the most moving speeches I have
ever heard. Together with a thousand Romanian citizens – this was
in the Ceaucescu era – and some fifty foreigners from a dozen
countries, we were standing in front of a monument commemorating the victims of Nazi Germany. We were in Sighet, Romania, where
exactly forty years before the Jews had been deported to Auschwitz.

The speaker was Elie Wiesel, born and raised in Sighet. He told
us about his native town, a place with happy children and religious
studies, with joy and debates, with rabbis and revolutionaries. But
that town of love and learning was destroyed forever when the Jews
of Sighet, the majority of the people, were marched from the ghetto
to the railway station. And no one came to their help. No one
opened his door or showed any compassion or took any risk for their
sake. The Jews of Sighet were alone.

"The opposite of love," said Elie Wiesel, "is not hate. The opposite
of love is indifference."

These words are also the message of Raoul Wallenberg. His deeds
still tell us that even under the most dangerous circumstances, a
human being has responsibilities that he or she should not escape.
If you are in a position to save lives, you have to try. Just to stay safe,
in neutral territory, closing your eyes or complaining about the
cruelties outside your own haven, is not enough. You have to take a
stand and a risk when civilization is at stake. If you don't, you are
part of the process of destruction. "The opposite of love is not hate.
The opposite of love is indifference."

So, maybe Elie Wiesel's and Raoul Wallenberg's messages to humanity are almost the same. There was no Wallenberg in northern Transylvania, so all the Jews there were forced to leave. The survivor from Sighet and the one who helped so many to survive in Budapest have both proved to us that if we do not resist evil, it might be the end of everything we believe in.

Raoul Wallenberg, however, has never been able to tell us about his conclusions. He is a man who, after having fought one of the two worst tyrannies of our time, immediately fell victim to the second one. He disappeared in the Gulag, and to this day we do not know his fate. Alive, he would now be eighty years old.

But we can still hear the voice of the one and only common citizen of Canada, the United States, Israel, and Sweden. Miriam Herzog was seventeen years old when she was saved by Wallenberg at one of the death marches from Budapest to the Hungarian border. Years later, in Israel, she told us about her surprise when she heard Wallenberg saying, as he was distributing the one hundred protective passports he had that day, "I feel I have a mission to save the Jewish nation, and so I must rescue the young ones first."

"To save the Jewish nation." What would be Raoul Wallenberg's reaction to the world almost fifty years later?

May I ask this question in a somewhat different context and postpone my guess about his reaction? Wallenberg today – if alive and living in Stockholm – might now and then listen to a regional radio station, called Radio Islam. It has nothing to do with Islamic studies. Instead, Radio Islam has conducted the most vicious anti-Jewish campaign in Europe since the Third Reich: "It lies ... in Judaism's nature to corrode, weaken from the inside and ravage ... Judaism, the Torah and the Talmud stink of racism and contempt for other peoples ... Each and everyone who reads *The Protocols of the Elders of Zion* will be astonished that mostly everything there has come to pass ... If Hitler had liquidated *all* the Jews, we would in fact not have the problem we now have in the Middle East." And so on and so forth.

The first two trials of Radio Islam went on for almost four months. The editor who was responsible, Ahmed Rami, from Morocco – now, unfortunately, a Swedish citizen – was found guilty on seventeen counts of defaming the Jewish people. He was sentenced to half a year in prison, and Radio Islam was closed down for one year.

However, in the last two years Radio Islam has been on the air again. Its incitement to racial hatred has escalated. "The Jewish power is like a cancer, an AIDS, which we cannot defend ourselves against ... Like the German people, which rose against the Jews in the thirties and forties, the Western people will rise again ... I welcome, I welcome a new Hitler ... Judaism is an illness ... To be a Jew is a provocation ... When Jews come together they become a criminal Mafia." And so on.

Last month, we had a third trial against this radio station. The new so-called responsible editor, a member of a Nazi organization in Sweden, was sentenced to four months in prison. Radio Islam was again convicted of defamation, this time on nine counts. Again, it will be closed down. Of course, we in the Swedish Committee Against Anti-Semitism recommend legislation that will make it possible to definitively shut down radio stations that are attacking and libelling ethnic minorities.

But except for the legal system of my country, the reaction against this neo-Nazi propaganda was minimal in the eighties. More shocking than the anti-Jewish campaign itself was the indifference toward it. Indifference from most major newspapers and all political leaders. Indifference from writers, journalists, and others who often pretend that they represent the conscience of their nation.

For eight years, our committee had to struggle against an increasing number of anti-Semitic articles and statements; we did not get support from mass media or politicians. But now, during the last year, there has been a change of attitude. The new cabinet has come out forcefully against anti-Semitic slander. A TV documentary about neo-Nazi movements triggered a broad political debate. When anti-Jewish agitation is linked to the Nazis, people start getting worried. And suddenly we have allies everywhere – in the press and in government and in the churches.

For how long? And why did they not show up before?

Well, it is much easier and more tempting to fight the battles of yesterday. Raoul Wallenberg tried to teach us the opposite: to fight the Jew-hatred of the present, what he saw in his times. He did not just remind us of the Dreyfus Affair, or condemn the pogroms of tsarist Russia at the beginning of this century, or analyze the expulsion of the Jews from Spain five hundred years ago. These events are, of course, extremely important – they deepen our knowledge about mechanisms which come into the open when anti-Semitism takes over. However, Wallenberg fought the enemy of the day: the Nazis and the Arrow Cross in Budapest in the summer and fall of 1944.

In Europe today, most people think that anti-Semitism is always wearing the same face. Anti-Semitism to them is still what was seen in Europe in the thirties and forties – Wallenberg's environment and what he fought: stone-faced SS officers rounding up Jews for transportation to death camps. When anti-Semites enter the stage pretending that they only express solidarity with oppressed Palestinians, most Europeans do not recognize them. But when Jew-haters openly link their behaviour to Nazi traditions, people start to understand what they are watching. The astonishing thing with anti-Semitism, though, is its flexibility. It cannot change its goal – to attack the Jews – but it can change its face, its strategy, and part of its vocabulary.

This old-new anti-Semitism has again become a plague, especially in Western Europe, to which I limit my comments. The breakthrough was the summer of 1982, after the Israeli invasion of Lebanon. That war did not, of course, create anti-Semitism but, rather, released it. It gave the Jew-haters a feeling that now they could go public again and launch their terror. Bombs have been thrown at synagogues, Jewish schools, and institutions. Jews and Jewish shops and restaurants have been attacked by extremists of different political colours. Again, Jewish cemeteries are being desecrated. This has happened in many European cities, and I here refer to the so-called old democracies, meaning areas liberated in 1944 or 1945: Antwerp, Paris, Rome, Vienna, London, Copenhagen, Berlin, Munich, Marseilles, Brussels, and several other places. They try to kill or frighten Jews just because they are Jews.

Not least scary today is, of course, the rightist mob violence in many parts of Germany: almost two thousand attacks on immigrants have taken place, there is ongoing destruction of Jewish graves, and the museum on Nazi atrocities in Sachsenhausen was burned down. The chancellor of Germany did not even have time to attend the demonstration held later, and thus prove the determination of his country to resist the new Nazis of Germany.

Disturbing also has been the tendency in Western Europe to judge attacks on Jews as part of an almost legitimate warfare against the State of Israel. When many people were killed or wounded in Paris in the bombing of the synagogue on Rue Copernic, the then prime minister of France, Raymond Barre, complained that the bomb also killed "innocent Frenchmen" – not only Jews. When the Antwerp synagogue was attacked, a Belgian insurance company claimed that the damages were not to be covered, as the incident was not a criminal act but an "act of war." If you kill Jews, it might be deplorable, but it is not criminal, as there is a war against Israel in the Middle East.

This link between anti-Semitism and anti-Zionism is established also on other levels. Since the Lebanese war, a wave of anti-Semitic articles has reached newspapers and magazines in our countries. Again, we can read that the Bible tells the Jews to oppress other peoples, and that there is a conspiracy among Jews everywhere to seek power and to dominate mass media. Et cetera, et cetera.

In the mainstream West European press, not seldom, the same old lies are printed again, in letters to the editor and in sly innuendos squeezed into articles about the conflict in the Middle East. Not that the mainstream West European press has become anti-Semitic, but its tolerance toward anti-Semitism has risen dramatically. Articles which were thrown in the wastebaskets all those years after the Second World War may be read again.

We have seen for a decade how the old stereotypes directed against the Jews have returned, now often directed against the Jewish state. In the United Nations, this pattern – to go after the collective Jew, the state itself – was very obvious in the years following the Six Day War. The anti-Israel campaign often dominated the agenda of the United Nations and its agencies, always poisoning their work and compromising their ideals. For years, Israel was repeatedly condemned, branded as aggressor and oppressor, and picked as a scapegoat for almost anything. There was an automatic majority of communist dictatorships, Muslim countries, and a number of Third World non-democratic nations, which conducted a campaign against the Jewish nation, while, of course, there never was any complaint about massacres, torture, warmongering, and terrorism among Israel's enemies. When the history of the first forty-five years of the UN and its agencies is written, the anti-Zionist hysteria will probably be regarded as the most disgusting chapter. Luckily, the collapse of the Soviet empire and the liberalization of several Third World countries have, to a large extent, changed this climate of ideological pogrom which surrounded Israel at the UN and lasted for about two decades.

Naturally, I do not regard criticism of Israel as anti-Semitism. It is as legitimate to oppose certain Israeli policies as it is to scrutinize any other nation. For a number of years, I publicly criticized several decisions of Likud-dominated governments, not least their attitudes toward the future of the West Bank. I am delighted by the political and diplomatic openings of the present Labour-led cabinet of Israel. We must be careful not to automatically label harsh words about Israel as anti-Semitism.

However, anti-Zionism has become very similar to anti-Semitism: anti-Semitism is discrimination or hostility against the Jews; anti-Zionism is discrimination or hostility against the Jewish state.

Traditional anti-Semites, in their most extreme form, claim that Jews have no right to exist; anti-Zionists say that the Jewish state has no right to exist.

Anti-Semites reject the right of the Jewish people to express their opinions, culture, and religion; anti-Zionists reject the right of the Jewish people to have a national consciousness expressed in the State of Israel.

Old-fashioned anti-Semitism told us that Jews were a threat to other peoples and creeds and thus had to be fought; the new anti-Semitism tells us that Zionism is racism and therefore has to be struggled against.

Auschwitz did not start at Auschwitz. It started with systematic attempts to make Jews illegal, to isolate the Jews from others, to prepare public opinion for the future destruction of the Jewish people. What we have seen on the international scene for years are systematic attempts to delegitimize the Jewish state and to isolate Israel in a way that, in fact, prepares world opinion for its future destruction. Fortunately – and I repeat this – with the fall of the Soviet Union this strategy of isolation of Israel has, to a large extent, failed.

Sometimes anti-Zionists claim that they are not against Jews but *only* against the Jewish state. Suppose that someone said, I am only against the existence of Great Britain but I am *not* anti-British! Or if somebody told me, I love Swedes, but Sweden should be abolished. No one would take such statements seriously. It is hard to love a people and hate their state.

Anti-Zionism is also the perversion of language. It is often exploiting words which have always been connected to Jewish suffering but is now turning them against the Israelis and the Jews. The war in Lebanon was a "holocaust." The struggle against the PLO is "genocide." Israel aims at the "extermination" of the Palestinians. West Beirut is the new "Warsaw ghetto." The Star of David is reshaped into the Swastika.

This parallel between the Nazis and the Israelis was the main theme of the most aggressive anti-Semitism that existed for more than thirty years in the former Soviet Union. For decades, the Soviets equated Israel and Nazi Germany, and published cartoons with Israeli leaders dressed like SS officers.

In the last decade, this language has also spread to Western Europe. Sometimes even leading politicians there make the parallel. This comparison is both a trivialization of Nazism and a demonization of the Israelis. It is also an attempt to deny our responsibility for the past. Now the Jews have proved that they themselves are as bestial as their former oppressors! Now the victims and the children of the victims of the Holocaust are doing to others what was done to them!

Part of the explanation for why this language has swept through some of our nations has to do with guilt. In some countries, people are aware of the fact that a large number of their fellow citizens *did* collaborate with the German occupiers. In other countries, like my own, guilt is rooted in the fact that Sweden did *not* take part in the efforts to defeat Nazism. By equating the murderer and the victim, we wash our hands; we free ourselves from the guilt or responsibility for the disasters of the past.

But, as Raoul Wallenberg proved, it is not enough to resist the anti-Semitism of the past. In the forties, the most dangerous anti-Semites were those who tried to make Europe *judenrein* – free of Jews. In our days, the most dangerous anti-Semites might be those who want to make the Middle East *judenstaatrein* – free of a Jewish state.

If Wallenberg had been with us today, my guess is that he would agree. That man would probably have recognized the links between an anti-Semitic belief, which led to the extermination of a people, and an anti-Zionist conviction, which aims at the annihilation of a state.

Of course, I admit that besides anti-Zionist fanaticism in parts of the Arab and Muslim world, anti-Semitism in the former Soviet empire is the most obvious threat to Jews today. I here refer to a number of speeches by Professor Irwin Cotler, an expert on anti-Jewish tendencies of the post-Soviet era. He has itemized ten dynamics in that region, including the threatening development of nationalist movements, the emerging culture of anarchy, the economic melt-down of some of the new states, how *Glasnost* becomes a cover for anti-democratic excesses, the *Pamyat* phenomenon, the anchorage of anti-Semitism amongst intellectual and cultural elites in the Russian Republic, the theological anti-Semitism in the Orthodox church, and the Islamization of the southern republics – all of these trends constitute immediate or long-term dangers for the Jews of this vast area.

I can add to that the growing anti-Jewish propaganda in Romania, Hungary, and Slovakia. And, of course, we always have to observe the deep-rooted Polish prejudice, which has now, when almost all the Jews there are gone, become an anti-Semitism without Jews. But my following observations regarding Eastern Europe are limited to the Baltic states.

On 25 August of last year, a few hours after the statue of Lenin was finally cut down and removed from its pedestal, I made a speech at a rally on the site of the Big Choral Synagogue of Riga. Now, remember the impact of those days: the coup attempt in Moscow, the violent attacks on the emerging independence of the three Baltic states, the resistance by Boris Yeltsin and thousands of Moscow citizens, and the surprisingly quick defeat of the hard-line communists. That was a week that changed the world.

Of course, the Baltic Jewish Festival, which was to have been held with some six hundred participants from a dozen countries, was cancelled when the Soviet military machine tried to take over. But I already had a visa for Latvia and went there to be with friends in those days of grief and anguish.

By the time the plane touched down at the Riga airport, Latvia was already liberated. The Soviet tanks and soldiers had withdrawn to their barracks. The news from Moscow made them understand that the coup had failed.

The people who met me at the airport were all smiling: you may recognize or imagine the sort of smile from deep within, which is not only an expression of joy, kindness, or friendship, but the visible sign that something fundamental has happened in one's life. People started to understand that finally, after half a century of occupation, the nightmare might be over.

These people had decided to veto the cancellation of the Jewish Festival. So, the next day the festival began, and people from all the countries around the Baltic Sea tried to rebook their air tickets to Riga. Again: remember the *Jewish* history of these countries. More than 95 per cent of the Jews there were slaughtered during the Holocaust – the large majority in 1941 – usually with active assistance from Estonians, Latvians, and Lithuanians. We were there to celebrate the rebirth of these same three nations.

I am a non-Balt and a non-Jew. However, two causes have been with me all my adult life. One was the struggle for decades to break the silence about the right to independence for the Baltic states. The other one is the right for the Jewish people to live without persecution either in Israel or in the Diaspora. These two causes were converging right there at the opening of the Jewish Festival in Riga.

The terrible fate of Latvia, Lithuania, and Estonia is unique. Never before have three former democracies – yes, they had been parliamentary democracies in the twenties – been occupied, annexed, and colonized. For decades, Latvia belonged to a totalitarian planet; it was now returning to the family of free nations. To support the re-emerging democracies was and is an obligation for all of us, Balts and non-Balts.

The fate of European Jewry is also, to say the very least, unique. Never before had it been a goal of a big, industrialized, and well-educated country to kill everyone who belonged to the Jewish people for the simple crime that they were Jews. Latvia had been one of the worst areas of mass murder; the number of survivors was arguably the lowest of Nazi-conquered Europe – always bearing in mind that what happened to the Jews fifty years ago is an obligation for all of us, Jews and non-Jews.

The summer before, in 1990, I had visited Latvia with one of the few survivors, George Schwab, now a professor of history in New York City. We went to the ghettoes of Liepaja and Riga, the former concentration camp of Kaiserwald, the killing fields of Rumbula, and other places. I was shocked by the lack of memorials commemorating the suffering of Latvian Jews, astonished by the lack of adequate teaching about the Holocaust in Latvian schools, struck by the lack of official recognition of the tragic fact that thousands of Latvians had been part of the terror machine.

Hence, Professor Schwab and I met with Foreign Minister Janis Jurkans, urging his government to take action, and in September two years ago the Latvian Parliament issued the historic statement condemning everyone who had taken part in the genocide of more than eighty thousand Latvian Jews. The declaration expressed deep regret for the fact that Latvian citizens had assisted the Germans. It promised that Latvia would forever keep alive the memory of the victims and would fight against any future expression of anti-Semitism.

The Latvian government has now to live up to its promises. Just two weeks ago, I again visited Riga, this time with two members of the British Parliament, Greville Janner and David Sumberg. We met with the president of Latvia, Gorbunovs, and several other leading politicians. They again promised that the new textbooks – the first history books issued by free Balts since the twenties – would not hide the horrendous facts of the Holocaust for new generations of Latvians. This should also be the case in Estonia and, of course, Lithuania, where about a quarter of a million Jews were exterminated.

If the future textbooks tell the truth, people around the world will increase their support for the Baltic nations. I will feel even more proud than today to be regarded as a friend of the Balts. But if they fail, if the new books of history evade the painful facts about Baltic involvement in the murder of Jews fifty years ago, it will be a sad sign that the Balts are still not ready to live in truth.

So, let me return to the morning of 25 August last year. For about nine hours, the Latvians tried to tear down the Lenin statue. Thousands of Latvians were surrounding the place. I went around watching their faces. There was not much joy, and not much hate either. They were just waiting, looking extremely tired, the smiles of previous days gone. It was as if the terrible truth had suddenly overwhelmed them: that two or three generations of Balts have been distorted, humiliated, and reduced in numbers, first by communist cruelties and deportations, then by Nazi tyranny, and finally, again, by Soviet determination to wipe out Baltic national consciousness. They were waiting for hours, until the very symbolic moment when the statue of the founder of Bolshevism was torn down in the centre of Riga.

Then we went to the site of the Big Choral Synagogue, which had been burnt down with many Jews inside fifty-one years before. On that place, on that morning, I again quoted Elie Wiesel. "Let us remember," said Wiesel, "let us remember the heroes of Warsaw, the martyrs of Treblinka, the children of Auschwitz. They fought alone, they suffered alone, they lived alone, but they did not die alone, for something in all of us died with them."

What died with them? My answer is: what died was the creed that there are limits of human cruelty. Now we know: THERE ARE NO LIMITS. The Holocaust proved that evil ideology combined with total power could bring our societies to unimaginable atrocities.

I come from a country which did so little in the thirties and the first years of the Second World War to save Jewish lives; it is the darkest chapter of modern Swedish history. But Sweden is also the native country of Raoul Wallenberg, who proved that one man could make a difference.

Wallenberg was not the only one. Yes, in Latvia thousands of citizens took part in the slaughter of Jews. Some of them even started harassing and beating Jews before the Germans had arrived. But Latvia was also the native country of Janis Lipke, who, by the most daring operations, saved dozens of Jews from being killed.

Lipke was a worker. For more than three years, he risked his own life in efforts to rescue Jews by smuggling them out of the Riga ghetto, one by one, and then hiding them in different locations, keeping them alive for many, many months in a most hostile environment. He survived the war and passed away only a few years ago. He saved about fifty Jews and was honoured by *Yad Vashem* in Jerusalem. Janis Lipke is a Latvian hero, who proved again that one man can make a difference.

To my mind, Raoul Wallenberg is the greatest Swede ever, and Janis Lipke is the Wallenberg of Latvia. For the last thirty months, I have urged the Latvian government and Parliament and the City Council of Riga to honour Lipke: to tell the Latvian people about his actions and idealism, to name a major street or a square or part of one of the great parks of Riga after him, and on that spot erect a statue of him. Tell the world that you realize that those Latvians who saved Jewish lives also saved Latvia's belief in its own future.

It is tremendously important, especially for young people, to be given and to see and study examples and ideals. It is not enough to condemn what the murderers did and to complain about what indifference led to. We also have to prove to new generations that there are lights even in the history of darkness, that there is an alliance of rescuers and people who realize that ideals are nothing if not supported by actions. The names of Wallenberg and Lipke and Schindler and Pastor Trocmé of Le Chambon and Father Niccacci and the Lubberts and Perlasca and Langlet and Rotta and Lutz and many others make us stronger because they give us back our belief in ourselves, and in the potential of goodness.

Wallenberg is not related only to those disasters where Jew-hatred is the driving force. His deeds should not become an inspiration exclusively to individuals, but also to governments and organizations. It would not be too difficult to speculate about "a Wallenberg reaction" – if I may say so – to the ethnic cleansing of Bosnia and the deliberate and systematic killing of civilian populations in this part of the former Yugoslavia. It would be even easier to define obligations for our countries and citizens when it comes to the ongoing catastrophe of Somalia: the destruction of hundreds of thousands of people by drought and war. With the whole world watching, numerous small children are suffering, starving, and literally shrinking to death every day. In the name of Wallenberg, we should urge our governments quickly to overcome bureaucratic and practical obstacles in order to create an organization efficient enough to transport food and medicine to those Somalians who could still survive.

As a Swede, I want to use this opportunity to thank the devoted people of Canada for what you have done to transform the fate of Wallenberg into a memory of great moral significance for the free world. I see Wallenberg as a most un-Swedish character. Sweden, like Switzerland, often symbolizes the idea of staying neutral. Wallenberg is the personification of the idea of breaking out of neutrality when crucial values are at stake.

Sweden is a most orderly country, where we play by the rules: we try to play it safe. Wallenberg discovered that in Budapest there were no rules. You, yourself, had to invent new rules, as the old ones were already broken by the murderers. His obsession was: There is no safety on the European continent. Only by astonishing and dangerous action could safety for some possibly be achieved.

Thus, to me, it is no enigma that the Swedish government after the Second World War did so little, or nothing, to intervene on Wallenberg's behalf. Our then foreign minister was mostly irritated by efforts by Wallenberg's family and friends to press his case. In the fifties and sixties, Swedish officials were astonished by Wallenberg's growing fame abroad. That fame was partly the reason that my country later, maybe too late, became more active in trying to find out what had happened to this Swedish diplomat.

Yes, Wallenberg and other rescuers make us all feel stronger. Inspiring others is also the case with those citizens today who devote most of their lives to the protection of democracy, tolerance, human rights, and the rule of law. There is an alliance of people around the world who are always strengthening others to do more for these ideas. They make us understand that government by the people and by free speech is the core of our civilization.

Let me finally arrive at the denial of the Holocaust. It could be summed up in a question, which in itself is blasphemy: Was Raoul Wallenberg just *lying* about what he saw and the crimes he tried to stop? Were all the other witnesses of the genocide also lying, including those murderers who have confessed after the war? Are the tens of thousands of documents in German and other archives just frauds, made by Jews in order to deceive the world? Are the remnants of the extermination camps only Potemkin villages? Are the hundred of thousands of survivors a mass conspiracy? Are the great scholars just bluffing? Are the mass graves staged, and the pictures smart tricks, and the trials of the war criminals show trials, and the gas chambers unfounded rumours, and the disappearance of six million people a gigantic illusion? Just asking these questions is perverse. And yet that is what a growing movement in a number of countries seeks to do.

The attempts to rehabilitate Nazism do not have to be that primitive. More than anything else, I think, the banalization of the Holocaust is becoming a major danger. Let us notice that the most subtle version is by those who are not denying what actually happened in the death camps. In the heated debate among German historians in the eighties, Professor Ernst Nolte presented a theory which denies the uniqueness of the "Final Solution." Nazi annihilation policies, says Nolte, were a copy of the Bolshevik original. What came first, he asks, the Gulag or Auschwitz? "Auschwitz is not primarily a result of traditional anti-Semitism. It was ... above all a reaction born out of anxiety of the annihilation occurrences of the Russian revolution."

We understand the psychological background: millions of Germans seek a theory that would diminish the significance of Nazi atrocities. By blaming the Soviet Union for the Holocaust, they transform German history of this century to sort of an unfortunate reaction against communist cruelties. By ruling out anti-Semitism as a major driving force of the Holocaust, they also try to minimize the dangers of the new anti-Semitism.

Less subtle is Jean-Marie le Pen, the leader of the National Front in France. Most of the dead in World War II were non-Jews, he says. Whether one million or six million Jews died is a topic for discussion – a detail – and details should be researched by historians, not politicians. Without explicitly saying that the Holocaust is a bluff, le Pen first denies the facts (the number of victims, etc.), second its moral meaning (it is a *detail*), and third questions the entire Holocaust (let the historians investigate this). Le Pen's approach gives French anti-Semites a feeling of being acquitted: now they know how to come out of the shadow of both Vichy and Auschwitz.

Then we have the Third World version. What happened to European Jewry is similar or identical to what happened to many peoples in wars of liberation – for example, what the French did to the Algerians in the fifties. The defender of the SS officer Klaus Barbie, Jacques Vergès, at the trial in Lyon openly insulted the Holocaust survivors present in the courtroom by deploring the fact that he did not see any survivors there from Sabra and Chatilla. The Vergès approach states, first, that all killing has the same moral, political, and historical significance and, second, that the Israelis are the successors of the Nazis in the business of murder.

But the most extreme form of the so-called revisionists are the outright deniers. They have nothing to do with serious academic research; they are neo-Nazis trying to destroy memory in order to remove that shield of protection for the Jews. There were no gas chambers, they say. The Holocaust is a Jewish invention in order to create compassion and guilt in the West and to squeeze money out of the Germans. Today, denial of the Holocaust is an industry of lies. It can be found in most countries in the Western world: Faurisson in France; Butz, Leuchter, and the so-called Institute For Historical Review in the United States; David Irving in the United Kingdom; Zundel in Canada; Bennett in Australia; Felderer and Rami in Sweden; and so on and so forth.

There are now hundreds of books pretending that the Holocaust is a hoax. The denial of the *Shoah* is becoming the nucleus of the neo-Nazi propaganda. In the future, the survivors of the Holocaust – those who can convey the truth to new generations – will disappear, while the deniers will most likely increase in numbers.

Again, the perversion is obvious. First, the anti-Semites take Jewish lives; a few decades later, they take their deaths from them too. They claim that these Jews have never been killed. But they are evidently not alive. The conclusion: six million European Jews have never been here on our planet – the ultimate annihilation!

The deniers try to destroy memory. By pretending that the Jews themselves have invented the Holocaust in order to deceive non-Jews, they transform the crime into an allegation against the victims.

The denial of the Holocaust might seem, to some of you, too absurd to become a real threat. I emphatically reject that optimism. The revisionist propaganda is gaining strength, as Professor Yehuda Bauer at the Hebrew University in Jerusalem has written, "precisely because the Holocaust is too horrendous a reality to be accepted ... and any theory denying it may find fertile psychological ground." Bauer gocs on to say that such revisionist propaganda aims at the destabilization of democratic societies, first in order to justify Nazi Germany and second to create a society in its image.

We must never forget that those who deny the crimes of the Nazis are those most likely to repeat them. They deny the Holocaust for exactly the reason that they themselves are inclined to complete what Hitler did not have the time to accomplish.

Let us therefore bear in mind that anti-Semitism remains a disease in the gentile society. Yes, anti-Semitism is a disease among many non-Jews; it makes Jews suffer and die. However, Jews are not the only victims. Anti-Semitism always starts with the Jews. It never stops with the Jews. Jew-hatred, if not contained, almost always develops into assaults on other groups and minorities and finally destroys democratic institutions and the rule of law.

As a non-Jew I realize that when anti-Semites, disguised as anti-Zionists or not, attack the Jews, they attack all of us. Let us therefore prove that we understand at least part of the Wallenberg legacy and try to live up to it. Let us, Jews and non-Jews together, with all our energy and strength, fight this old-new anti-Semitism in unity.

War Crimes Justice – Five Years Later

NUREMBERG LEGACY:
THE UNITED STATES FIVE YEARS LATER
ELIZABETH HOLTZMAN

Five years after McGill University's important Conference on the legacy of Nuremberg, it is just as important as ever to bring Nazi war criminals to justice. Sadly, the growth of anti-Semitism and other forms of hatred over the last five years has made it even more urgent that we keep alive the truth of the Holocaust.

Indeed, one of the most disturbing developments over the last five years has been the growth in serious attention paid to people trying to deny that the Holocaust ever occurred. The educational value of putting Nazi war criminals on trial to teach new generations about the awful deeds is justification enough for continuing to pursue these criminals.

Sadly, the issue of exposing anti-Semitism is not academic. With the fall of communism, too many in the former Soviet Union and Eastern Europe have returned to old hatreds, including the hatred of Jews. This is true even in areas such as Poland, where few Jews remain. In Yugoslavia, attempts at "ethnic cleansing" provide a chilling demonstration that the Nazis' ideas and tactics are still with us today. In Germany, we see the rise of new neo-Nazi groups, their violent attacks on foreign immigrants, and the weak response of the German government.

The end of the Soviet Union has not brought only bad news. The opening of Soviet files on the Nazis has provided an important new source of information that will aid in pursuing and bringing to justice many war criminals. Previously, there was little information about the fate of Jews in Soviet territory invaded by the Germans, and it was believed that the German army was not heavily involved with killing Jews. The files show that in fact the German army was active in rounding up and massacring Jews. The new data indicate that more Jews may have died in the Holocaust than currently estimated.

Here in the US, there have also been some advances in opening up old files and bringing to light more information about the sordid history of US government aid to Nazi war criminals after the Second World War. In March, 1992, I wrote a letter requesting that the Central Intelligence Agency open to the public its files on Nazi war crimes. In September, 1992, the CIA agreed to open its files. While I welcome this historic agreement, I have already learned that the CIA's performance must be closely monitored. The agency at first claimed that it could not find its files on some specific war criminals, and only "discovered" them after some prompting from my office.

I am proud of the continuing accomplishments of the US Office of Special Investigations (OSI), which was set up as a result of legislation, I drafted when I was in Congress. The OSI has investigated sixteen hundred people, filed more than eighty cases, stripped forty-two people of US citizenship, and expelled thirty-one people. Much of that activity has come in the last five years, despite the opposition of the Republican administrations under which the office was working.

There have been some advances in other countries. The United Kingdom and Canada have set up groups modelled after the OSI, though they have not filed many charges yet. Australia set up a unit, which filed a very small of cases, and then closed it down again.

These times do not call for face-saving gestures; they call for a determined effort to bring all Nazi war criminals to justice. We must teach a new generation the peril of indifference and the importance of fighting any form of bigotry. And we must show a new crop of bigots that there is a price to be paid for acting on their hatred.

WAR CRIMES: AN AUSTRALIAN UPDATE
JUSTICE MICHAEL KIRBY, AC, CMG

New War Crimes Legislation. Following the conference in 1987, there have been a number of important developments affecting war crimes in Australia and also affecting the associated topic which I chose to consider, the apparent conflict between the belated prosecution of alleged war criminals and the fundamental right to a fair and speedy trial.

The War Crimes Amendment Act 1988, which came into force in 1989, almost entirely repealed and replaced the War Crimes Act 1945. As amended, the act contained a new preamble reciting concern which had arisen "that a significant number of persons who committed serious war crimes in Europe during World War II may since have entered Australia and become Australian citizens or residents"; a determination that it was appropriate that such persons should be brought to trial "in the ordinary criminal courts in Australia"; and the acceptance that "it is also essential in the interests of justice that persons so accused be given a fair trial with all the safeguards for accused persons in trials in those courts, having particular regard to matters such as the gravity of the allegations and the lapse of time since the alleged crimes."

Following the passage of the foregoing amendments to the War Crimes Act, the first prosecution was initiated. It involved Mr Ivan Polyukhovich, an Australian citizen and a resident of South Australia. It was alleged that between 1942 and 1943 he had committed war crimes in the Ukraine, then in the Soviet Union under German occupation. Mr Polyukhovich was charged on 25 January 1990 with nine offences under the Act. Subsequently, the information was amended and a total of thirteen charges were laid. They alleged the commission of war crimes involving the wilful killing of approximately twenty-five people, some being Jewish and others Ukrainian. Most of the victims came from the village of Serniki; others came from the nearby village of Alexandrove. Mr Polyukhovich was also charged with war crimes, alleging that he was knowingly concerned in the wilful killing of approximately eight hundred and fifty people known as "the Jews of Serniki."

Virtually immediately, Mr Polyukhovich brought proceedings in the High court of Australia (the highest court in Australia) claiming a declaration, binding on the federal authorities, that the War Crimes Amendment Act 1988 was invalid or that specified provisions of the 1945 Act were invalid, as amended. The Chief Justice of Australia (Mason CJ) referred to the Full Court of the High Court of Australia the question whether the Act, as amended, was invalid in its application to the information laid against Mr Polyukhovich.

War-Crimes Legislation Upheld. On 14 August 1991, in a decision of very considerable constitutional importance beyond the issue of war crimes, the High Court of Australia upheld the constitutional validity of the amended federal legislation. (See *Polyukhovich* v. *The Commonwealth of Australia & Anor.*[1]) The majority (Mason CJ, Deane, Dawson, Gaudron and McHugh JJ) held that, to the extent the amending legislation operated upon conduct that took place outside Australia and at a time when Australian legislation was not in force as later enacted, making such conduct a criminal offence in Australia at the time it was charged, the law was nonetheless one with respect to Australia's "external affairs." Under s.51(xxix) of the Australian Constitution, the federal Parliament may make laws with respect to "external affairs." The majority held that the fact that the law operated on the past conduct of persons who, at the time of the commission of that conduct, had no connection with Australia, did not in any way detract from its character as a law with respect to Australia's "external affairs" at the time it was enacted. Various arguments were rejected by differing combinations of judges of the court. Thus, the argument that the amendment usurped the exercise of the judicial power of the Commonwealth was dismissed. So was the argument that the retrospectivity of the operation of the amendment was unconstitutional. Nevertheless, the judges warned that the separation of powers inherent in the Australian Constitution would invalidate a law that inflicted punishment upon specified persons without a judicial trial, because such a law would involve the usurpation by Parliament of the judicial power reserved to the courts.

In a short note such as this, it is impossible to do justice to the complexity of the arguments and issues raised by Mr Polyukhovich in objection to the legislation under which he was charged. It is sufficient to note that (with Brennan J alone dissenting) the Act, as amended, was held to be valid. Accordingly, the prosecution of Mr Polyukhovich, and later other persons charged, went ahead.

Prosecutions under the Act. Committal proceedings against Mr Polyukhovich commenced in the Adelaide Magistrates' Court in South Australia on 28 October 1991. The taking of evidence concluded on 20 May 1992. During the hearing, a total of forty-seven witnesses were called by the prosecution to give evidence. Of these, thirty-six came from overseas countries, including the Ukraine, Israel, the United States, Canada, Germany, Russia, and Czechoslovakia.

Following completion of the evidence, the prosecution further amended a number of its charges. With respect to five charges as laid, the prosecution no longer sought committal because relevant witnesses had been unable to attend. Some of them had died after the commencement of the proceedings. Some were too ill to travel the long distance to Adelaide. In one instance, the sole witness gave evidence significantly inconsistent with the information that he had previously given to the federal director of public prosecutions. These charges were dropped.

Upon the remaining charges, on 5 June 1992, the magistrate in Adelaide committed Mr Polyukhovich to stand trial, but only upon two counts. Those counts alleged the killing of a total of six persons. On the remaining charges, except for one, Mr Polyukhovich was discharged. Those charges included the charges alleging his complicity in the murder of the Jews of Serniki. With regard to the remaining charge, the magistrate made no orders of committal. This was a charge in the alternative to the individual charges on which orders had been made committing the accused to stand his trial.

On 5 July 1992, the federal director of public prosecutions, as entitled to under his statute, filed an *ex officio* indictment in the Supreme Court of South Australia. Notwithstanding the committal by the magistrate, the indictment alleged five counts against Mr Polyukhovich and required that he be brought to trial upon those counts. They included the two counts on which he was committed and added counts alleging his complicity in the murder of the Jews of Serniki.

On 27 July 1992, Mr Polyukhovich was arraigned before the Supreme Court of South Australia. He pleaded not guilty to all five counts of the indictment presented to him. The conduct of the trial was delayed because Mr Polyukhovich instituted proceedings in the Supreme Court of South Australia to have the indictment quashed and the proceedings permanently stayed. His application in that regard has been set down for hearing in that court on 30 November 1992.

Other Prosecutions and Their Outcomes. Two other persons have been prosecuted under the amended war-crimes legislation. Mr Mikolay Berezowski, also a resident of South Australia, was arrested and charged on 5 September 1991 with a war crime alleging that he was knowingly concerned in the wilful killing of approximately one hundred and two Jewish people described as the "Jews of Gnivan." Gnivan is a town in the Ukraine. It was alleged that Mr Berezowski's offences occurred between 1 March 1942 and 31 July 1942. The committal proceedings concerning him commenced in the Adelaide Magistrates' Court on 22 June 1992. They concluded a month later. The magistrate discharged Mr Berezowski. A total of twenty-five witnesses were called by the prosecution to give evidence. Twenty-two of them came from overseas countries, including the Ukraine and the United Kingdom. It is open to the director of public prosecutions, notwithstanding the order of discharge, to file an *ex officio* indictment requiring that Mr Berezowski be brought to trial. That right has been upheld by the High Court of Australia.[2] However, it does not appear that such an *ex officio* indictment will be laid. The Berezowski case appears to be closed.

The third prosecution in the series involves Mr Heinrich Wagner, again a resident of South Australia. He was arrested and charged in September, 1991. His offences were alleged to have been committed between May and July of 1942 and to have involved the wilful killing of approximately one hundred and four Jewish adults and the further wilful killing of approximately nineteen Jewish children. The victims came from the village of Izraylovka in the Ukraine. Mr Wagner was further charged with a war crime involving the murder of a Ukrainian construction worker. This was alleged to have occurred near the village of Ustinovka in the Ukraine in 1943.

The committal proceedings concerning Mr Wagner commenced in the Adelaide Magistrates' Court in June 1992. Proceedings have continued over many months. They have involved the calling of thirty-seven witnesses, of whom twenty-seven came from overseas countries including the Ukraine, the United States, the United Kingdom, Germany, Austria, France, and Russia. The evidence of one overseas prosecution witness, a historian, was given by way of satellite link between Australia and the United States. The proceedings concerning Mr Wagner are part-heard at the time of this note. Thus, after massive litigation, reaching to the highest courts, only two persons are presently under active prosecution. One has been arraigned to stand trial. The other is still before the committal inquiry.

Right to Fair Trial Upheld. Australia has no constitutional guarantee of a speedy trial of criminal charges. Nevertheless, the common law provides certain guarantees against delay in the prosecution of alleged criminal offences. The issue of whether the common law stepped into the silences of the Constitution and statutes to provide an effective right to speedy trial was considered in my own court (the Court of Appeal of New South Wales) in *Jago* v. *The District of New South Wales & Ors*.[3] This was also a decision delivered after the McGill conference. By majority (Samuels JA and myself), it was held that there was no common-law right to a speedy trial, although there was a common-law right to a fair trial. Fairness would include consideration of any undue delay in a prosecution. One of the judges of the court (McHugh JA), who was later elevated to the High Court of Australia, held that the common law did provide, in Australia, a right to a speedy trial.

The decision in *Jago* went on appeal to the High Court of Australia. That court in *Jago* v. *The District Court of New South Wales & Ors*[4] laid down the rule now binding in Australia. Although expressed in terms of New South Wales circumstances, the state from which the appeal came, the principle would appear to apply throughout the Commonwealth. The High Court held that there was no common-law right to the speedy trial of a criminal charge separate from the right to a fair trial that is protected by such remedies as relief against abuse of process.

All of the justices of the High Court of Australia emphasized the high significance of delay in bringing criminal charges to trial in determining whether the trial would or would not be fair. The court reaffirmed the power of the judicial branch of government, in defence of the integrity of its own processes, to provide a permanent stay where a belated prosecution would amount to an abuse of legal process. In short, whilst the executive branch of government, in the form of the director of public prosecutions or otherwise, might, in the name of the Crown, prosecute offenders, the judicial branch reserves to itself the inherent right to stay such prosecutions if they could not take place without relevant unfairness to the person accused. Obviously, long delay, the loss of vital witnesses, lapse of memory, and other such considerations pertinent to war-crimes prosecutions would be relevant to the determination of a stay application. Clearly, the decision in *Jago* will be at the forefront of the pending application in South Australia to have a permanent stay provided against the prosecution of Mr Polyukhovich in 1992 for offences in which he was allegedly involved fifty years earlier and for which he was not charged for another forty-eight years. The outcome of the stay application remains to be determined.

Abandonment of Prosecutions. Australia, like Canada and other countries, is going through a period of severe economic difficulty. Pressure is exerted upon governments at every level to cut expenditures deemed inessential. In June, 1992, it was publicly announced that the federal attorney general (Mr Michael Duffy) had decided to close down the War Crimes Special Investigation Unit from 30 June 1992. From that date, approximately twenty of the original fifty staff members of the unit were transferred to a so-called War Crimes Prosecutions Support Unit. The federal director of public prosecutions in Australia understands that the responsibility of this smaller unit is to provide the support necessary for the conclusion of the war crimes prosecutions presently being conducted, viz. those against Mr Polyukhovich and Mr Wagner. The unit, so diminished, is not to have an investigative role. In accordance with public announcements, the current prosecutions will be concluded but no further prosecutions will be initiated.

The announcement has been the subject of public criticism most especially by, but not confined to, representatives of the Jewish community in Australia. Nevertheless, the decision appears irreversible. In a sense, the decision reflects the particular difficulty in a democracy governed by the rule of law in pursuing, so belatedly, such major war-crimes prosecutions. Consistently with modern perceptions of procedural fairness, it is incumbent upon society itself to provide the best possible legal assistance to those accused. It is necessary to bring witnesses, at a very considerable expense, from distant corners of the world. Alternatively, it is necessary to establish expensive telecommunications links. The array of counsel in cases up to the highest court of the country and in protracted committal and interlocutory proceedings demonstrates the special problem of bringing such proceedings to a successful conclusion. In the end, the large unit of staff members, the very small number of identified offenders, the great costs, and the apparently limited success persuaded the politicians that there were, on balance, more important targets for the scarce resources available to them.

The war-crimes saga has not concluded in Australia. Even the legal principles resulting from the prosecutions may be still further elaborated. But a further five years on, not a single war criminal has been convicted under Australia's amended legislation. Huge public funds have been expended. A large unit of prosecuting lawyers and support staff has been kept very busy. Witnesses have flown a million miles and more. Public attention has lapsed.

There are some who will say that the rule of law has been vindicated by these proceedings: important constitutional decisions have been laid down; a principle has been established for the future; war criminals are beyond immunity and cannot escape vindicating justice. Others will say that it would have been better to have spent the money on the famine victims in Somalia or perhaps to have built a hospital in the Ukraine to help the children who are victims of Chernobyl as a more enduring memorial to those who have suffered in war crimes. Each reader must decide.

NOTES

1   (1991) 172 CLR 501.
2   See *Director of Public Prosecutions Act* 1983, s. 6(2d) and s. 6(2e). See also *Kolalich* v. *Director of Public Prosecutions (NSW)* (1991) 66 *ALJR* (HC), 27; *R.* v. *Duffield & Dellapatrona*, Court of Criminal Appeal (NSW), unreported, 1 October 1992, where the adverse comment on this practice, as it has developed in Canada, was noted. See editorial "Indictment" (1966) 28 *Cr L Q* 129, 130.

3 (1988) 12 NSWLR 558 (CA).
4 (1989) 168 CLR 23.

WAR-CRIMES LEGISLATION IN THE UNITED KINGDOM: THE CURRENT POSITION, OCTOBER 1992
THE HONOURABLE GREVILLE JANNER, OC, MP

Since my speech at the historic conference at McGill University, "Nuremberg Forty Years Later," much has changed for war criminals resident in the UK. The Parliamentary War Crimes Group, of which I remain honourary secretary, spearheaded the campaign and lobby to have war-crimes legislation enacted. In May of 1991 the War Crimes Act was passed. The government then set up a police War Crimes Unit at New Scotland Yard and an equivalent unit in Scotland, and these two groups of officers are currently investigating atrocities and the evidence of involvement by suspects.

The Home Secretary announced in February, 1988, that he was setting up an independent inquiry into war crimes to be chaired by Sir Thomas Hetherington, a former director of public prosecutions, and William Chalmers, a former Crown agent in Scotland. The inquiry's terms of reference included the following instructions:

1 To obtain and examine relevant material ... relating to allegations that persons who are now British citizens or resident in the United Kingdom committed war crimes during the Second World War.
2 To interview persons who appear to possess relevant information relating to such allegations.
3 To consider ... whether the law of the United Kingdom should be amended in order to make it possible to prosecute for war crimes persons who are now British citizens or resident in the United Kingdom.
4 To advise Her Majesty's Government accordingly.

The Hetherington-Chalmers War Crimes Inquiry Report was presented to the House of Commons and Lords in July, 1992, and the Home Secretary said of it, "We are impressed by the force of argument that led the inquiry to its clear conclusion that legislation was required, but we want to hear the views of Parliament before taking a final view on the principles of legislation."

In the next few months, the War Crimes Group organized a mass rally in Manchester, attended by over four hundred people, and an international conference on Nazi war crimes in London. The conference brought together the heads of governmental war crimes units in the US, Australia, and Canada. Sir Thomas Hetherington was the keynote speaker. A public rally was organized to immediately follow the conference and was addressed by the heads of the American, Canadian, and Australian war crimes units. Over seven hundred and fifty people attended. The following day, a student lobby of Parliament was organized – one hundred and fifty Jewish students participated.

In December, 1989, the House of Commons took its first vote on the issue. A resolution noting the Hetherington-Chalmers War Crimes Inquiry Report and endorsing "the need for legislation" was passed by three hundred and forty-eight in favour and one hundred and twenty-three against.

After the legal committee of the War Crimes Group met the Home Secretary, David Waddington, the War Crimes Bill was presented to Parliament in March, 1990, supported by the Prime Minister and Her Majesty's Government. The Home Secretary announced the Bill as giving "Effect to the principal recommendation of the War Crimes Inquiry that British courts should be given jurisdiction over offenses of murder, culpable homicide and manslaughter committed as war crimes in Germany or German-occupied territory during the period of the Second World War, by persons who are now British citizens or resident in the United Kingdom."

The Commons passed the second reading of the bill in March with two hundred and seventy-three members of Parliament in favour and sixty against, and the final reading in April by one hundred and thirty-five votes to ten – both large margins. However, in June the House of Lords defeated the War Crimes Bill. In its place they passed the following amendment: "This House declines to give the Bill a Second Reading because the Bill would afford retrospective legislation under which criminal charges could be brought in respect of war crimes committed over forty years ago outside the United Kingdom by persons who owed no allegiance to the Crown; there being no reasonable assumption of a fair trial and no appropriate punishment on conviction." Two hundred and seven Lords voted for the amendment with seventy-four against.

In December, the new prime minister, John Major, reaffirmed the government's commitment to the legislation, and the bill passed through the Commons for the second time in March, 1991. In the following month, the Lords again tried to use its powers of delay but were overruled by the government. The Leader of the House announced, "The Government, both through myself and the Home Secretary, made it clear in the procedure debate and on the Second Reading of the War Crimes Bill in March of this year that, if a dispute remained between the two Houses, we would expect, as the Parliament Acts do, to ensure that the views of the elected Chamber ultimately prevailed over those of the other House."

On 9 May 1991, the bill became the War Crimes Act 1991. The Act follows the principal recommendation of the Hetherington-Chalmers War Crimes Inquiry Report. It gives British courts jurisdiction over crimes of murder and manslaughter committed as violations of law and customs of war in Germany or German-occupied territory during the Second World War. Those who were not British citizens or residents at the time are now liable to the same charges that British citizens always were. Central government is authorized to meet the cost of investigations and proceedings. Legal aid is to be made available to defendants under usual procedures.

The Act also provides for the procedure of transfer to the Crown Court without committal proceedings. This is already available in serious fraud cases. The defendant's rights are safeguarded by the right to appeal for dismissal of the charges. If the judge considers there to be insufficient evidence to secure a conviction, the case will be closed.

The Metropolitan Police War Crimes Unit and the Scottish Unit were set up, with immediate effect. The units are investigating alleged atrocities, but so far have not begun a prosecution.

Other changes in the law essential for war crimes trials have been passed in other legislation. For example, it was essential that the option of using television evidence transmitted by satellite from abroad be available for war crimes trials. Some witnesses will be too elderly or frail to be able to travel to the UK. This was not introduced to the legal system in England until the Criminal Justice Act 1988. It remains for the moment outside the Scottish legal system, which is entirely independent of the English system.

But the Prisoners and Criminal Proceedings (Scotland) bill will introduce the option of live video links in Scotland. This bill passed through the House of Lords, which introduced an amendment excluding video links in war crimes trials only. However, the government – supported by the Opposition – has now announced that it will overrule the Lords' amendment. The necessary legislation now looks certain to pass.

In my speech at McGill, I spoke of the Gecas case. In July, 1992, Gecas lost a libel suit that he had brought against Scottish television. The television station produced a programme in 1987 called "Crimes of War," which alleged that Gecas had participated during the war in the execution of large numbers of Jews and other innocent civilians in Lithuania and Byelorussia during the Second World War. The programme was broadcast to the nation. Amongst his conclusions, the Judge Lord Milligan stated the following: "I am clearly satisfied on the evidence as a whole upon the standard of proof agreed to apply to this case that the pursuer [Gecas] participated in many operations involving the killing of innocent Soviet citizens, including Jews in particular ... The pursuer committed war crimes against innocent civilians of all ages and both sexes." The difference between the burden of proof in a libel case and that in a war crimes case is the difference between "on the balance of probabilities" and "beyond a reasonable doubt."

Now that the Gecas libel suit is over and the House of Lords' outlawing of video links in war crimes trials will probably be overruled shortly, we can expect prosecutions for war crimes in the near future – although not necessarily of Gecas himself. All will depend upon the Crown's assessment of the strength of the evidence and hence of the likelihood of convictions.

CANADA: FIVE YEARS LATER
DAVID MATAS

Since the conference in 1987, there have been dramatic developments. The Criminal Code has been amended to allow for the prosecution in Canada of war criminals and criminals against humanity.[1] The Immigration Act has been amended to prohibit admission into Canada of war criminals and criminals against humanity.[2] The Citizenship Act has been amended to prohibit the granting of citizenship to war criminals and criminals against humanity.[3]

Immigration forms have been amended so that everyone who now applies for admission to Canada is asked if he or she has ever committed a war crime or crime against humanity. Citizenship forms have been amended so that everyone who applies for citizenship is asked if he or she has ever committed a war crime or crime against humanity.

War-crimes units have been set up in the Justice Department, for prosecution, and in the RCMP, for investigation. Six cases have been launched: four prosecutions, one denaturalization and deportation, and one deportation.

Superficially, everything has changed. Practically, little has changed.[4] None of the criminal prosecutions has succeeded. Imre Finta was acquitted of crimes committed in Hungary. The Crown appealed to the Ontario Court of Appeal and lost. The Crown has now appealed to the Supreme Court of Canada.

The Crown stayed charges for crimes committed in Russia against Michael Pawlowski after the preliminary motions judge, Mr Justice Chadwick, refused the Crown permission to collect videotape commission evidence against Pawlowski from witnesses living abroad. The Crown entered an acquittal against Stephen Reistetter, who had been charged with the commission of crimes in what was then Czechoslovakia, because, so the Crown said, the evidence had deteriorated since the laying of the charge: two witnesses had died, one had become mentally infirm, two others refused to testify.

The fourth prosecution, that of Radislav Grujicic, charged with war crimes in the former Yugoslavia, was launched in December, 1992. It has not come to any conclusion at the time this update was written.

The denaturalization and deportation of Jacob Luitjens and the deportation of Arthur Rudolph succeeded in the result, but with significant failings along the way. The Luitjens case took far too long. The denaturalization judge, Mr Justice Collier, took almost two and a half years after the completion of the evidence to hand down his judgment. The judgment came down only after a complaint had been made to the Canadian Judicial Council about the judge because of the delay. The government took another eight months after the Luitjens citizenship was taken away to get a deportation hearing going. Canada never acted upon the extradition request from Holland for Luitjens, first made in 1981, and renewed periodically since then. Luitjens eventually did go to Holland, and is now there in jail serving a sentence imposed for his crimes. But he went to Holland on his own, after the deportation order was issued but before all his Canadian avenues of appeal had been exhausted.

Arthur Rudolph never lived in Canada. Deportation proceedings began against him after he came for a visit. The adjudicator who ordered Rudolph deported gave him a partial exoneration for the crimes charged against him, deciding to believe the testimony of Rudolph, even when it contradicted documentary evidence in court.

And that is the sole result of more than five years of work. The legislation amending the Criminal Code, the Immigration Act, and the Citizenship Act received royal assent on 16 September 1987. The results to date are not much to show for that length of time.

The experience Canada does have teaches us a lesson. It is that civil remedies are working and criminal remedies are not. The reason for failure in each of the criminal cases has been different, but the bottom line is the same. Courts have been prepared to denaturalize and deport. They have not been prepared to convict.

It is worth noting that in the Luitjens case, the judge ruled that the standard of proof required for denaturalization would be a high degree of probability. Counsel for Luitjens had argued for a criminal standard, proof beyond a reasonable doubt. Mr Justice Collier of the

Federal Court Trial Division held that the civil standard, a balance of probabilities, would apply, but that the standard of proof would be strict nonetheless.[5] As well, in denaturalization proceedings, the technical rules of evidence apply, including the hearsay rule.[6] In spite of the high standard of proof and the application of the technical rules of evidence, Luitjens was denaturalized.

Prosecution has been touted as a made-in-Canada solution. And indeed it is. While many other countries prosecute Nazi war criminals, no other country has a universal jurisdiction statute like the Canadian one. In Canada, a person may be prosecuted for a war crime or crime against humanity no matter what the nationality of the accused or victim, no matter where the *locus* of the crime, provided only that the accused is found in Canada. The United Kingdom and Australia both have Nazi war crimes universal jurisdiction statutes, but both were passed subsequent to the Canadian one. At the time the Canadian law was passed, Canada was the leader in the field. As well, both the British and Australian laws are limited to the prosecution of Nazi war criminals. The Canadian law extends to all war criminals who are found in Canada, whenever and wherever the crimes were committed.

What makes prosecution a made-in-Canada solution, though, is not so much that the Canadian legislation is unique. It is that the offence is dealt with entirely in Canada. The accused at no time falls under the sway of a foreign justice system. Canadians, applying Canadian standards, dispose of the case in its entirety.

For decades, Canada did nothing about bringing Nazi war criminals to justice. There are various reasons for this inactivity, but prime among them was a desire to do nothing, insularity, and the feeling that Canada should do nothing because these cases had nothing to do with Canada.[7] Going from doing nothing to doing everything has just been too much of a leap to make. Feelings of insularity remain widespread. The attitude that Canada should not be involved continues, both within the judiciary and among potential jurors. Denaturalization and deportation, by foisting the war criminal and the problem onto another country, is more consistent with prevalent Canadian sentiment, despite the new legislation.

When the made-in-Canada solution was announced, one motivating factor was that many of the accused came originally from Eastern Europe. Deportation would mean deportation back to Eastern Europe, then under communist rule. Communist regimes would try returning Nazi war criminals unfairly. The communist system of justice did not meet Canadian or international human rights standards. Deportation back to communist regimes was not just legally questionable. It was politically impossible. Ethnic communities in Canada from Eastern Europe bridled against the possibility of having someone from their community sent back to the clutches of a communist regime they opposed.

Why were Finta, Reistetter, Pawloski, and Grujicic prosecuted, and Luitjens and Rudolph deported? The reason, I suggest, is that the four who were prosecuted came from Eastern Europe. The two who were deported came from Western Europe. It was the dictates of the Cold War that chose the remedy.

Whatever the logic or persuasiveness of the reluctance to deport to Eastern Europe, it has totally disappeared with the disappearance of communism itself in Eastern Europe. Indeed, today communists are treated more harshly in many countries of Eastern Europe than they are in Canada. Insofar as the made-in-Canada solution was founded on the existence of communist regimes in Eastern Europe, that foundation has disintegrated.

Now we are faced with a converse logic. There is an argument that we should be prosecuting rather than deporting, not because the regimes of Eastern Europe will treat returning Nazi war criminals too harshly. Rather, the fear is that the present regimes of Eastern Europe will treat returning Nazi war criminals too kindly. Those returned will walk away scot-free on return.

Lithuania and Latvia have engaged in a system of blanket pardons for those convicted by the predecessor communist regimes after the Second World War. Over one thousand of the pardons granted in Lithuania were issued to those convicted of Nazi war crimes. The Lithuanian government claims that these people were convicted in unfair trials with falsified evidence. Yet the Simon Wiesenthal Centre, in Los Angeles, has identified several of those who were pardoned as people who had confessed to participating in the mass murder of Jews. Their confessions had been corroborated by witnesses.

In Ukraine, there exists a rehabilitation programme that has granted blanket amnesties to large numbers of Ukrainian nationalists convicted by Soviet courts. There are no mechanisms to check whether those being given amnesties are guilty of Second World War atrocities.[8]

Franco Tudjman, president of Croatia, is reported as being "utterly unrepentant about the atrocities committed by the Croatian Ustasha during the Second World War, especially the massacre of Jews and Gypsies."[9] In a book that Tudjman wrote, he asserts that the figure of six million Jews killed in the Holocaust was based on "emotional, biased testimony and exaggerated data."[10]

In Hungary, an estimated half the members of Parliament of the governing Hungarian Democratic Forum back Istvan Czurka. Czurka has written about an international conspiracy of Jews, Bolsheviks, and world bankers smothering Hungary's development.[11] And one could go on.

The fear that Nazi war criminals returning to Eastern Europe will escape prosecution is a legitimate one. If the Canadian criminal justice system were working, that fear would be persuasive argument for pursuing the made-in-Canada solution. But the criminal justice system is not working. We do not face a choice between convictions in Canada and deportation without conviction abroad. Instead, the choice is between, on the one hand, waiting indefinitely for the Crown to prepare perfect criminal cases that never materialize, acquittals from juries that do not believe in the law, road blocking from judges on technicalities and, on the other hand, denaturalization and deportation.

If that is our choice, and, based on present realities, it seems to be, then the decision to be taken is clear. As long as Canada is serious about bringing to justice Nazi war criminals in some form or other, as long as we accept the principle that some remedy for the crimes of the Holocaust is better than no remedy, the option of denaturalization and deportation must be pursued, and given first priority.

"Given first priority" does not mean pursued exclusively. I do not propose that prosecution be dropped as an option. On the contrary, prosecutions should continue.

Right now, the War Crimes Unit in Justice exercises a choice of remedies: an accused is either prosecuted or brought to denaturalization and/or deportation proceedings. It is this choosing that is wrong.

Remedies should be pursued in combination rather than alternatively. A person in Canada guilty of war crimes should be both convicted and deported.

The cumulative pursuit of remedies is elsewhere commonplace against immigrants. Immigrants are routinely prosecuted for working illegally and directed to immigration inquiries for working illegally. They are prosecuted for entering by misrepresentation and directed to immigration inquiries for misrepresentation. And so on.

It is not double jeopardy to both convict and deport someone for the same offence. Double jeopardy means trying someone in criminal court twice for the same offence. But citizenship and immigration proceedings are not criminal proceedings. They are civil proceedings. Denaturalization and deportation are not punishment for an offence. They are the regulatory consequences of fraud on entry. When there are cumulative proceedings and a person is both convicted and ordered deported, typically, the person serves his or her sentence in Canada. Then the deportation order is executed.

It is only here, in the war-crimes area, that special, onerous rules apply. It is only here that a combination of remedies is avoided and a choice is made. And the favoured choice has been the option least likely to succeed, prosecution. Given the track record, if a choice is to be made, denaturalization and deportation would be the far better choice. But even better than that would be to make no choice at all but instead to pursue every remedy possible.

The minister of justice has taken the position that simultaneous criminal and civil proceedings against war criminals would be an abuse of process. It is true that the courts will enter a stay of one proceeding where civil and criminal proceedings raise substantially the same issue.[12] However, it is also the law that the courts will be slow to interfere unless it is clear that the civil and criminal proceedings really raise in substance the same issue and, if one proceeding succeeds, so, necessarily, must the other proceeding.[13]

However, that is obviously not the case for simultaneous civil and criminal war-crimes proceedings. The issue for denaturalization and/or deportation proceedings is whether or not the person committed fraud on entry to Canada. The issue for criminal proceedings is whether or not the person committed a war crime or crime against humanity. The issues raised in the two proceedings would not in substance be the same. A criminal conviction for war crimes or crimes against humanity does not mean that a denaturalization and/ or deportation effort must necessarily succeed. Denaturalization and/or deportation does not mean that a criminal prosecution for war crimes and/or crimes against humanity must necessarily succeed. To suggest that a challenge for abuse of process might prevail in this situation is far-fetched.

For Nazi war criminals in Canada, the stumbling block is that the preferred option of the government, at least for Eastern Europeans, is prosecutions instead of denaturalization and/or deportation. For non-Nazi war criminals in Canada, the problem is the reverse. Although the law is general and makes no distinction between Nazi war criminals and non-Nazi war criminals, the practice is quite different. For non-Nazi war criminals, the government commences deportation proceedings, but does not prosecute.

That option, deportation without prosecution, creates its own problems. Those who enter, in effect, get a free ride. They get a temporary stay in Canada. They get a chance of exoneration, should the system fail and not be able to prove that they are war criminals. And if they should lose, they are free to move on.

For the Canadian system to function effectively as a deterrent, there must be prosecution for these people, as well as deportation. There should be civil and criminal proceedings for Nazi war criminals and non-Nazi war criminals alike. Only then will we have an effective system that brings war criminals in Canada to justice.

There is a technical point that has to be made here. A distinction has to be made between those who entered Canada before and after 30 October 1987, the date of the coming into force of the immigration provisions of the new war crimes law. The change in the immigration law, in 1987, did not reach back into the past like the change in the criminal law. A person in Canada can be prosecuted for a war crime or crime against humanity whether or not the crime was committed before the passage of the law, as long as the act was a crime at international law or was criminal according to the general principles of law recognized by the community of nations at the time it was committed. A person cannot, however, be removed from Canada for commission of a war crime or crime against humanity unless the person entered Canada after 30 October 1987. Prior entries can be removed only on the basis of misrepresentation at the time of the original entry.

For people who do enter Canada now, there is some scope for the abuse-of-process argument. If the government simultaneously prosecutes someone for a war crime and attempts to remove the person on the ground that there are reasonable grounds to believe that the person has committed a war crime, the person would have a solid argument for a stay of the criminal proceedings. If the accused succeeds in the civil proceedings, then the criminal proceedings must necessarily fail. It would be impossible for one court to find the person guilty of a war crime beyond a reasonable doubt, after another court had found that there are no reasonable grounds to believe that the person had committed a war crime. For post-October 1987 arrivals, civil and criminal remedies should proceed sequentially rather than simultaneously, with civil remedies first. What should not happen is what is happening – the Crown's proceeding with civil remedies only. That amounts to an abdication of justice.

NOTES

1 Section 7(3.71).
2 Section 19(1)(j).

3 Section 20(1)(c) and (d).
4 See David Matas, *Nazi War Criminals in Canada: Five Years After* (B'nai Brith Canada 1992).
5 (1989) 2 FC 125.
6 *Federal Court Act*, Section 53(2).
7 See David Matas and Susan Charendoff, *Justice Delayed: Nazi War Criminals in Canada* (Summerhill Press 1987).
8 Canadian Jewish News, 10 Oct. 1991.
9 John Cruickshank, *Globe and Mail*, 13 Dec. 1991, p. A19.
10 "Wastelands – Historical Truths," quoted by Paul Lungen, *Canadian Jewish News*, 30 Jan. 1992, p. 7.
11 *Globe and Mail*, 3 Nov. 1992, p. A8.
12 See *Amalgamated Dairies and Provisional Milk Marketing Board* (1984) 14 CCC (3d) 421 (PEI Supreme Court, Chadwick J.).
13 *Weight Watchers International* v. *Weight Watchers of Ontario* (1972) 25 DLR (3d) 419, (FCTD Heald J.).

Freedom of Expression and Freedom from Expression: Five Years Later

HATE SPEECH: UNITED STATES UPDATE
ALAN DERSHOWITZ

In the five years that have passed since the McGill Conference on Nuremberg and its legacy, I have become even more certain of my commitment to freedom of speech and my opposition to laws that would ban Holocaust denial and other hate speech. We live in an age in which the volume has been turned up by all sides. Abortion advocates and opponents regard each other with hate. Gay rights advocates and gay rights opponents see each other as hateful. Black radicals, Arab radicals, Jewish radicals, feminist radicals and Islamic radicals all resort to this epithet. None of this is desirable. But what would be far more dangerous than the rhetoric of hate is the empowerment of any government to pick and choose among speakers.

The advent of thought police on college campuses and the imposition of censorship in the name of political correctness poses a serious problem to academic freedom. Examples abound of paternalistic censorship run amuck.

The answer to false speech is true speech. The answer to hate speech is thoughtful rebuttal. The answer to censorship is debate. The Holocaust was not caused by free speech. Indeed, if anything, an atmosphere of censorship made it impossible for dissenters in Nazi Germany to respond to hate speech. Even today there is a direct correlation between nations that censor and nations that repress other freedoms. There is also a direct correlation between nations that recognize freedom of speech and those that respect the rights of minorities.

Let us show faith in our citizens to pick and choose for themselves what is true and what is false, to separate the good ideas from the bad ideas, and to live in the spirit of liberty.

PRINCIPLES AND PERSPETIVES ON HATE SPEECH,
FREEDOM OF EXPRESION, AND NON-DISCRIMINATION:
THE CANADIAN EXPERIENCE AS A CASE STUDY IN
STRIKING A BALANCE
IRWIN COTLER

The five years since the Nuremberg Conference have witnessed an explosion of racial and religious incitement in democratic societies in Europe, Canada, the United States, Latin America, and Asia against vulnerable minorities in their midst. The legal remedies invoked to combat such incitement have been the object of constitutional challenges in regions around the world, triggering a series of *causes célèbres* in the nineties: the *Le Pen* case in France, the *Radio Islam* case in Sweden, the *Smirnov-Ostashvilli* case in the former Soviet Union, the *David Irving* case in England, the Minnesota "Cross-Burning" case in the United States, and the historic trilogy in Canada – for which the *Keegstra*[1] case is metaphor and message – to name but a few.

Indeed, this article is being written against the backdrop of the most celebrated litigation involving hate speech, freedom of expression, and non-discrimination in the history of Canadian jurisprudence. In December 1989, three cases[2] involving freedom of expression and hate propaganda were joined for hearing before the Supreme Court of Canada. The hearings revolved around challenges to the constitutionality of Canada's anti-hate legislation as an unconstitutional infringement of the freedom of expression guarantee of the Canadian Charter of Rights and Freedoms.[3] Interestingly, these cases represent the watershed of the "freedom of expression versus hate speech" debate that animated both the Nuremberg Conference and the courts five years ago.

In each of these cases there were two central issues before the court, issues that are likely to be the central concerns of any court in a democratic society called upon to decide a racial incitement case. First, whether the Charter protection of freedom of expression includes incitement to racial hatred, and, second, even assuming that racial incitement is *prima facie* protected speech, whether it can nonetheless be subject, in the words of the balancing principle

under Section 1 of the Charter, to "reasonable limitations prescribed by law as can be demonstrably justified in a free and
democratic society."

An appreciation of this incredible array of litigation reveals a
little-known but compelling socio-legal phenomenon: that Canada
– particularly since the Nuremberg Conference – has become an
international centre for racist/hate propaganda litigation in general
and Holocaust denial litigation in particular. This does not mean
that Canada is a world center for the Holocaust denial movement;
rather, it is the result of racist/hate propaganda in Canada being
met by one of the most comprehensive sets of criminal and civil anti-
discrimination remedies in any society.

The Canadian experience has generated one of the more
compelling and instructive sets of legal precedents respecting this
genre of litigation in the world for a variety of reasons. First, the
dynamic and dialectical encounter between the rise in racist hate
speech and the existence in Canada of a comprehensive legal regime
to combat it not only mirrors this phenomenon elsewhere but is a
case study of the validity and efficacy of legal remedy. Second, the
encounter emerges not just as a legal one but as a profoundly
philosophical or existential one. What is at stake is not only the
validity and efficacy of legal remedies but the balancing, of two
fundamental normative principles: on the one hand, freedom of
expression as the lifeblood of democracy, of the autonomy of the
individual; and, on the other, the right of vulnerable minorities to
protection against group-vilifying speech and its related humiliation,
degradation, and injury. Third, the Charter emerges as a double-
edged constitutional sword – invoked by both hatemonger and
victim alike. The hatemonger shields himself behind the free speech
principle; the victim shields himself behind the right to protection
against group-vilifying speech. Finally, the Supreme Court of Canada
has articulated a series of principles and perspectives that may help
to pour content into what First Amendment scholar Fred Schauer
has called the "multiple tests, rules, and principles" reflecting "the
[extraordinary] diversity of communication experiences,"[4] a matter
of particular importance as the rise in racist hate propaganda is now
an international and not just domestic phenomenon.

What follows is a distillation of some of these interpretive
principles and perspectives that should be useful to advocates,
activists, judges, and scholars in appreciating the considerations that
ought to be factored into any analysis of hate speech, freedom of
expression, and non-discrimination and, correspondingly, into any
attempt to strike a balance between competing normative principles.

Principle One: "Chartering" Rights: The Constitutionalization of Freedom of Expression – The "Lifeblood of Democracy." The adoption by Canada of the Canadian Charter of Rights and Freedoms in 1982 was regarded by the then minister of justice, Mark MacGuigan, now a judge of the Federal Court of Canada, as the "most significant legal development in Canada in the second half of the twentieth century." The present chief justice of the Supreme Court of Canada, the Right Honourable Antonio Lamer, characterized the enactment of the Charter as a "revolutionary" act, parallel to the discoveries of Pasteur in science. Indeed, it transformed the ethos of the free speech debate in Canada from a power process or "jurisdictional" one to a rights process or normative one. In pre-Charter law the question was which jurisdiction has the power to legislate respecting free speech; in post-Charter law the question is whether the legislative exercise of power is in conformity with the Charter.

Section 1 sets forth the fundamental premise for balancing competing rights and interests: "The Canadian Charter of Rights and Freedoms guarantees the rights and freedoms set out in it subject only to such reasonable limits prescribed by law as can be demonstrably justified in a free and democratic society." Section 2(b) constitutionalizes freedom of expression. It guarantees "everyone ... freedom of thought, belief, opinion and expression, including freedom of the press and other media of communication."

In the words of the Court, the rights and freedoms guaranteed by the Charter, such as freedom of expression, are to be given "a generous and liberal interpretation," as befits constitutionally entrenched rights. The Constitution, said the Court, in its paraphrase of Paul Freund, "should not be read like a last will and testament, lest it become one."[5]

This by no means suggests that the Canadian experience is irrelevant to societies that do not have an entrenched Charter of Rights. As stated by the Supreme Court, "[The notion] that freedom to express oneself openly and fully is of crucial importance in a free and democratic society was recognized by Canadian Courts prior to the enactment of the Charter ... freedom of expression was seen as an essential value of Canadian Parliamentary democracy."[6] In other words, freedom of expression was regarded as a "core" right even before the advent of the Charter, a perspective that ought to be instructive for societies without a constitutionally entrenched Bill of Rights.

What the Canadian experience demonstrates is that a constitutionally entrenched Charter of Rights invites "a more careful and generous study of the values informing the freedom,"[7] and therefore commends itself to those concerned with a more enhanced promotion and protection of human rights generally. But while the Charter regards freedom of expression as "the lifeblood of democracy," it acknowledges that this freedom may be subject to reasonable and demonstrably justified limits; and, as will be seen below, this balancing act involves existential as well as legal questions – rights in collision as well as rights in balance. On the one hand, there is the "fundamental" right of free speech, a core principle; on the other hand, there is the right to protection against group-vilifying speech – also a core principle. What is at stake is the litigation of the values of a nation.

Accordingly, one cannot say that those who challenge anti-hate legislation are the only civil libertarians, or the only ones promotive of free speech; or that those who support anti-hate legislation are not really civil libertarians, or are against free speech. Rather, there are good civil libertarians and good free speech people on both sides of the issue. In a word, one can adhere to the notion of free speech as the lifeblood of democracy and still support anti-hate legislation.

Principle Two: Freedom of Expression – Fundamental – but Not an Absolute Right. Freedom of expression, then, as Professor Abraham Goldstein has put it, "is not absolute, however much so many persist in talking as if it is."[8] Indeed, in every free and democratic society certain forms and categories of expression are clearly regarded as being outside the ambit of protected speech. Even in the United States, certain categories of speech – obscenity, personal libel, and "fighting words" – are not protected by the First Amendment. Such utterances, said the US Supreme Court in *Chaplinsky*, "are no essential part of any exposition of ideas, and are of such slight social value as a step to the truth that any benefit ... is clearly outweighed by the social interest in order and morality";[9] while some American scholars argue that *Beauharnais v. Illinois*,[10] which upheld the constitutionality of a group libel ordinance, is still good law.

In a word, all free and democratic societies have recognized certain limitations on freedom of expression: for example, limitations in the interest of national security, such as prohibitions against treasonable speech; or limitations in the interest of public order and good morals, such as prohibitions against obscenity, pornography, or disturbing the public peace; or limitations in the interest of privacy and reputation, such as prohibitions respecting libel and defamation; or limitations in the interest of consumer protection, such as prohibitions respecting misleading advertising; and so on.

Principle Three: The Scope of Freedom of Expression and the "Purposive" Theory of Interpretation. In the view of the Canadian Supreme Court, the proper approach to determining the ambit of freedom of expression and the "pressing and substantial concerns" that may authorize its limitation is a *purposive* one. This principle of interpretation was set forth by Chief Justice Dickson (as he then was) in the *Big M. Drug Mart Ltd.* case as follows: "The meaning of a right or a freedom guaranteed by the Charter was to be ascertained by an analysis of the purpose of such a guarantee; it was to be understood, in other words, in the light of the interests it was meant to protect."[11]

In the *Keegstra* case, the Court reiterated the three-pronged purposive rationale for freedom of expression that it had earlier articulated in the *Irwin Toy* case as follows:

1 seeking and attaining truth is an inherently good activity;
2 participation in social and political decision-making is to be fostered and encouraged; and
3 diversity in forms of individual self-fulfilment and human flourishing ought to be cultivated in a tolerant and welcoming environment for the sake of both those who convey a meaning and those to whom a meaning is conveyed.[12]

Hatemongering, however, according to the Court, constitutes an assault on these very values and interests that freedom of expression seeks to protect. First, hatemongering is not only incompatible with a "competitive marketplace of ideas which will enhance the search for truth," but it represents the very *antithesis* of the search for truth in a marketplace of ideas.[13] Second, it is antithetical to participation in democratic self-government and constitutes a "destructive assault" on that very government.[14] Third, it is utterly incompatible with a claim to "personal growth and self-realization"; rather, it is analogous to the claim that one is "fulfilled" by expressing oneself "violently."[15] Citing studies showing that victims of group vilification may suffer loss of self-esteem and experience self-abasement,[16] the Court found that incitement to racial hatred constitutes an assault on the potential for "self-realization" of the target group and its members. It is not surprising, then, that the Court anchored its reasons for judgment in the "catastrophic effects of racism."[17]

Principle Four: Freedom of Expression and the "Contextual" Principle. A fourth principle of interpretation – or "building block"[18] as Madame Justice Bertha Wilson characterized it – is that of the "contextual" principle. The contextual principle, as with the purposive principle, is relevant both in the interpretation of the ambit of a right and in the assessment of the validity of legislation to limit it.

As the Supreme Court put it in *Keegstra*, "it is important not to lose sight of factual circumstances in undertaking an analysis of freedom of expression and hate propaganda, for these shape a court's view of both the right or freedom at stake and the limit proposed by the state; neither can be surveyed in the abstract."[19] As Wilson J (as she then was) said in the *Edmonton Journal*, referring to what she termed the "contextual approach" to Charter interpretation:

a particular right or freedom may have a different value depending on the context. It may be, for example, that freedom of expression has greater value in a political context than it does in the context of disclosure of the details of a matrimonial dispute. The contextual approach attempts to bring into sharp relief the aspect of the right or freedom which is truly at stake in the case as well as the relevant aspects of any values in competition with it. It seems to be more sensitive to the reality of the dilemma posed by the particular facts and therefore more conducive to finding a fair and just compromise between ... competing values.[20]

In a recent retrospective on the case, Justice Wilson commented that "there was, for example, no point in assessing the value of freedom of speech for balancing purposes in the context of our political institutions if it had come before the court in the context of advertising aimed at children."[21]

One might equally argue – as will be seen through the prism of the principles below – that it makes all the difference in the world if the freedom of expression principle at issue comes before the court in the context of political speech or in the context of hate speech aimed at disadvantaged minorities. As Justice Wilson concluded on this point, "a contextual as well as purposive interpretation of the right was required for purposes of Section 1 balancing."[22] In the matter of hatemongering, then, whether the principle of interpretation adopted is the purposive or the contextual one, both interpretations converge in favour of the right of disadvantaged minorities to be protected against group vilification, while maintaining an "expansive" and "liberal" view of freedom of expression itself as a core right.

Principle Five: Freedom of Expression in a Free and Democratic Society. According to Supreme Court doctrine, the interpretation of freedom of expression must involve recourse not only to the purposive character of freedom of expression (section 2(b)) but "to the values and principles of a free and democratic society." This phrase, as the court put it, "requires more than an incantation ... [it] requires some definition ... an elucidation as to the values and principles that [the phrase] invokes."[23]

Such principles, said the court, are not only the genesis of rights and freedoms under the Charter generally, but also underlie freedom of expression (Section 2b) in particular. These values and principles include "respect for the inherent dignity of the human person ... [and] respect for cultural and group identity";[24] accordingly, anti-hate legislation should be seen not as infringing upon free speech but as promoting and protecting the values and principles of a free and democratic society.

Principle Six: Freedom of Expression in Comparative Perspective. In determining whether incitement to racial hatred is a protected form of expression, resort may be had not only to the values and principles of a free and democratic society such as Canada but to the legislative experience of other free and democratic societies. An examination of the legislative experience of other free and democratic societies clearly and consistently supports the position that such racist hate speech is not entitled to constitutional protection.[25]

Indeed, by 1966, the Cohen Committee on Hate Propaganda had already recorded the existence of legislation in a number of countries which sought to proscribe incitement to group hatred. The countries concerned were demonstrably "free and democratic."

Moreover, the legislative pattern since 1966 in these and other free and democratic societies supports the view that not only is such legislation representative of free and democratic societies but its very purpose is to ensure that such societies remain free and democratic. Indeed, free and democratic societies in every region of the world have now enacted similar legislation, including countries in Asia, the Middle East, and Latin America, as well as the countries of Scandinavia and Western Europe. Such legislation can also be found in the countries of Eastern Europe and the former Soviet Union.

Principle Seven: Freedom of Expression in the Light of "Other Rights and Freedoms." The Supreme Court has also determined that the principle of freedom of expression must be interpreted in the light of other rights and freedoms sought to be protected by a democracy like Canada. In the words of the court: "The purpose of the right or freedom in question [freedom of expression] is to be sought by reference to ... the meaning and purpose of the other specific rights and freedoms with which it is associated."[26]

It should be noted that the purpose, if not also the effect, of hate speech is to diminish, if not deny, other rights and freedoms, or the rights and freedoms of others; indeed, such hatemongering is the very antithesis of the values and principles underlying these rights and freedoms. Accordingly, any reading of freedoms of expression in the light of other rights and freedoms admits of no other interpretation than that such hate speech is outside the ambit of protected expression.

Principle Eight: Freedom of Expression and the Principle of Equality: Hate Propaganda as a Discriminatory Practice. If freedom of expression is to be interpreted in the light of other rights and freedoms, a core – and underlying – associated right is that of equality. The denial of other rights and freedoms – or the rights and freedoms of "the other" – makes freedom of expression, or group defamation, not just a speech issue but an equality issue. In the words of Professor Kathleen Mahoney: "In this trilogy of cases, the majority of the Supreme Court of Canada articulated perspectives on freedom of expression that are more inclusive than exclusive, more communitarian than individualistic, and more aware of the actual impacts of speech on the disadvantaged members of society than has ever before been articulated in a freedom of expression case. The Court advanced an equality approach using a harm-based rationale to support the regulation of hate propaganda as a principle of inequality."[27]

Principle Nine: Freedom of Expression, Group Libel, and the "Harms-Based" Rationale. According to the Supreme Court in *Keegstra*, the concern resulting from racist hatemongering is not, "simply the product of its offensiveness, but stems from the very real harm which it causes."[28] This judicial finding of the "very real harm" from hatemongering is not only one of the most recent findings on record by a high court but may be considered a relevant and persuasive authority for other democratic societies. The following excerpt from the *Keegstra* case is particularly instructive in this regard, while anchored in the analysis and findings of the Cohen Committee: "Essentially, there are two sorts of injury caused by hate propaganda. First, there is harm done to members of the target group. It is indisputable that the emotional damage caused by words may be of grave psychological and social consequence ... A second harmful effect of hate propaganda which is of pressing and substantial concern is its influence upon society at large."[29]

The Supreme Court's conclusion on this point – relying as it does on the conclusions of the Cohen Committee itself – is particularly relevant today. In the words of the court: "The threat to self-dignity of target group members is thus matched by the possibility that prejudiced messages will gain some credence, with the attendant result of discrimination, and perhaps even violence, against minority groups in Canadian society. With these dangers in mind, the Cohen Committee made clear in its conclusions that the presence of hate propaganda existed as a baleful and pernicious element, and hence a serious problem, in Canada."[30]

Again, in the words of the Cohen Committee as quoted by the Supreme Court of Canada:

The amount of hate propaganda being disseminated [is] probably not sufficient to justify a description of the problem as one of crisis or near crisis proportion. Nevertheless the problem is a serious one. We believe that, given a certain set of socio-economic circumstances, such as a deepening of the emotional tensions or the setting in of a severe business recession, public susceptibility might well increase significantly. Moreover the potential psychological and social damage of hate propaganda, bot to a desensitized majority and to sensitive minority target groups, is incalculable. As Mr. Justice Jackson of the United States Supreme Court wrote in *Beauharnois v. Illinois*, such "sinister abuses of our freedoms of expression ... can tear apart a society, brutalize its dominant elements, and persecute even to extermination, its minorities.[31]

Principle Ten: Freedom of Expression, Hate Propaganda, and International Law. In the words of the Supreme Court, international law may be regarded as "a relevant and persuasive source"[32] for the interpretation of rights and freedoms under the Charter. Moreover, as Chief Justice Dickson (as he then was) wrote in *Keegstra*, "no aspect of international human rights has been given attention greater than that focused upon discrimination ... this high concern regarding discrimination has led to the presence in two international human rights documents of articles forbidding the dissemination of hate propaganda."[33]

Accordingly, reading the freedom of expression principle in light of international human rights law generally, and under these two international human rights treaties in particular,[34] requires that such racial incitement be excluded from the protective ambit of freedom of expression. Any legislative remedy prohibiting the promotion of hatred or contempt against identifiable groups on grounds of their race, religion, colour, or ethnic origin would be in compliance with

Canada's international obligations, and, indeed, would have the effect of implementing these international obligations.

Accordingly, reasoned the Supreme Court in *Keegstra*, after a review of international human rights law and jurisprudence, "it appears that the protection provided freedom of expression by CERD and ICCPR does not extend to cover communications advocating racial or religious hatred";[35] and, it concluded, which is of crucial importance in assessing the interpretive importance of international human rights law, "CERD and ICCPR demonstrate that prohibition of hate-promoting expression is considered to be not only compatible with a signatory nation's guarantee of human rights, but is as well an obligatory aspect of this guarantee."[36]

Principle Eleven: Freedom of Expression and the Multicultural Principle. Freedom of expression must be read in light of Canada's status as a multicultural democracy; accordingly, it should be interpreted, to quote S.27 of the Canadian Charter of Rights and Freedoms, "in a manner consistent with the preservation and enhancement of the multicultural heritage of Canadians."

This interpretive principle admits of no other reading than that hatemongering is not only an assault on the members of the target group singled out on grounds of their identifiable race or religion but is destructive of a multicultural society as a whole; as such, it falls outside the protection of freedom of speech. Conversely, and again to paraphrase Mr. Justice Cory in *Smith and Andrews*, anti-hate legislation is designed not only "to protect identifiable groups in a multicultural society from publicly made statements which wilfully promote hatred against them," as Justice Cory observed, but is designed to "prevent the destruction of our multicultural society."[37]

Principle Twelve: Freedom of Expression and the Principle of "Abhorrent Speech." It is important that one distinguish between political speech – where the government, its institutions, and public officials are the target of offensive speech – and abhorrent, racist speech, intended to promote hatred and contempt of vulnerable and targeted minorities. The hatemongering at issue in *Keegstra* – and in analogous cases – is not the libel of public officials as in the *Sullivan* case,[38] or directed against "the world at large" as in the *Cohen* case,[39] but is hatemongering wilfully promoted against disadvantaged minorities with intent to degrade, diminish, vilify. This is not a case of a government legislating in its own self-interest regarding its political agenda, but an affirmative responsibility of governments to protect the inherent human dignity – and equal standing – of all its citizens.

Principle Thirteen: Freedom of Expression, and the "Slippery Slope." Those
who reject anti-hate legislation on the grounds that such group libel
legislation leads us inevitably down the "slippery slope" to censorship, ignore a different "slippery slope" – "a swift slide into a
marketplace of ideas in which bad ideas flourish and good ones
die."[40] I submit that the more that hateful speech is tolerated, the
more likely it is to occur. As Karl Popper put it, the "paradox of
tolerance" is that it breeds more intolerance – so that the tolerance
of hateful speech results in more, not less, hate speech, in more,
not less harm, and in more, not fewer hateful actions. For tolerance
of hate speech risks legitimizing such speech on the grounds that "it
can't be all bad if it is not being prohibited." The slippery slope is
there – but it may lead not in the direction of more censorship –
which has not occurred in Canada – but in the direction of more
hate – which has occurred in other countries.

CONCLUSION

The wilful promotion of hatred may be said to be composed of a
number of characteristics whose collection is itself representative, if
not determinative, of a genre of expression that is beyond the ambit
of protected speech. These characteristics, taken together, provide
a set of indices warranting the exclusion from the ambit of protected
speech of such a genre of expression; or if such expression is to be
considered *prima facie* protected speech, then such anti-hate
legislation as is designed to combat it should be regarded as a
reasonable limit prescribed by the law as can be demonstrably
justified in a free and democratic society. These indices are:

a. Where the genre of expression involves not only the communication of hatred – "one of the most extreme emotions known to
   humankind"[41] – but the wilful promotion of such hatred against
   an identifiable group, an incipiently malevolent and violent act
   constituting an assault on the inherent dignity of the human
   person.
b. Where it involves not only an assault on the inherent dignity and
   worth of the human person but on the equal worth of all human
   beings in society. For the systematic, public promotion of hatred
   against an identifiable group has the effect of reducing the
   standing and respect of that group and its members in society as
   a whole, while resulting in the self-abasement of each.
c. Where such hatemongering not only does not preserve, let alone
   enhance, a multicultural society such as Canada but is destructive
   of it. In the words of Cory, J (as he then was), "what a strange and

perverse contradiction it would be if the Charter of Rights was to be used and interpreted so as to strike down a law aimed at preserving our multicultural heritage."[42]

d. Where the constitutionalization of the wilful promotion of hatred would not only constitute a standing breach of Canada's international obligations under treaties to which it is a party but a standing breach of its obligation to implement domestic legislation to prohibit such expression. To paraphrase Justice Cory, "what a strange and perverse contradiction it would be if freedom of expression was to be used and interpreted so as to undermine Canada's conformity with international human rights law."[43]

e. Where such hatemongering is not only destructive of the values and principles of a free and democratic society – and opposite to the legislative experience of other free and democratic societies – but constitutes a standing assault on the values and interests – and the purposive rationale – underlying protected speech.

f. Where the hatemongering not only constitutes an assault on the very values and interests underlying freedom of expression, but is destructive of the entitlement of the *target* group to protection from group defamation.

g. Where the hatemongering not only lays the basis for discrimination against, and debasement of, members of the target group but engenders, if not encourages, racial and religious discord, while causing injury to the community as a whole.

h. Where such hatemongering not only does not partake in the conveyance of ideas or meaning of any kind, but is utterly without any redeeming value whatever.

NOTES

1 *R.* v. *Keegstra* [1991] 2 WWR 1 (SCC), [1990] 3 SR 697.

2 *R.* v. *Keegstra* [1991] 3 SCR 697; *R.* v. *Andrews & Smith* [1990] 3 SCR 870; *Human Rights Commission* v. *Taylor* [1990] 3 SCR 892.

3 Canadian Charter of Rights and Freedoms, Part I of the Constitution Act, 1982, being Schedule B to the Canada Act 1982 (UK), 1982, c. 11.

4 F. Schauer, Book Review, 56 *Univ. Chicago L. Rev.* 397, 410 (1989).

5 *Hunter* v. *Southam* [1984] 2 SCR 145, 155.

6 *Keegstra, supra* note 1, p. 27.

7 Ibid.

8 Abraham Goldstein, "Group Libel and Criminal Law: Walking on the Slippery Slope." Paper presented at the International Legal Colloquium on Racial and Religious Hatred and Group Libel, Tel Aviv University, 1991, p. 3.

9 *Chaplinsky* v. *New Hampshire,* 315 US 568, 571–2 (1942).

10 *Beauharnais* v. *Illinois* 343 US 250 (1952).

11 *R.* v. *Big M. Drug Mart Ltd.*, [1985] 1 SCR 295.

12 *Keegstra*, 28.

13 *R.* v. *Zundel* (1987), 580 R (2d) 129 at 155–6, and quoted with approval on this point in *R.* v. *Andrews and Smith* (1988) 28 OAC 161, to the effect that "the wilful promotion of hatred is *entirely antithetical* to our very system of freedom" (emphasis added).

14 *R.* v. *Andrews and Smith*, Ibid., per Grange JA at 181–4.

15 See *Irwin Toy Ltd* v. *A.-G. of Quebec* [1989] 1 SCR 927, 970.

16 See empirical date respecting the harm to target groups as summarized in Report of Special Committee on Hate Propaganda in Canada (1966), pp. 211–15; findings of the Ontario Court of Appeal in *R.* v. *Andrews and Smith*, supra note 2, per Cory, J., at 171; and empirical data cited in M. Matsuda, "Public Response to Victim's Search: Considering the Victim's Story," 87 *Michigan L. Rev.* 2320 (1989).

17 *Keegstra, supra* note 1, 51.

18 See Justice B. Wilson, "Building the Charter Edifice: The First Ten Years," conference paper, Tenth Anniversary of the Charter (Ottawa, April 1992), p. 6.

19 *Keegstra*, 35.

20 *Edmonton Journal* v. *Alta.* (AG), [1989] 2 SCR 1326 at 1355–6.

21 Supra, note 18.

22 Ibid.

23 *Keegstra*, 34.

24 *R.* v. *Oakes* (1986) 24 CCC (3d) 321 (SCC) at 346.

25 See, for example, the "Study on the Implementation of Article 4 of the International Convention on the Elimination of All Forms of Racial Discrimination" (a report on the United Nations Committee on the Elimination of Racial Discrimination, submitted in May 1983) A/CONF. 119/10 18 May 1983.

26 *R.W.D.S.U.* v. *Dolphin Delivery Ltd.*, [1986] 2 SCR 573, per McIntyre, J. at 583.

27 K. Mahoney, "*R.* v. *Keegstra*: A Rationale for Regulating Pornography?" 37 *McGill Law Journal*, p. 242.

28 *Keegstra*, 42.

29 Ibid., 43.

30 Ibid.

31 Ibid, 44.

32 *Reference re Public Service Employees Act* (Alta) (Dickson CJC dissenting, but not on this point) (1987) 1 SCR 313 per Dickson CJ at 349. See also *R.* v. *Videoflicks*, (1984) 14 DLR (4th) 10 (Ont. CA) at 35–6.

33 *Keegstra*, 45.

34 *International Convention on the Elimination of All Forms of Racial Discrimina-*

tion. See especially Article 4 (a) of the convention; and *International Covenant on Civil and Political Rights.* See especially Article 20(2) of the convention.

35 *Keegstra*, 46.

36 Ibid., 48.

37 *R. v. Andrews and Smith* (1988) 43 CCC (3d) 193 (Ont. CAO at p. 211).

38 *New York Times* v. *Sullivan*, 376 US 254 (1964).

39 *Cohen* v. *California*, 403 US 15 (1971).

40 This principle and perspective fine expression in A. Goldstein, supra, note 8.

41 *R.* v. *Andrews and Smith* (1988) 20 OAC 161 (Ont. CA), per Cory J (as he then was) at 178.

42 Ibid., 176.

43 Ibid.

Against Injustice

PERFECTABILITY AND CORRUPTIBILITY:
TOWARDS A POST-APARTHEID, NON-RACIAL,
DEMOCRATIC SOUTH AFRICA
ALBIE SACHS

The Dilemma

I start with two poignant sayings which I brought back with me after years of exile in Africa.

The first is: "The beautiful people are not yet born." It is the deeply sad observation by a Zimbabwean poet on the disappointments of independence in his country.

The second is even harsher: "A rich man's fart smells sweet." The Kenyan writer Ngugi felt this phrase was so apposite to the situation in his country that he used it several times in a recent novel. Young Kenyans could not imagine that the Father of the Nation, Jomo Kenyatta, patriarch, autocrat, and amasser of fortunes, had once been a famous freedom fighter who had spent a decade in prison for opposing British colonial domination.

Will the post-apartheid generation feel the same about us?

We who have spent all our lives fighting power, now suddenly face the prospect of exercising it. Many of us are as fearful of the prospect of finding ourselves in office as those presently there are alarmed about giving it up. At the moment when we are about to see the achievement of what we dreamt of, a kind of sadness rather than joy settles upon us. Where there should be a feeling of elated accomplishment, there is an emotion of disenchantment, in some cases even of cynicism. Can it be that apartheid, by depriving us of the satisfaction that should go with its overthrow, will win its last victory?

If preparing ourselves for freedom is difficult, preparing ourselves for power is proving even harder. Some people run for office. Some run from office. I must acknowledge that I am from the latter group. When elections for the national Executive of the ANC were held last year, someone asked me: Where is your constituency? "The flowers, the mountain and the sea," I answered. He rushed off to make speeches, shake hands, and caucus. I was paralyzed, muted by the idea of even a little bit of power. (I might mention that I was elected, he was not – the fynbos have their representative).

We cannot recapture the elan and conviction of the earlier period. We should not even try. It is as though the political and social pluralism that we now acknowledge in a diverse civil society, reflects itself in a corresponding deconcentration and dispersion of our joy. There is not moment of victory, no VE day, no 4th or 14th of July, not to speak of a November 7th. We move with emotional difficulty from the heroic project of insurrection on a certain day, to the banal scheme of creating good government over a period of time. Is this what all the dreams and pain were for?

Were we wrong in the dark and bitter days of the 1960s and the 1970s to declare: "No middle road"? Today we are on the middle road, we help to construct it, eager to demonstrate the broadness of our vision. We even accept it as praise to be called flexible, though we might still flinch a little at being referred to as moderate.

Not that there is any logical contradiction involved. To have opted for a middle road in conditions of racist power would have meant choosing subordination not equality; in the context of absolutist racial domination, the only way of keeping the democratic ideal alive was through the revolutionary project. Yet many of us cannot make the transition from being in the opposition, accountable only to the future, to being in authority, answerable to the present. Our psychology, our whole being, has been driven by the impulse of opposition.

It is scant consolation that members of the ruling party, and whites in general, have so shaped their personalities by being the boss that they have even more trouble moving from power to opposition than we do moving from opposition to power.

What is it about power, one asks, that makes people so reluctant to give it up? We are constantly reminded by those in office of how burdensome and exhausting it is. Yet they insist on shouldering rather than sharing their load. They gaze timidly at the Rubicon, insisting that nothing less than a Titanic is necessary to carry then across.

And what is it about authority that causes so many of us to turn our backs upon it? The truth is that a great number of us are as fearful of winning as we are of losing. We are confronted with crises of life style. We find ourselves torn from old networks and plunged into new ones. We discover that we are defending when formerly we were attacking. We can no longer identify ourselves in terms of what we oppose because our enemies are even more confused and all-over-the-place than we are.

We are the world's leading experts on how to boycott elections but know little about how to win them. We gained considerable experience in making the country ungovernable in conditions of racist autocracy, but have yet to master the art of making the country governable in the context of democracy.

What is it that we are afraid of? Each one of us has a different personal itinerary, and each one of us has a different anxiety. I will mention mine.

To begin with, I refer to some of the things that do *not* worry me.

It is *not* inappropriate that our leaders should move into well-appointed houses and be supported by secretaries, drivers, and security staff. It is due only to the psychology of underdevelopment on the one hand, and the habits of arrogance on the other, that they say they must forever live in the backyards of cities and ride around on mopeds in old suits carrying battered briefcases.

Indeed, it is important that our leadership should not be distracted by constant financial concerns and that it be able to receive guests in conditions of reasonable comfort as internationally understood. Rich might not be beautiful, but neither is poor. We must reject the kind of revolutionary asceticism that equates purity with poverty and that requires bland, soulless leaders who move around as part of a collective jelly without personalities of their own. The choice is not between ostentation and abnegation. The day may come when a leader says that to have a gold bed or diamond-studded toilet paper holder is to support local industry, but I rather doubt it. Our corruption, should it come, would be of a more sophisticated kind, as befits a developed country.

Similarly, responding to the needs of those thousands of persons who dedicated themselves body and soul to the struggle for democratic rights should not be considered as in any way corrupt. The highest reward for a freedom fighter is not office or honours but to be able to live in a world that he or she has helped to make free. Yet people live not by freedom alone. If those who divided up our country, lined their pockets, and organized assassination, torture, lies, and disinformation can receive pensions, then surely years of full-time service in the interest of non-racial democracy should also be recognized.

Nor is the question of the general competence of the future government personnel a matter for concern. Having seen leaders from all parties engaged in intense intellectual karate at CODESA, I have no doubt that government can only be invigorated and made more sophisticated by the large-scale introduction of people from what I call "our side."

It might be that "their" soldiers are better killers than ours, and their propagandists better liars, but otherwise we can more than hold our own. A local pro-government newspaper calls for negotiators that coo like doves and have the cunning of serpents: in the group in which I participated, the leading government negotiator cracked up completely and his colleague ended up voiceless, showing the cunning of a dove and cooing like a snake.

When it comes to sense of humour, we are, of course, way ahead. We can draw on the wit and subtlety of all cultures rather than being forced to rely on the dourest aspects of one – but, alas, stiff necks seem to be worth more than quick tongues or fanciful imaginations in our country, so this might have to be counted as a minus.

One can envisage a short phase where our new incumbents in the Union Buildings are still searching for the toilets while the old crowd carry on running the country. Yet in general terms I think we possess people who are more widely read, more travelled, and more open-minded – we certainly do not object to hearing the prayers of all faiths. We speak more languages and in political terms have had much greater exposure to the great – and the little – ideas of our times.

Exile has some advantages. We not only read about and listened to theories on life in Africa, the Soviet Union, the USA, India, or Sweden. We went there, studied, worked, and argued there, saw the rise and fall of governments and leaders. While people here lived on the rather thin pro-nutro gruel of Verwoerd, Vorster, Botha, and de Klerk, we experienced at first hand the richer diet of Nyerere, Nasser, Machel, Palme, Mitterand, Gorbachov, Gandhi, Wilson, Thatcher, and Reagan.

Above all, we come from all of South Africa. Our roots are planted in every part of the country and are nourished by every community. We can call upon the life experience, wisdom, and expertise of all our people, not just one section. And we are proud of the dedicated and vibrant persons in our ranks from that one section as well. (viva Antje, viva Hein, viva Jannie, viva)

In any event, only a crazy person or someone born into the ruling class would actually prefer to run the country entirely on their own. Since we are neither mad nor second-generation rulers, the chances must be good that we will draw in the best people from all backgrounds to help get the country going again.

We believe that the overwhelming majority of our compatriots are only too eager to see non-racial, non-sexist democracy work. The idea of a government of national unity to deal with the tasks of transition and to lay the foundation of future advance is not for us an imposition but an opportunity. Nor do I give any credence to the cartoon Pik-anin visions of an intolerant, demagogic, and power-hungry crowd taking over the reins, attempting to impose unrealistic and unacceptable policies on the country and then trying to stamp out all dissent.

There are both subjective and objective reasons for not being fearful of such a scenario.

Perhaps I am unduly influenced by the fact that ever since, as a student at this University, I took part in the Defiance of Unjust Laws Campaign forty years ago, the movement I have been associated with has been lead by such humane and thoughtful persons as Albert Luthuli, Oliver Tambo, and Nelson Mandela. In all that time, even when under strong pressure to do so, they never abandoned non-racial policies, nor did they move away from the basically tolerant, dignified, and democratic vision of the Freedom Charter. There is no reason for them to do so now, no advantage at all.

The objective factors might be even more compelling. In South Africa we have long had democratic institutions. We have had parliaments since the last century. We are used to general elections, the idea of opposition parties, of a critical press. In other parts of Africa, these institutions were not deeply implanted during the colonial period, and the general population was not familiar with them. They came with independence in the context of fragile post-colonial states, and often did not last very long.

In our country, the problem has not been the absence of these institutions, but their restricted nature. Our demand is not basically for the introduction of new and unfamiliar concepts and structures, but to make those that already exist operate in a democratic fashion.

Secondly, we have a level of economic development and a degree of economic interdependence unequalled on the continent. Despite apartheid, notwithstanding the immense inequalities, and independently of our cultural diversity, we are more tied together as a people in a common society and more susceptible to common citizenship than are the citizens of any other part of Africa.

At the same time we possess highly developed organs of civil society that cut across the racial and ethnic cleavages and that provide important counterweights to the state and to political parties. The fact that by and large they have also been involved in the general struggle against apartheid gives them considerable popular authority. Not only are there the churches and other religious bodies, such as exist elsewhere on the continent, but there is a powerful trade union movement, and there are important community, students, business, sporting, cultural, and youth organizations throughout the country.

The subjective and objective factors are interrelated, each reinforcing the other. The pro-democracy movement in various parts of the continent, together with the ending of the cold war, are also propitious for us. South Africa is not only ripe but over-ripe for democracy. It should have come years ago.

What, then, are the dangers?

The dangers as I see them are of a far more subtle kind, as befits a country that is really far more sophisticated than one would believe from the bizarre caricatures of our people that still unfortunately seem to inhabit the imaginations of most whites.

I worry that the years of protracted struggle will have made us intellectually weary, so that our principal objective will become that of getting into office and little more.

We should not, of course, underestimate the symbolic value of simply having a government based on majority rule. It is the visible embodiment of the achievement of our slogan: freedom in our lifetime. It is the foundation for allowing a proper country at peace with itself to evolve. It is the key to South Africanizing South Africa. Indeed, for many of us, taking part in the first democratic elections will be the highpoint of our lives.

Yet voting and even winning elections is not enough.

We need a program, not just the words of a program but an actual program, a coherent program based on a clear vision, one that will function and that will proceed rapidly and systematically to improve the lives of those who have suffered the most under apartheid.

I fear for intellectual fatigue, a loss of imagination and elan, a gradual descent into ad hoc-ism and improvisation.

We are correctly concerned about not making promises that we cannot fulfil. Perhaps this is the good that comes out of disaster, that emanates from the collapse of unsustainable dreams of perfection. Yet the poor are still poor, the oppressed still the oppressed.

We enter the Union Building and take our places in Parliament, sing the longest anthem in the world, with verses from Nkosi Kikelele and Die Stern, win debate after debate, pass law after law, and still the poor remain poor and the oppressed oppressed.

We become masters and mistresses of defending our positions, explaining away our inability to tackle the problems of the country. We refer quite correctly to the terrible legacy of apartheid and the continuing resistance of the civil service, the selfishness of the business sector and the drag on progress imposed by all the many conservative elements in the country.

Deprived of the vision that we had once thought would solve everything at a stroke, and reluctant to replace it with what we had formerly rejected as reformist solutions, we end up with nothing, and the poor remain poor and the oppressed oppressed.

We commemorate days of heroic memory, give each other decorations of one sort or another, remind the people of the years of struggle and sacrifice, launch campaign after highly publicized campaign to deal with all the problems of the country, and the poor still stay poor and the oppressed oppressed.

Having resisted the bullets and bombs of lead, we now face the bullets and bombs of sugar, and slowly we succumb to their sweetness. A job for a friend here, a place for a relative there. Advance knowledge of government decisions, buying up land, directing contracts. After all, the Nationalists did it to a great effect, not to help themselves, of course, but to assist the Afrikaner people ... The biggest employment agency in the country, namely the AB (Afrikaner Broederbond), becomes the NRABSB (the Non-Racial Afrikaner Broeder and Suster Bond) and we replace it with ...

Now-it's-our-turn-ism takes over from ad hoc-ism. There is no form of corruption that we will be inventing, every variety will have already been used in what will be referred to by some as the good old days. We will simply be carrying on the well-tried practices of previous governments. If all power corrupts, then people's power corrupts in a popular way. A *lucre continua!*

The poor become angry, the oppressed chafe. We point out that it is not through adventurist actions that they will get their rights, that they must take their place in the queue like everybody else. They are obstinate, occupy land, go on strike, refuse to pay taxes. We send in the police, lock up the persons who are agitating them ... Appeal for national unity. Remind them of the struggle.

We have achieved a great victory. We have de-racialized oppression. We have done something that apartheid never succeeded in doing – we have legitimized inequality.

Re-Posing Some Basic Questions

Neither kings nor freedom fighters have any divine right to rule. That is why we have constitutions.

Constitutions both express and tame power. They are built not on trust but on mistrust, and not just of the other side but of ourselves.

The rich talk a lot about constitutions but have little need for them, since they have other ways of defending their power. The poor say little about constitutions but have a great need for them, since they can provide secure means of empowerment.

Good principles do not constrain good people, they free them to act.

One should not be surprised that the debate about riches and power in the future South Africa should be dominated by the rich and powerful. Yet one is. The very way constitutional issues are posed presupposes certain answers. The result is that we do not grapple with the hard problems, we simply defend positions.

Such debate as exists focuses almost exclusively on office, only slightly on rights, and hardly at all on process.

Perhaps it is understandable that those who tremble at the prospect of having to give up power should spend all their intellectual energies on constructing defensive constitutional redoubts for themselves. They are part of the equation and we have to negotiate with them. This is difficult but not impossible, provided we remember that the golden rule of negotiations is "don't expect bananas from a mango tree."

Yet there is no excuse for the rest of us, and particularly for university people, keeping our vision so narrow.

By allowing questions to be posed in terms of the preoccupations only of the rich and powerful we empty the debate of its core problems and deprive it of its true creative potential. Ideas advance not so much when good and bad notions clash but when beautiful concepts collide with each other. Banal questions, on the other hand, get banal answers.

One result of restricting the debate is the overcrowding of what must be the most highly populated territory in South Africa, namely, the high moral ground. Everyone is jostling to claim occupation. In one sense this is a positive phenomenon. It encourages reference to universal language and takes us out of the narrow framework within which we normally present our arguments. Yet it has its disadvantages. The objective of debate is merely to be seen to come out well and to score points against the other side. It is not to confront and resolve hard questions.

Let us be less fearful of being viewed by others as toppling from the high moral ground and let us be less concerned about possibly arriving on the sacred soil a few seconds later than our opponents. Let us rather concentrate our attention on establishing principled and realisable positions that will last into the future. If we succeed in this endeavour, we might find that the high moral ground comes to us, or, rather, that we have been standing on it all the time.

Let us as a nation not fall out of the rule of the Broederbond into the realm of Saatchi and Saatchi.

These thoughts emerge when one looks at some of the principal issues underlying constitutional debate in South Africa at this stage. Four examples may be given. First, the question on the regions is put as one of how to achieve regional autonomy when it really should be one of how to ensure regional development. Second, we are asked how it is technically possible to fit social rights into the constitution instead of being confronted with the question; "what does the constitution have to say about the massive indignities from which the majority of our people suffer?" Third, the issue of freedom of association is presented mainly in negative terms, that is, in relation to freedom of disassociation, or freedom to opt out of non-racial democracy, when it should be tied in with creative constitutional principles relating to an active role for community organizations and other organs of civil society. Finally, many questions are asked about guaranteeing rights for minorities, while there is almost total silence on what should be the central issue: how can we secure meaningful rights for the majority?

REGIONS: THE RIGHT TO ISOLATION OR THE RIGHT TO DEVELOPMENT. What the people in the regions are really demanding is not autonomy but development. They want to break out of the poverty into which they were plunged by the migrant labour system. They want roads, water, electricity, schools, clinics, and sports fields. They want to be part of the mainstream, not isolated and dependent backwaters. As they say, they are sick and tired of being sick and tired.

They demand not the right to isolation but the right to development. Far from development frustrating their culture and personality, it helps strengthen them. The people of the regions have been marginated for too long. They are not a third world folk living on the periphery of a first world nation, waiting with cap in hand to receive aid. They are South African citizens who have suffered greatly over the decades. They have claims to share in the bounty of the country which they have helped to build up.

We appreciate that there are people who as a matter of constitutional principle favour the maximum devolution of power consistent with the state holding together. The real question they have to face is whether constructing walls round the regions will promote liberty or consolidate autocracy.

Our fear is that it will do the latter.

The great majority of those who favour the creation of semi-independent states do so because they wish to resist rather than promote democracy. They envisage systems of rural autocracy sustained by local police and para-military formations answerable in a feudal way to local personalities. We would be living in a world of constitutionalised warlordism. Protection there would be, but of the feudal rather than the equal kind.

Federalism has as result become a dirty word for many people. It is associated with diversiveness, isolation, and disempowerment. It is seen as a guarantee of continuing subordination and inequality.

The number of people who can claim consistent and honourable espousal of the federal principle as a bulwark against over-centralized power, and who have not stood personally to gain from it, is small indeed. The main thrust for federalism today comes from those who in the past supported the highest degree of collaboration with the central authorities in cracking down on those fighting for non-racial democracy, coupled with the most emphatic attempts to disperse the pro-democracy movement itself.

The homeland system and the creation of the TBVC states is linked in the public mind with authoritarianism, corruption, underdevelopment, and marginalisation, not with interdependence, autonomy, freedom, and pride. In those cases where indigenous local popular pressure proved stronger than the people of Pretoria and new administrations more accountable to the people emerged, the demand is not for isolation from national life but integration into it.

The general rule today is that the more independent of Pretoria an administration is, the more likely is it to support being part of the mainstream. The closer it is to the central government and its security apparatus, the more probable its demand for federalism.

The debate is further bedeviled by the fact that the most extreme demands for territorial autonomy come from the most determined opponents of freedom and equality. The ultra-right expressly declare that their objective is to create an Afrikaner state in which white domination prevails, and then to link up with what they call black states in a confederal scheme.

The motives for federalism therefore vary considerably, with the libertarians forming a tiny minority of those who favour it. In my view, we have to look at the issue on its merits, independently of who supports and who opposes any particular position.

I have long urged that we avoid trying to deal with the question in terms of definitions. The Federal Republic of Germany is far more united in structure and functioning than the United States of America. Let us work out the boundaries and powers of the different tiers of government in an objective way, taking into account the basic needs of the country, and then allow the university professors to tell us what we have arrived at.

The real question is not what term we use (unitary state, federation, unitary state with federal feature, a united South Africa with regionalism). What matters is how government in the country can be organized so as to promote the great objectives of the Constitution: freedom, equality, democracy, and development.

Once we establish the essentially undivided character of South Africa, once it becomes clear that the real objective of territorial subdivision is to empower rather than disempower the people in the regions and in the country as a whole, once the fear of ethnic divide and rule is eliminated, then we can fully explore the true possibilities and pitfalls of regional government.

In a large country like South Africa with different centres of economic activity, the need for central government to be complemented by regional and local government is obvious. Whereas the provinces of Natal and the Orange Free State could both effectively serve as bases for regional government, the Cape is far too vast and the Transvaal far too populous to do so.

The Development Bank of South Africa has proposed nine regions, the ANC Constitutional Committee ten. Other suggestions including building up from strong metropolitan and county government to produce weak regions and a strong centre.

Whatever form is finally decided upon, government at all levels should be democratically based rather than appointed. Furthermore, whatever powers and functions are given to the regions, the Bill of Rights, including the principles of non-racism and non-sexism, must apply throughout the country.

It is also almost universally accepted that the central government should have exclusive powers over certain issues, such as external affairs and basic fiscal and monetary policy. The only real difference is in relation to whether the regions should have exclusive competence in certain matters or whether its powers should be concurrent with and not repugnant to those of the centre.

A number of us who support the idea of a unitary state for South Africa recently visited the Federal Republic of Germany. We found that the relationship of the Laender to the centre was in fact very similar to what we were envisaging for a united South Africa, namely, that with two relatively small exceptions, the regional governments and the central government had concurrent powers, with the centre having the last word in the case of conflict.

We were also impressed with two measures that had been taken in order to overcome the extensive inequality that had existed at the time the Basic Law was adopted, namely, the burden-sharing tax and the principle of regional equalization, in terms of which a higher proportion of state funding went to the poorer than the wealthier regions.

Looking back on South African history, we discover that the old provinces had similar powers to those that we are proposing today. Our best advocate is General Jan Smuts. With his holistic vision, he saw that it was precisely because South Africa was such an amalgam of communities that union was necessary. The interior was dependent on the coastal regions, and vice versa. He wanted Boer and Briton to come together; we want all the people of our country to feel they are part of one evolving nation.

The Provincial Councils that came into being with the Union of South Africa in 1910 were directly elected and, until abolished by the Tricameral system in 1983, had the power to pass ordinances with the force of law. Such ordinances would be harmonized wherever possible with national legislation, but could not be repugnant to it.

The two differences are that we propose ten regions instead of four provinces, and we suggest that their right to function be written into the constitution so that they cannot be abolished, as they were by the Tricameral constitution.

We recognize the difference between nation-forcing and nation-building. Yet just as balkanizing the Balkans did little to create stability in southern Europe, so we feel that balkanizing ourselves will not bring peace to southern Africa. What we need is a shared national revulsion against violence, oppression, and racism, and mutual acknowledgment of our interdependence. We want neither forced unity nor artificial diversity. With our history of apartheid it is only on the basis of mutual acceptance of the principle of unity and equality that diversity can freely express itself and not be associated with domination.

THE QUESTION OF SOCIAL RIGHTS. If some natural calamity destroyed the homes, livelihoods, and expectations of millions of people, everyone would accept the need for immediate disaster relief. When, however, misfortune is the result of human agency, we paradoxically accept it as natural: any moves towards special expenditure to overcome the effects of the calamity are condemned as involving undue state interference, even, may we be preserved, as socialism.

The real issue is not how to package social rights to be able to squeeze them into the constitution, but how to formulate the constitution so that it takes account of the immense social indignities created by apartheid. The majority of South Africans have lived for too long beyond the pale, disregarded, shunted around, the objects of policy, without a say in their own fate. They have not only been politically voteless but socially disenfranchised.

The essence of a constitution is that it speaks with equal voice to all, recognizing neither high nor low, haughty nor humble, rich nor poor, settlers nor natives, just people, human beings, citizens. As such, any impediments or barriers to the voice of the constitution being heard by anyone in the land become anti-constitutional. Constitutionalism and colonial-type thinking are mutually antagonistic.

Equal citizenship means more than the formal removal of legal barriers to equality. It requires universal franchise, but does not stop there. It is based on an undifferentiated nationality, but goes further. Equal citizenship presupposes equal status and equal dignity.

Double standards have been applied as a matter of avowed policy. The rationalisations have changed. Discrimination was justified, first, between Christian and non-Christian, then between European and non-European, then between civilized and non-civilized, and then between culturally different groups. More recently we have begun to hear of the necessity to distinguish between First World and Third World people. It is not all that long ago that a South African government official could declare on TV that two things he could never get used to were "a Bantu woman driving a car and a Banto man carrying a briefcase."

In a modern and relatively well-developed state like South Africa, the status and dignity of persons cannot be separated from how they live, their state of health, degree of education, access to employment, and involvement in public life. The fact that constitutions are eminently official documents setting out the highest official pronouncements on the nature of society does not restrict their impact to the officialized world only. Long after the formal impediments to equal status are removed, the informal barriers remain. In some ways they are even more pernicious because the official version is that they are non-existent, while the lived reality is that they are still very much there.

Contrary to what the Law Commission has declared, a person's health in our country is not related to what the Creator gives or takes away (how unjust to blame the Creator for diseases of apartheid-provoked starvation), but to the status granted or denied by years of discrimination. Literacy and illiteracy are status questions, not questions of learning. Homelessness is a status matter. Unemployment is largely a status issue.

The fact that millions of people exist in unliveable conditions is an affront to their dignity and an injury to the constitutional notion of equal protection. Having to live in a country where these conditions exist is an affront to all of us; rich or poor, we are all assailed by the odour of oppression and we all have the right to breathe the clean air of justice. Only by guaranteeing at least the basic minima of a decent life to all will the colonial-type status divisions in our country be eliminated. Being without homes, jobs, schooling, health facilities, food, and recreational facilities is part of the status of being black. Taking all these things for granted, regarding them as so non-problematic as not to necessitate constitutional regard, is part of the status of being white.

Constitutionalism is offended by the existence of these crudely real status divisions in our society. Constitutionalism cannot turn away from massive affronts to basic dignity of citizens.

It is against this background that the proposal is made to include in a future Bill of Rights provisions requiring an expanding floor of minimum rights for all South Africans. The proposal recognized that the rate of expansion should be conditioned by the availability of resources, and that the constitution should not hold out false promises.

Making these allowances, it represents an attempt to give flesh and blood to the concept of equal protection. It establishes the foundation of public responsibility for the securing of the basic minima of a decent existence for all. It is a concrete means of evening up the real as opposed to the nominal status of persons in South Africa. It is an acknowledgment that the total package of rights and duties involved in the concept of citizenship includes the responsibility of government to ensure that, within the limits of its budgetary possibilities, it gives priority to providing an equal start in life for all.

There are weighty arguments against constitutionalizing social rights, and they have to be considered on their merits. Yet it is not an exaggeration to say that the future of constitutional government in this country is bleak unless we find a principled and efficacious way of dealing with the enormous social disparities that divide us. It is not enough to point to the technical difficulties that might be encountered when applying the concept of an expanding floor of minimum rights. Critics of the idea should either advance a better means of ensuring that we overcome the problem, or else help us refine the principle.

In the end, the real issue is whether there should be constitutionalized indifference or constitutionalized concern. Where social
misery is both government-created and remedial, the argument for
constitutional concern is overwhelming.

FREEDOM OF ASSOCIATION AND CULTURAL, RELIGIOUS, AND LANGUAGE
RIGHTS. At one stage, much is being made of the principle of
freedom of association, not as a means of guaranteeing that people
should be able to associate, but to ensure that they could associate.
The objective was to allow for privatized apartheid. Whites were to
be permitted to use the principle of freedom of dissociation to
establish racially "pure" neighbourhoods, with their own schools,
sports facilities, hospitals, and so on. The constitution was to give
them the freedom to discriminate, subject only to the proviso that
no state institutions or funding would be involved.

Today we hear less of this idea. Perhaps it was rejected on
principle. More likely, the authors consulted their calculators and
decided that it would be just too expensive.

In fact, freedom of association has the potential to be one of the
richest and most meaningful principles of a new Bill of Rights, of
special but by no means exclusive relevance to the dispossessed. Not
only would it guarantee the classic rights of opposition or dissident
political groups to function, it would promote important new ideas
about the nature and role of the constitution. In particular, it would:

• acknowledge that the constitutional universe was populated not
  simply by the state and individuals, but by a variety of social
  formations that were more than mere aggregates of individuals,
  groupings that possessed their own personality, character and
  internal organization;
• give space for the existence and functioning of such bodies in a
  way that neither required them to receive official sanction nor
  permitted them to violate the general laws of the land; and
• recognize that these bodies had interests both of a substantive
  and of a procedural kind that deserved to find a place in the total
  arrangement of the constitution.

Since the dispossessed live largely outside of the beneficence of
state institutions, their capacity to organise and to represent
themselves has special meaning for them.

The issue is of direct relevance to the poor and oppressed in two
other ways. In the negative sense, the present owners of property
and holders of power use the just concept of protecting minority

rights in order to pursue the unjust objective of defending minority privilege. Built-in vetoes in Parliament are said to be necessary to preserve cultural interests when their real objective is to maintain a monopoly of economic and social power. In the positive sense, the millions of people marginalized by apartheid society will need their community, cultural, and religious organisations to give them a sense of pride and participation, as well as to put pressure on a government to attend to their needs.

The challenge now is to get away from the deadlock-producing debates on minority vetoes and to deal on their merits and with appropriate mechanism with the real cultural, religious and linguistic questions facing us.

The whole question of giving constitutional recognition to the cultural, linguistic, and religious diversity of South African life requires sensitive provisions of a far-reaching nature in the Bill of Rights. Such clauses must not only prevent discrimination against anyone because of religion, culture, or language, but must in a positive way affirm the right of people to associate freely so as to be able to express their rights in a meaningful manner.

The constitution is the fundamental law of the country. Nothing is beyond its purview. Nothing that agitates the population, that provokes anxiety or anger, that touches on the profound concepts of self that the people might have, should go unnoticed by it.

Not that the constitution seeks to solve all problems or even to prescribe the way to resolve all questions. Rather, it establishes the framework of principles and procedures in terms of which power is to be exercized and rights expressed. Just as the constitution cannot be indifferent to the massive inequalities and social misery in the land, so it cannot turn its back on religious, cultural, and linguistic diversity of our society. The way it should do this, however, is not through open or veiled forms of group rights in the organs of public power, but by means of guaranteed rights of freedom of association and expression in the non-governmental sphere.

The earlier debate on group rights obscured the issue centred around whether groups should have the right to be represented as such in the organs of state power. In South African conditions such as representation would have meant the permanent racialization of politics and government. It would also inevitably have led to attempts to give inordinate powers to the white minority as against the black majority.

The group rights idea was trounced in its initial form. The South African Law Commission probably made its major contribution to constitutional debate by pointing out the problems that the group rights concept posed for the creation of an acceptable Bill of Rights for the country. Negotiations over a new constitution could not have taken place if the notion of entrenched political rights for ethnic, language, or religious groups had not been removed from the agenda.

Considerable space must exist for establishing mechanisms and procedures for ensuring that language, religious, and cultural rights are not violated. Further, since these are by their nature not merely negative rights which the state should not infringe but positive rights which people wish to enjoy in a collective manner, the means should be furnished to encourage free association and expression.

One can envisage that interest groups would have the right not only to exist but to function actively and to make such contribution to solving national problems as they might wish to do. Attention would have to be paid to achieving five objectives simultaneously:

- the right of these bodies to exist and to function actively with the requisite degree of autonomy;
- their right to cooperate with each other and with the government to achieve the objectives of the constitution;
- the right to receive certain backing or benefits when undertaking activities that promote the national interest;
- the right not to be co-opted or muzzled when cooperating with the government; and
- the right to be consulted and to be involved in the process of elaborating new legislation that touches their areas of interest, and to monitor the laws and ensure that they are applied in a just and effective manner.

At the same time, the normal checks and balances of a multi-party democracy must operate to prevent oppression or abuse of political minorities. A sensitive Bill of Rights, backed up by appropriate enforcement mechanism, should be established to ensure that the diversity of the country receives appropriate acknowledgement.

The people affected by these two principles might be the same, but the two sets of mechanisms are quite different in character and should not be confused. Once the two ideas have been separated, there is nothing that stands between South Africa and democracy, except, of course, simple ambition and the refusal of incumbents to give up office.

MINORITIES AND MAJORITIES: ALL CHECKS AND NO BALANCES. According to the principle that bad ideas never die but simply reappear in new forms, the group rights notion is now resurfacing, and doing so in rather bizarre form. The claim is made that, in order to overcome what is castigated as simple majoritarianism, there should be special representation in the legislature and the executive for political minorities.

In other countries, political minorities have a clearly defined role in constitutional life, They are known as the Opposition and they are protected by important constitutional safeguards, such as the right to criticize the government and to campaign freely to become themselves the government in future. In South Africa, however, the demand is made by the erstwhile group rights-ists that political parties that are poorly represented in the lower house should have their electoral disappointments assuaged by receiving over-representation in the upper house.

South Africa has the distinction of being the only country in the world where legislative impasse is seriously proposed as a positive constitutional principle. In most countries, constitutions are designed to avoid or at least minimize legislative paralysis. In South Africa, the reverse applies.

This is not quite as irrational as might at first sight appear. For those who have been in office for decades, prolonged paralysis is a desirable outcome. The have's continue to have and the have-not's to have-not. The problem of whether to have minority rule or majority rule is solved: there is no rule at all. The status remains very much quo.

The idea of an upper house being constituted on the basis of disproportional representation makes it a mathematical certainty that the two houses will be reverse images of each other. We would thus have a democratically chosen lower house being counterbalanced by its undemocratic upper house alter ego. If the upper house has powers not only to delay but to veto proposed legislation, the result will be that no legislation could be adopted without the concurrence of parties that lose the elections.

It is one thing to say that there must be checks and balances to prevent the majority party from abusing its power, or from suppressing minority views, or from denying fundamental rights of individuals or groups. It is quite another to say that winners and losers of elections should all come out equally. The result of the adoption of this scheme would be to mock the whole democratic process. Elections would be meaningless, the concept of government empty, and the idea of opposition absurd.

The need is acknowledged for checks and balances against simple majoritarianism, but how does one even begin to introduce checks and balances against what has been called simple majoritarianism?

Once more, preoccupation with a constitutionally grotesque attempt to protect minority privileges under the guise of securing minority rights distracts attention from important and difficult questions that should be asked.

The hard question is, how can one secure majority rights when minority has been behaving like a majority, and the majority have been treated like a minority? Is the only solution for the majority to declare itself a minority, and then seek protection as such?

Some people seem to think that the majority do not need rights, they have power. The way the debate proceeds, the only constitutional question worth discussing is how to curb that power. The implication is that majorities are always greedy, insensitive, and grabbing, while minorities are made up of kind folk simply wanting to be left to their own devices. South African experience does not bear this out.

The concept of minority rights protection has an honourable history. Most proponents of minority rights throughout the world had no difficulty in giving their wholehearted support to the anti-apartheid struggle, even though it was being conducted by the majority not minority. Normally, it is minorities that require special protection against suppression of their culture, marginalization of their language and beliefs, extinction of their personality, denial of their history, and general exclusion from the middle and higher reaches of society.

In South Africa it was the majority that was the minority. In some respects assimilation was forced, in other ways segregation was imposed, but in all cases people were denied their own voice and their own participation in decisions affecting their lives. It was the minority that interiorized the majority, that suppressed and falsified its history, sent its leaders to jail, and pushed its members to the margins of the cities, the margins of the country, and the margins of public life. The beneficiaries of minority protection should accordingly be not the offending minority but the victimized majority.

With great generosity and common sense, and with a view to securing advancement for all and enduring the perpetual cycles of domination and subordination, the majority have indicated their willingness not to do unto the minority what the minority did unto them. Through their organisations they have shown that they are willing, indeed anxious, to live under a new constitution that guarantees equal rights to all and prevents the subordination or harrassement of any.

They accept all the checks and balances that have been worked out in different parts of the world to prevent the overconcentration of power. They have no problem with acknowledging cultural, linguistic, and religious rights. They recognize that there are real fears amongst the privileged groups that the processes of transformation might lead to the collapse of government, the extinction of the rule of law, and a new form of racial dispossession. As Bloke Modisane might have put it, the majority have been assiduous students at the table of constitutional good manners.

Yet constitutional debate never seems to revolve around the aspirations and fears of the generous majority, but invariably focuses on the anxieties and demand of the selfish minority. The majority also have rights. They have struggled and suffered to achieve those rights. They have undergone all the marginalization and suppression normally reserved for minorities. Even now that they are about to get the vote, they are told that they must be constitutionally disempowered and deprived of the capacity to effect changes which will rescue them from subordination.

The minority rules, OK? It decides the agenda, focuses the debate on its own pre-occupations, and builds in mechanisms to ensure that it will always have a voice equal to that of the majority.

There are all sorts of checks and balances that can ensure that minorities are not oppressed. That is not the real issue. The real question at the heart of all constitutional argument in our country is, will a party that has lost elections give up office? Will the president step down if the electorate prefer someone else? Or will the party be in office forever, and the president be president for life?

If it were a matter of a minority requiring special protection so as to enable it to overcome imposed disadvantage, a case could be made for possibly granting it a disproportionate say in relation to matters directly affecting its interest. A coherent argument could also be made out of consociational modes of power-sharing if the constitution were formally to acknowledge the existence of racial, linguistic, religious, or other cleavages in society and structure government accordingly.

As has been pointed out, however, the explicitly recognition of group rights in the South African constitution has, for good reasons, been rejected. No one demands it any more. Even the right-wing persons who reject non-racial democracy on principle declare that they want sovereignty in a separate state and not group rights in a unified state.

In South Africa's case, however, it is the majority not the minority that seeks to overcome disadvantage. It wishes to use its about-to-be acquired voting rights to adopt legislation which will give it the chance of enjoying equal rights with members of the minority. It seeks the right to the reality of equal status. It wants to be free to use its languages and express its beliefs and personality. It wishes to move from the margins to the centre of public life and society. It claims education, houses, jobs, adequate food, electricity, clean water, rubbish collection, clinics.

This is not domination. This does not mean abuse of the rights of minorities. It implies using the power of legislation to secure the basic demands for a decent life of people who have for decades been dispossessed.

What the minority are asking for, on the other hand, is not the justified right to prevent domination by the majority but the unjustified power to block the process by ending their privilege. Minority vetoes are normally justified as being necessary to prevent departures from the principle of equality; here they are intended to exclude the achievement of equality.

In conclusion, there must be checks and balances even between checks and balances. Defenders of the status quo, reluctant rather than enthusiastic signatories of the principles of non-racialism, want all checks and no balances. They do not want mechanisms to ensure that majority rule functions in a secure, considered, and manifestly fair way. They seek to have all the checks and balances weighted to one side to be heavier than majority rule. If the centre-piece is wiped out of the whole edifice crumbles. There is nothing left to check, nothing there to balance.

Majority rule is the core principle of democracy. It is right and necessary to encase it in a Bill of Rights so that it cannot be used to oppress either minorities, the majority, or individuals. It is fit and proper that the cultural, religious, and language rights of the people, whether of majorities or minorities, should be entrenched against possible tampering by the majority. It is appropriate that the constitution should guarantee political minorities the right to oppose the majority and to campaign to become the majority at a future election.

We need all the checks and balances that a modern democracy has to prevent overconcentration of power in the hands of a few. We have to have separation of powers, a constitutional court, active regional and local government. We support an electoral system based on proportional representation that encourages broad representativity and electoral alliances. We prefer executive government headed by a president who is largely answerable to Parliament. We can be in favour of voluntary coalitions when the national interest so demands. Yet we cannot eliminate or go back on the principle of majority rule.

Tying Up the Themes

THE REVOLUTIONARY POTENTIAL OF CONSERVATIVE IDEAS. What, it might be asked, have the sighs and doubts of a rather fatigued freedom fighter got to do with the great constitutional issues of the day?

Will the poor remain poor and the oppressed continue to be oppressed, whatever the constitution says?

A cynic might declare that we have had the year of the killer and the year of the liar, and are now in the year of the constitutional lawyer. Yet we dare not be cynical. We have to fight as resolutely and honestly over the terms of the constitution as we did against assassination and disinformation. Scepticism is good, necessary, but to be cynical now is to absolve apartheid and disarm opposition to it.

Perhaps we now face the greatest battle of all, the one not against an external enemy but against our own selfdoubt and failure of confidence. We honour our past and all those who died and the many who supported us, not by insisting on maximalist demands but by using our imaginations and combativity to insist on what was always our core objective, namely, the helping of the poor and the oppressed to achieve decent and dignified lives for themselves. If the constitution does not respond to that challenge, if it answers only to the anxieties of the rich, it is not a proper constitution.

Many of us at one stage believed that it was only through a system of people's power that the poverty and humiliation of the majority could be ended. We saw constitutionalism not as a defender of people's rights in itself but as a means of institutionalizing people's power previously won through insurrectionary activity. Today, we speak more of people's rights than we do of people's power.

We are discovering the full potential for our country in the application of universally held concepts of human rights. We are finding that principles which might be conservative in other countries are transformatory, even revolutionary in ours.

Political pluralism, representative democracy, the rule of law and the notion of good government have all been seen in other contexts as conservative doctrines designed to reinforce the power of the ruling elite. In South Africa they have the potential to undermine existing power relations and to open up the way to substantial social, economic, and political advance by the majority.

Representative democracy gives the mass of poor people who have been shunted from pillar to post a chance to articulate demands, to get information, and to exercise direct pressure on local, regional, and national organs of government to attend to their needs.

The rule of law provides a framework for dealing with the violence and the warlordism that has plagued our country. It helps to abolish all the areas of feudal type domination, whether on farms or in zones under warlord control. It is a major instrument for dealing with *baasskap*, hit squads, corruption, and nepotism. It goes hand in hand with tolerance, for which the people are aching.

Good government requires breaking down the present caste-like character of bad government and replacing it with a system of public administration that serves the public, the whole public and nothing but the public.

Some countries are abnormally normal. In these parts of the world, self-satisfied repetition of virtuous and anodyne slogans of daily life can be stifling. The unravelling of taken-for-granted meanings and the discovery of real relationships behind glib words can be liberating. Democracy can even be strengthened by putting it under strain, forcing it to justify itself and not merely to be taken for granted. Yet in an abnormally abnormal country like ours, to achieve the banal and artificial verities of other countries can be liberating. It is not democracy but autocracy that is taken for granted. The exclusion of the majority from the most elementary regard by previous constitutions means that their inclusion today opens the way to dramatic advance in every area of life.

What we have to avoid (those of us who identify with the grass roots and community organisations) is not the application of these potentially liberating and tranformatory principles, but their aridisation (desertification). We need to beware of emptying phrases like democracy, freedom, and national unity of real meaning. We have at all times to be careful not to officialize and institutionalize them, nor to triumphalize their surface while we trivialize their substance.

We are not required cynically to accept that politics is the art of the manipulatable. Rather, we make our contribution by ensuring that the majority are active and conscious agents in the process of transforming their lives. The very thing that most alarms defenders of the status quo, namely mass involvement in the process of change, is, in fact, the main guarantee that constitutionalism has real meaning for the country.

The process of fighting against injustice, of institutionalizing a just system of rights and establishing an honest system of responsibilities, and then of implementing the new ideas, is a continuous one. The same people who resisted the injustice of apartheid in the past must be the main participants in the creation of the post-apartheid constitutional justice of the future.

What distinguished our generation was its refusal to accept the inevitability of race conflict and race domination. Now we must display the same imaginative resoluteness in resisting the idea of the inevitability of corruption and the certainty of authoritarianism. Slowly we are achieving a democratic constitution. Slowly we will work towards securing a dignified life for all. This does not imply a monopoly of virtue, honesty, and integrity for ourselves or any particular group. No one has the right to attempt to appropriate universal values. There can be no closed way of achieving an open society. There is no copyright over progressive ideas.

Even reactionary ideas have their place in the constitutional debate. All of us need to look each other in the eyes, to discover who are the true democrats and who the natural authoritarians, and there might be a few surprises. The participatory role of constitution-making is the only one that will guarantee its fundamentally across-the-board universal character.

The philosopher kings of our epoch are far too street-wise to try to write constitutions on their own. Their wisdom and philosophy tells them to encourage the people themselves to write the constitution. Experts have their role to play in achieving the best formulations and in ensuring that the package of rights and duties is well assembled and presented. Yet the philosophy which binds a constitution together comes not from abstract learning but from the logic of experience.

Constitutions do not make people. People make constitutions. Yet they do so in their own best image. They try to avoid the pain and disaster of the past and to lay down a framework for the achievement of their best aspirations for the future. A good constitution is no guarantee of a good life, but it is an important element in securing it. The key factor is not just a general rights willingness, that is, a determination to assert rights. This willingness is most important amongst those most vulnerable.

Good constitutional principles are truly worth fighting for. The constitutional debate is not and should not be about who wins the first elections, or the second, or the third. The struggle over the constitution is a struggle over rights, not a struggle over power.

Political movements, even those we love most dearly, come and go. They keep their names and change their principles or keep their principles but change their names. Yet the people, and the people's suffering and longings, go on forever. A good constitution holds the promise of ensuring that real change takes place in our country and that it does so in an orderly and principled way. The terms of constitution can also be to some extent self-fulfilling, inasmuch as sharing in the process of agreeing on a basic law for the country might encourage a sense of shared commitment to the values that are so enshrined.

Two themes that run through constitutions are "never again" and "at the very least." They both have immense implications for the majority in this country. Never again will people be humiliated and insulted on the grounds of race. Never again will there be forced removals, pass laws, group areas, and job reservation.

At the very least, everyone should have a decent home, electricity, water, schooling, medical attention, and social security in old age. Life might be unjust and unfair in many ways, but at the very least everyone should be free to speak his or her mind, to vote for the party of his or her choice, and to lead a private life as he or she chooses.

At the very least, everyone should have equal protection under the constitution, be free to associate with others to defend his or her interests, and be entitled to the benefits of good government and the security of the rule of law.

EQUAL PROTECTION. If you woke up in the morning, and you were of a different colour, or a different gender, or spoke a different language, or were of a different faith, if you identified not with this party but with that one, would you still say that such and such a constitutional principle was the best one?

Equal protection is one of the few principles that manifestly meets the criterion of neutrality and moral independence. It should lie at the heart of any post-apartheid constitution. Its significance and ramifications are what constitutional debate in South Africa should really be centred on, not monstrous constitutional devices to ensure that somehow minority power can survive in pseudo-legitimate form.

It requires change, but insists that transformation takes place in a principled way. Equal protection says that if you are under-privileged, you will be given the chance to improve your situation, and if you are over-privileged, you will not be harassed or abused while the inevitable process of evening up takes place.

It also provides the means of resolving the tension between liberty and equality. It is through the idea of equal protection that the rights concept becomes central to the organization of modern society.

If the two great principles of liberty and equality can best be harmonized by means of a system of established and guaranteed

rights, this has implications for all countries, but especially important ones for South Africa. If ever a country needed to take rights
seriously, it is ours.

Equal protection relies on representative democracy, but goes
beyond simply having an equal franchise and equal freedom for all
from restraint or abuse. In its fullest sense, it provides the possibility
of achieving active popular participation in the democratic process
without compromizing either liberty or equality.

A strong system of guaranteed rights provides a framework for
ensuring that representative democracy is reinforced rather than
undermined by participatory democracy. In the past we have
bedeviled our thinking with the obstructive notion that an inherent
tension exists between representative democracy, with its potential
for manipulation and corruption, and participatory democracy, with
its liability to facilitate intolerance and authoritarianism. A resilient,
rights-based constitution should be able to contain both, and to do
so in a mutually enriching way. The poor and the oppressed can
really make a difference to their lives. At the same time, the rules are
not made by and for them alone, as would be the case under a
system of people's power.

What does equal protection imply?

In the first place, it means an end to discrimination. This requires
much more than simply scrapping all the laws and practices whereby
the state imposes overt discrimination. It means guaranteeing that
no citizen is debarred by virtue of race, gender, belief, birth, or
other irrelevant and unreasonable characteristic from enjoying basic
rights, whether in the public or in the private domain.

The law must provide remedies against the exclusion of persons
from schools, hospitals, hotels, or restaurants. It must ensure that
no one is prevented on these grounds from being employed or
promoted, or from buying a house or renting a flat. Naturally there
will be realm of intimacy and personal privacy where the law will not
intervene. The constitution cannot outlaw bigotry, but it can
intervene where authoritarian beliefs cease to be simply the rigid
world views of individuals and become the basis of actively preventing others from enjoying their basic rights.

The setting up of proper agencies to monitor discrimination in
our society and provide appropriate remedies, is a necessity. We can
learn from useful experience in countries like the USA, the United
Kingdom, and Australia. Bigots may dally, dance, drink, and debate
with whom they choose. They cannot prevent others from buying a
house, renting a flat, entering a public swimming pools, or expressing their views.

In the second place, equal protection requires that all spending by government, whether at the national, regional, or local levels, be done on an equal basis. The redistributory implications of this principle have barely been grasped. It means that instead of spending five times as much on every white school child or white patient as on each black one, expenditure should be the same for all.

It goes much further. It means that basic utilities, services, and infrastructures must be supplied to the poor on the same basis as to the better off. For the first time people living in the townships and squatter camps, in the homelands and the TBVC states, will receive services and benefits on the same basis as the whites have always done. Suddenly they will count.

It signifies that the same pension must be paid to an elderly person, whether he or she is black or white, and independently of whether he or she lives in Sea Point or Khayalitsha or in a rural part of the Ciskei. This would require extra funding. In most cases, however, it will not mean that more money must be found, but rather that the money that is available be spent on an equal basis. The whites will lose their subsidized services. Nothing that they already possess is taken away from them, but they will not continue to receive greater benefits from the rest of the population. Per capita rather than per race spending is of the essence of constitutionalism.

Thirdly, equal protection means that a person's chances in life should not be unduly affected by what part of the country that person is born in. Because of the way the Land Acts and the migrant labour system worked, certain zones of the country are extremely underdeveloped while others are relatively advanced. Without a constitutionally directed policy of regional equalisation there cannot be meaningful equal protection in South Africa. Many countries have a constitutional requirement that special portions of the central budget be made available for infrastructure development in poorer regions.

As has been said, what people in the overcrowded and under-developed regions want is not isolation from but participation in national life. The undignified dependence of the present regional structures on handouts from Pretoria must give way to a system of developmental entitlements directed towards integrating the zones concerned into the national economy as well as into the systems of health, education, welfare, and recreation. People in the rural areas need roads and telephones and reliable postal services; they need electricity, water, clinics, and schools; they need cinemas, swimming pools, and sportsfields.

Fourthly, equal protection necessitates the creation of a system whereby everybody is enabled to receive at least the minimum decencies of a dignified life. Equal protection does not mean that the standard of living for everyone should be the same. It does not make class division in society or social stratification unconstitutional. There might still be rich and poor for a long time; maybe it is the rich who shall always be with us.

The political parties will each campaign in terms of their own philosophies on how society should best be organized. What will be beyond argument, however, will the necessity for any government to attend to the basic needs of the whole population, and to do so in an equal way.

The question of entitlements needs to be re-visited. The concept of equal protection presupposes a system of equal entitlements arising directly from citizenship. These entitlements range from the right to vote, which presupposes polling booths and counters, to the right to education, which requires schools and universities, to the right to basic health services, which necessitates hospitals and clinics.

Entitlement is the mechanism that links the concept of rights to the practice of good government. It is law-based and principled. Yet people who themselves suffer from the problems of over-consumption hold forth about the necessity to prevent the poor from using the principle of entitlement to become consumers. The millions who have been forcibly dispossessed by apartheid are suddenly told that to enjoy the basic decencies of life they must now fend entirely for themselves. Any form of public intervention to secure elementary services is referred to as welfarism.

It needs to be repeated: rewards in our society are poorly related to energy, enterprise, or risk. If these were the criteria for success, then the so-called squatters would be the most rather than the least successful people in our society.

To say we want an active and hard-working citizenry is one thing. To argue that in South Africa everyone has an equal chance to be active and hard-working is quite something else. If some people are literate and others illiterate through no fault of their own, this is a constitutional question. If some people are forced to starve while others have problems of too much food, this is a constitutional matter. If some people are born in maternity homes while others come into the world in stables, this, in the third millennium AD, is a constitutional issue.

Equal protection demands finding the means to furnish the fundamental prerequisites for survival and the basic accoutrements of dignity for every citizen. Opinions can differ on how best this can be achieved. There seems to be little doubt, however, that the government will have to assume primary responsibility for establishing a basic platform of social, educational, and health entitlements for all.

The most developed proposal so far is that which states that the Bill of Rights should contain provisions for the creation of an expanding floor of minimum social, welfare, educational, and health rights. Such a program would be monitored by a Social Rights branch of a Human Rights Commission which would see to it that appropriate legislation was adopted to ensure that citizens could enjoy positive, directly enforceable rights in their spheres. Enforcement in the pre-legislative phase would be by publicity, public opinion, and Parliamentary procedure; in the post-legislative phase it would be in terms of rights created by the legislation.

Naturally, the program should not promise more than it can reasonably deliver. Constitutions are the most earthly of documents. They may permit pursuit of paradise in their prefatory preambles, but dare not promise the provision of panaceas in their preemptory paragraphs. The elements of affordability and enforceability would thus have to be built into the warp and woof of the original constitutional concept, not to undermine it but to give it real substance.

Finally, the principle of equal protection implies that affirmative action shall be undertaken where appropriate to accelerate equal access to opportunities. The issue of affirmative action will undoubtedly prove the most controversial of all the dimensions of equal protection. It is sufficient in the present context merely to mention that affirmative action should:

- be integrated into rather than detached from the principle of equal protection;
- complement the four other dimensions of equal protection rather than contradict them; and
- be governed by a sub-set of constitutional principles to ensure that it functions in a fair and effective manner.

One may thus propose that affirmative action be regulated by the following seven principles:

Responsibility: the nature of the imbalances and inequities must be such as to impute clear responsibility on the government to ensure redress. Against the background of officialized race and gender discrimination, this should not be difficult to prove.

Equity: the achievement of equitable results is not possible if the objectives and procedures are inequitable. Everyone concerned has the right to know precisely what his or her rights or responsibilities are. This entails that the criteria and procedures for affirmative action be set out in clear legislative terms.

Inclusiveness: the procedures must be such that all those with an interest in a particular program are given the opportunity to participate in trying to find solutions to problems that arise and to take part in implementing them.

Proportionality: the means used must be proportional to the ends to be achieved. This would affect the mechanisms employed, phasing, and time frames. Constitutionalism is concerned not only with recognising fundamental rights but with balancing the way these rights are exercised, especially when they are brought into competition with each other. Proportionality is the means of ensuring that equal protection is applied equally in conditions of inequality. It does not extinguish one right and exalt another, but regulates the area of interface between the rights. Proportionality in this context should not be confused with proportional representation. It refers to a rational, sensible, and workable relationship between the objectives to be achieved and the instruments to be used.

Accountability: the costs involved must be taken into account, and programs must be answerable to the persons directly affected, and to Parliament, the public, and the courts.

Flexibility: the means used to remove the barriers to advancement should be as well-tailored as possible to the actual situation, although the objective of removing these barriers must be rigidly adhered to. Wherever possible, the least onerous solution should be aimed at. The program should have a certain measure of adaptability built into them to take account of the real possibilities available and of subjective factors such as in-house culture – provided, of course, that doing so does not frustrate the whole enterprise.

A CONSTITUTIONAL ROLE FOR ORGANS OF CIVIL SOCIETY Government is neither the automatic enemy of the people, nor its inevitable saviour. How government functions depends in large degree on how society functions. If we are serious about the idea of bringing government close to the people, then we should not be fearful of bringing the people, in all their multiple formations, close to government. An active public opinion, which includes but goes well beyond the media, reinforces rather than undermines the constitution.

The more active the people, the quieter the constitution. The constitution is the back-up to people's rights, not their source. We do not need the courts when we are enjoying our rights. It is when we are not enjoying our rights that we need protection.

The top-down focus on the exercise of power rather than the bottom-up concentration on the enjoyment of rights has led to almost complete neglect of what should be the most creative aspect of constitutional planning, namely the role and functioning of organs of civil society. It is not a question of competition between the state on the one hand and organs of civil empowerment on the other. Strong organs of civil society make a strong state, not a weak one. The state can function more effectively if it does not try to do everything and if it operates in close injunction with the organs of civil society.

Thus the great tasks of providing schools and clinics and recreational facilities for everyone can best be undertaken if communities and educationalists and health workers and sports organizations are well organized and clear about what they want. The government can do more to promote language rights in an affirmative and not purely protective way if those who love a particular language are themselves active win its development.

Provided the broad non-racist and non-sexist principles of the constitution are always upheld, and general educational standards observed, there is no reason why people should not be active in developing community-based schools. The problem is to ensure active cooperation with, rather than antagonism towards, the relevant government department.

One envisages n.g.o.'s playing a much bigger role in the future than they have done in the past. Without necessarily being tied to any particular community structures they will have the possibility of encouraging community empowerment and local initiative, liaising with government where appropriate, and standing apart where necessary.

In the economic sphere one can expect the unions and business organizations to be far more active than they have been until now. A tripartite arrangement of labour-business-government offers greater possibilities of successful government policies than does legislation adopted uni- or bilaterally.

South Africa is unusual for the extent to which the poor are organized. The Civil Associations, formed in the struggle against apartheid, must now direct their energies to combatting the poverty inherited from apartheid. Their role is not to govern but to help make the country governable, not to replace the state but to ensure that government responds to the needs of the people on the ground.

Without a strong women's movement, the country's formal commitment to non-sexism is not likely to prosper. The government's task in fulfilling its constitutional commitment to overcoming sex discrimination and gender oppression can only be helped by the existence of a lively and independent movement that ensures that issues are constantly taken up and dealt with.

The more tenaciously bodies such as the Disabled People of South Africa fight for the rights of their members, the more likely is government to find the correct legislative and administrative answers to opening up opportunities for disabled men and women.

Accountability does not depend simply on making a reckoning after the event – it requires openness and pressure before the happening. Pressure on government is one of the essential ingredients of democracy, the more varied and the more active the better. What is important is that the pressure itself be accountable, that is, that it be open and honest.

In the not-so-distant past, whenever anyone from the oppressed majority tried to assert his or her ordinary rights, he or she was immediately referred to as cheeky. A vibrant civil society is in fact a cheeky society. People do not know their place because there is no fixed place for anyone. Where apartheid established place, the constitution acknowledges space.

It is the vocation of government to be constantly harassed and cajoled by those who chose it and in whose name it functions.

The constitution encourages people to be cheeky in relation to all forms of power, whether the power of government, or of the leading political party, or of economic giants, or of social institutions. Since the poor have as much right to be cheeky as the rich, the constitution facilitates the tugging of its own dugs, even by those who cannot read its terms.

Constitutions speak with equal volume to all, but their sound comes through more loudly to those who hear its beat than to those who merely follow the libretto. If the values they express are truly universal, then the illiterate will have no difficulty in understanding them and perhaps appreciating their inner music more fully than do the literate.

The term "organs of civil society" is gaining increasing currency in political circles, even it if hardly features in the constitutional debate. The number of associations covered by it is almost unlimited.

They included workers' organisations; religious bodies; women's groups; language promotion societies; unions of disabled persons; residents' associations; bodies for the defence of gay and lesbian rights; community organizations; burial societies; welfare organizations; self-help cooperatives; sporting, students', business, youth, cultural and scientific bodies; surfers clubs, and stamp collectors associations.

It is quite clear that in the case of some of these the constitution will speak in direct terms: religious, language, and cultural rights will require some degree of specific definition; workers' rights will have to be spelt out in a way that takes account of workers' struggles over the decades; and the question of rights for women has to be dealt with in response to what women are claiming as their just rights. The surfers and philatelists might not expect or even want the same degree of specific constitutional attention.

Whatever form these specific provisions take, certain themes will manifest themselves in all cases. The right to an appropriate degree of autonomy and self-expression will be common to all; the Constitution will guarantee the right of people to defend and promote their own interests, not just through political parties and elections, but directly.

It should be possible to make institutional arrangements which encourage active participation of interest groups, both large and small, in the processes of government. The case against corporate representation of trade unions, business interests, religious bodies, and so on in the legislature or executive is a strong one; they can support political parties if they so wish and get into office that way. This does not mean, however, that they should have no direct role in influencing processes of law-making and law-implementation.

The parliamentary system, whether at national, regional, or local levels, could be adapted to encourage direct participation of interest groups and the public in general in the legislative process. A system of public hearings could be organized to facilitate such participation. Public interest monitoring bodies could be established with strong rights to information and inspection and the power to hold hearings to which the public are invited. Parliamentary committees could be mandated to open questions to public debate. The stamp collectors society could have its day in the appropriate parliamentary committee room. All proposed legislation would have to be published in advance in a manner which would enable interested parties to be heard. A strong right to information would be central to the success of such a procedure.

The Constitution would be citizen-friendly. Instead of saying, "touch-me-not" it would say, "come-closer." In the legal sphere it would encourage class actions, that is, actions in court by groups whose interests stood to be affected by the outcome of a case, even if on the facts they might not be directly involved. In the electoral area it would promote the idea of referenda or direct citizens' involvement, independently of what the legislature might say. In the legislative field, it would support the notion of public hearings to enable interest groups to bring their influence to bear in an open way.

What would be envisaged, then, is a lively civil society directly acknowledged by the constitution, enjoying protected constitutional space within which to function and invited but not required to play an active role in public life. Even if all power did not go to the people, a significant degree of empowerment would.

PRINCIPLES OF GOOD GOVERNMENT. There is no idea, good or bad, that does not have its tradition in South Africa. We have a long tradition of well-organized and efficient public service, and an even longer one of corruption, deceit, and maladministration. We have had excellent and fair magistrates, police, and civil servants. The South African army fought valiantly against Hitler. We have also had cruel and corrupt magistrates, police, and civil servants, and soldiers who can hold their own with the most ruthless mercenaries in the world.

The system has always been at war with itself. It proclaimed an ethos of fairness and professionalism, yet it was always geared towards serving the interests of the few and suppressing the rights of the majority. Good government and apartheid were incompatible. There could never be an impartial way of administering partiality, nor could there be a just means of applying injustice. Similarly, there could never be good government based on bad laws.

Unfortunately, however, the reverse is not invariably true; good laws do not automatically make for good government. If the police, civil service, and army continue to function in terms of their worst traditions, we can anticipate new forms of corruption and authoritarianism replacing the old.

If, on the other hand, they succeed in retrieving all that was positive, if they are imbued with and guided by internationally accepted standards of correct functioning, and if they operate within appropriate constitutional principles, they can become a major force for helping to turn the country around.

Good government, often seen as the enemy of revolution, becomes a revolutionary force in a country like South Africa. Against the background of institutionalized bad government, constitutionalized good government becomes revolutionary.

Good government can help revolutionize attitudes, it can transform the nature of spending, and it can provide the security and tranquility necessary for deep social changes to take place.

We have been in opposition all our lives. Even if many of us would never till the day we expire let the phrase "defending law and order" pass our lips, we might just come to terms with the words "good government."

Against the background of bad government, good government is transformatory. It represents a move from sectionalism to broad South Africanism, from racism to non-racism, from sexism to non-sexism, from minority rule to democracy.

The people living in the informal settlements, in the backyards, and in the rural slums, who together form more than half the country's population, therefore have every reason to be interested in the concept of good government. It offers them not just formal citizenship and the right to vote but the right to be included on an equal basis in relation to all public spending. The commanding heights of local government might have more direct interest to them than the commanding heights of the economy.

South Africa is so backward in terms of its official institutions that concepts that are conservative in other countries become radical here.

The idea of good government is unassailable. It stabilizes and gives coherence to change. It is built on four principles, each of which has to be complied with on its own and all of which have to be followed together: representivity, competence, impartiality, and accountability. Representivity implies that the public administration reflects in its composition and functioning the diverse character of South African society. Competence means that everyone in the public service has the basic skills to perform his or her job. Representivity must not be achieved by disregarding qualifications, but neither must the concept of standards be manipulated to maintain present imbalances. If necessary, special training must be given to suitable persons to enable them to reach the necessary degree of competence. Impartiality signifies that the public servant attends with equal commitment to the problems of all. A diverse civil service means that the skills and life experiences to be found in all communities are represented but does not imply that civil servants look after the interests only of any ethnic, gender, language, regional, or religious group to which they might belong. Even less should they regard themselves as accountable to any political party. Accountability applies not only to hierarchical superiors, to financial auditors, to the Cabinet, to Parliament, and to the courts. There should be direct forms of accountability to the public.

The secrecy which until now has facilitated every kind of deceit and corruption must give way to a system of guaranteed openness. The public is entitled to know what government is doing in its name. It must be given every reasonable opportunity to intervene in areas where its interests are at stake. The constitution should enshrine this principle and indicate the mechanisms whereby it is to be enforced. Corruption and nepotism thrive on secrecy and arbitrariness. The tricameral system split corruption three ways. We must be careful when unifying the structures of government not to unify the structures of corruption.

The people must get their rights through open and legal means, not through knowing or getting to know someone in government. Re-distribution must take place through the law according to agreed-upon principles and criteria, not as a result of arbitrary handouts to favourites. The poor have never benefitted from corruption. They lack the money to bribe or the force to extort. What they need is rights and the means to enforce them.

It has been said that corruption makes tyranny bearable. If that is so, it makes democracy insufferable.

RULE OF LAW OR RULE OF WARLORDS?   There are two groups that argue that the masses (the people, the povo) should not be too involved in the question of constitution-making. The first believe that the constitution is too good for the people, the second that the people are too good for the constitution. Both are wrong.

The poor and the oppressed have been excluded for long enough from political rights. Now there are some who wish to exclude them from the constitutional debate as well. Those who have always had contempt for the majority will continue to do so. There is less excuse for persons who have always stood for democracy now assuming that concepts like good government and the rule of law belong only to the elite. No one should have greater interest in the rule of law than the dispossessed, who have suffered the most from lawlessness and from being excluded from the law's realm.

Their rights to property, to personal security, to freedom of movement and expression, have been more brutally violated than has been the case of any other section of the community. To this day, in the absence of the rule of law, many are forced to subject themselves to the rule of warlords. Millions of persons living on commercial farms are subject to the whims of the landowner rather than the provisions of the law. However kind and farsighted an individual *baas* might be, this is no substitute for enforceable legal rights. The same applies to the hundreds of thousands of persons employed as domestic servants, who are also entitled to legal protection against the arbitrariness of employers.

The rule of law extends to the home. It is true that the law cannot make people happy or even force them to live together. It can, however, prevent them from assaulting each other and imposing other intolerable indignities.

We need the rule of law in the streets and in the suburbs and townships. If people cannot walk freely for fear of being robbed or raped, the rule of law is violated. If we are unable to sleep tranquilly in our homes – whether modest or luxurious – the rule of law is absent.

Take away the right of the poor and oppressed to declare what they expect of the rule of law, and the concept will indeed be reduced to being little more than a prescription for securing the property rights and personal comfort of the ruling elite. Allow everyone to lay claim to the concept, however, and it can then respond to the claims of everyone.

In a country where the majority have been oppressed by both lawlessness and legalized tyranny, the rule of law allied to constitutionalism and equal rights becomes revolutionary. The constitution will have been brought about largely by the struggles and pain of the dispossessed. It will be up to them to claim that its terms be comprehensive and that its injunctions are followed.

It thus becomes all the more important for the voice of the dispossessed and the marginalized to be heard when the constitution is being framed. The rich and powerful have far less need of a constitution and the rule of law than do the poor and the oppressed. Their riches and their power give them the security that they require. They have every right to expect the law to defend them from arbitrary conduct, whether by the government or by private individuals. At the same time, their wealth and power does not give them the right to violate or ignore the rights of others.

No employer, no landowner, no chief, and no husband is above the law. The rule of law does not mean only that the rich are safe from arbitrary dispossession but also the poor.

If we are not to think of ourselves in a democratic South Africa as victors and vanquished, then we must try to find principles of government that have the broadest possible appeal. The rule of law is one of them. It signifies not only that the power of the state must be exercised in a lawful manner but that everyone is entitled to the protection of the law in going about his or her daily business.

The rule of law accordingly guarantees the exercise of constitutional rights in everyday life. It includes the right to be eccentric and dissident, but it goes much further. It covers protection from arbitrary conduct on the part of the state officials, but it is much more than that.

In a country where there is so much private power, so much fear, and so much abuse, the rule of law becomes a major instrument of social justice. In the context of what has been called the historic compromize in South Africa, it could be a principle that guarantees the advancement of the status of the majority without reducing the status of the minority. We might be sure that Dicey never had this in mind when he wrote about the subject for the upper middle class who had the vote in nineteenth-century England – but the rule of law in South African conditions can be quite empowering for the masses.

EMPOWERMENT TO THE PEOPLE. The slogan, "empowerment to the people" might not have the resonance of "power to the people," but it is both more feasible and wiser in our circumstances. As we used to say, "sometimes to be less revolutionary is to be more revolutionary."

What interest, one may, however, still ask, do the poor and the oppressed have in a constitution that most cannot even read, let alone feel capable of invoking?

First, their interest will depend on the extent to which they are involved in the process of constitution-making. This means not only that they must have the right to vote for the persons who will make up the constitution-making body but that they must understand the basic issues and make their pronouncements on them.

Secondly, the claims for human rights of those historically dispossessed must be clearly acknowledged in the constitution that emerges. If only the propertied classes and their representatives are involved in the process of writing the constitution, then the rights of the dispossessed are likely to be ignored.

Since our constitution will necessarily deal with the rights of both the possessed and the dispossessed, some kind of balance will have to be struck between the two. It will thus be in the interests of all of us for the constitution to acknowledge the difficulties involved in reconciling the competing claims; then, when it lays down the principles and procedures for dealing with them, it should do so in a way that gives appropriate weight to the necessity to overcome the injustices and inequalities of the past.

Thirdly, once the constitution has been adopted, its regard for the poor and the oppressed should be manifested in concrete actions. The vote, equal protection, remedies for discrimination, equal spending, regional equalisation, restoration of land rights, and affirmative action become powerful means of securing advancement. The space given to the organs of civil society should permit community and workers' organisations to keep up the pressure for change. Principles of good government and the rule of law provide the overarching context within which the claims are pressed.

The poor are not obliged to remain poor, the oppressed have means to deal with their oppression.

The rich man's fart smells sweet. May it never happen in South Africa that if a once noble veteran of struggle passes wind, the people declare, "What a victory!"

The beautiful people are not yet born. The Zimbabwean poet was right. He might have added, "nor will they ever be." Each generation struggles to produce its own beautiful people. We can inherit riches or poverty, power or oppression, but never beauty. We have to find it in ourselves, generation after generation.

Conference Participants*

Roderick Macdonald, Dean and Professor, Faculty of Law, McGill University.

Irwin Cotler, Professor of Law, McGill University, and Visiting Professor, Harvard Law School; Founder-Chair, InterAmicus; Legal Counsel, prisoners of conscience in the Soviet Union, South Africa, and Central America.

The Honourable David Crombie, MP, Secretary of State and Minister Responsible for Multiculturalism, including matters concerning human rights; first elected to the House of Commons, 1978; re-elected, 1979, 1980, and 1984; appointed Minister of National Health and Welfare, 1979, and Minister of Indian Affairs and Northern Development, 1984; Mayor of Toronto, 1972–78.

The Honourable Herbert Marx, MNA, Minister of Justice and Attorney-General for Quebec; formerly Professor of Law, Université de Montréal; author (with François Chevrette) of *Droit constitutionnel* and (with Irwin Cotler) of *Law and Poverty in Canada*.

David Johnston, Principal, Vice-Chancellor, and Professor of Law, McGill University; Chair, Committee of University Presidents; former Dean, Faculty of Law, University of Western Ontario, 1974–79; Commissioner, Ontario Securities Commission, 1972–79.

*   In order of proceedings; bios are as of November 1987.

The Honourable Claire L'Heureux-Dubé, Justice, Supreme Court of Canada; former Justice, Quebec Court of Appeal; Past President, International Commission of Jurists, Canadian Section; President, Quebec Association for the Study of Comparative Law; Vice-President, International Society on Family Law.

The Honourable Jules Deschênes, Chief Justice, Quebec Superior Court, 1973–83; Consultant, United Nations Centre for Social Development and Humanitarian Affairs; Member, United Nations Sub-Commission on Prevention of Discrimination and Protection of Minorities; Vice-President, World Association of Judges, Chair, Commission of Inquiry on War Criminals.

The Honourable Ramon Hnatyshyn, MP, Minister of Justice and Attorney-General for Canada; first elected to the House of Commons, 1974; Minister of Energy, Mines and Resources and Minister of State for Science and Technology, 1979; Government House Leader, 1984; President of Privy Council, 1985.

Elizabeth Holtzman, District Attorney, Kings County, New York; Congresswoman, 1973–80; Member, House Judiciary Committee; Drafter of "Holtzman Amendment" making possible revocation of US citizenship for Nazi war criminals; Member, US Citizens' Committee on Helsinki Accords; Member, Lawyers' Committee on International Human Rights.

Michael Meighen, partner, McMaster, Meighen; Counsel, Commission of Inquiry on War Criminals; Chair, Council for Canadian Unity; National President, Progressive Conservative Association of Canada, 1974–77.

Svend Robinson, MP, Member of Parliament for Burnaby, BC; Justice Critic, New Democratic Party; NDP spokesman on war criminals and Human Rights matters.

Greville Janner, MP, Member of Parliament, United Kingdom (Labour); Convenor, UK Parliamentary War Crimes Group; Founder, Trustee and former Chair, All-Party Committee for Homeless and Rootless People; Vice-Chair, All-Party Committee for Release of Soviet Jewry; Founding Member, International Committee for Human Rights in the USSR.

Serge Klarsfeld, Counsel for the Plaintiffs in the trial of Klaus Barbie;

responsible, with wife Beatrice, for the discovery of Barbie in Bolivia and for Barbie's extradition to France for trial; author.

Allan Ryan Jr, General Counsel, Harvard University; Former Director, Office of Special Investigation, US Department of Justice; author, *Quiet Neighbours.*

The Right Honourable Pierre Elliott Trudeau, Counsel, Heenan, Blaikie; Prime Minister of Canada, 1968–79, 1980–84; Founding Member, Montreal Civil Liberties Union; Albert Einstein International Peace Prize, 1984; former Member, Committee on Hate Propaganda.

David Matas, Author, *Justice Delayed*; Counsel, League for Human Rights of B'nai B'rith, Commission of Inquiry on War Criminals; Legal Coordinator, Amnesty International.

The Honourable Walter Tarnopolsky, Justice, Ontario Court of Appeal; Professor and Director, Human Rights Centre, Faculty of Law, University of Ottawa, 1980–83; Member, United Nations Human Rights Committee, 1977–83; Commissioner, Canadian Human Rights Commission, 1978–83; President, Canadian Civil Liberties Association, 1977–81.

Benjamin Ferencz, Executive General Counsel, Nuremberg Military Tribunal; Chief Prosecutor, *S.S. Einsatzgruppen* trial; Professor of International Law, Pace Law School.

Goshu Wolde, former Minister of Foreign Affairs, Ethiopia.

Gisèle Côté-Harper, Professor of Law, Laval University; Member, Quebec Human Rights Commission; former Member, United Nations Committee on Human Rights.

Judge Maxwell Cohen, Judge (ad hoc), International Court of Justice; Senior Scholar, Faculty of Law, University of Ottawa; former Dean and Professor Emeritus, Faculty of Law, McGill University; Chairman, Special Committee on Hate Propaganda, 1965–66; Chairman, Canadian Section, International Joint Commission, 1974–79; President's Award, Canadian Bar Association, 1986.

Ram Jethmalani, Member and Past President, Indian Bar Association; former Member of Indian Parliament; Vice-President, World Association of Peace through Law.

Alan Dershowitz, Professor of Law, Harvard Law School; Author, *The Best Defense*; former Director, American Civil Liberties Union; leading American civil liberties lawyer.

André Tremblay, Professor of Law, Université de Montréal; Director, Centre for Research in Public Law; Constitutional Advisor, Government of Quebec.

Arthur Chaskelson, Founder-Director, Centre for Public Interest Law in South Africa; litigated major cases involving apartheid "law"; former defense counsel to Nelson Mandela; Visiting Professor, Columbia University Law School.

Paul Boateng, MP, Member of Parliament, United Kingdom (Labour); first Black elected to UK Parliament, 1987; Member, Greater London Council, 1981–86; Executive, National Council on Civil Liberties, 1980–86; Member, Labour Party Sub-Committee on Human Rights; Member, Home Secretary's Advisory Council on Race Relations.

The Honourable Michael Kirby, Chief Justice, Court of Appeal, New South Wales, Australia; former Chair, Australia Law Reform Commission.

The Honourable Rosalie Abella, Judge, Provincial Court of Ontario, Family Division; Chair, Ontario Labour Relations Board; Sole Commissioner, Royal Commission on Equality in Employment; Director, International Commission of Jurists (Canadian Section).

His Excellency, Ambassador Stephen Lewis, Canadian Ambassador to the United Nations; Special Advisor on Africa to the Secretary-General of the United Nations; former leader of the Ontario Democratic Party and leader of the official opposition in the Legislature, 1975–78.

Sylvia Litvack, Partner, Chait, Solomon (Montreal); Trustee, Robert Litvack Memorial Award in Human Rights.

Carmen Quintana, Chilean human rights activist; victim of army brutality; first recipient, Robert Litvack Memorial Award in Human Rights, 1987.

OTHER CONTRIBUTORS

Per Ahlmark, distinguished poet, author, journalist, social critic, and parliamentarian, was the youngest person ever elected to the Swedish Parliament. After twelve years in Parliament, during which time he became deputy prime minister and minister of labour in the coalition government, he retired from political life to devote himself to family, community, and the pursuit of social justice. He served, *inter alia* as president of the Martin Luther Foundation, member of the Council of Europe, and chairman of the Swedish Commission against Racism and Antisemitism, while authoring works of poetry and politics.

Albie Sachs is a South African civil rights activist, author, and lawyer. In 1965 he was detained under the Internal Security Act and kept in solitary confinement for 180 days. He wrote of this period in *The Jail Diary of Albie Sachs*, which was later dramatized by the Royal Shakespeare Company and broadcast by the BBC. Sachs was told on his release that he could leave South Africa, provided he did not return. He accepted a scholarship to the University of Sussex where he obtained a PHD. His thesis was on the administration of criminal justice in South Africa. Between 1970 and 1976 Sachs taught at the University of Southampton, England. While there, he revised his thesis for publication and co-wrote *Sexism and the Law*, the first book in the Commonwealth to examine the forms of discrimination encountered by women. In 1976 Sachs was asked by the Mozambique government to draft a new Civil Code and to set up a system of legal education in that country. In 1988, his work in Mozambique came to an abrupt end – he survived a bomb blast orchestrated by the South African government. Sachs has been a law lecturer at the University of Southampton, Eduoardo Mondlane University in Mozambique, and Columbia University. He is currently director of the South African Constitution Studies Centre at the University of London; a teacher/administrator in the Community Law Centre, University of the Western Cape; and a member of the Constitutional Committee of the African National Congress and advisor in Working Group 2 (Constitutional Principles) at CODESA.

RESOURCE FACULTY

Irving Abella, Professor of History, York University; author, *None is Too Many*.

Christopher Amersinghue, Department of Justice, Ottawa.

Gérald-A. Beaudoin, Professor of Law and Director, Human Rights Research and Education Centre, University of Ottawa; Chair, CBA Committee on War Criminals.

Alan Borovoy, General Counsel, Canadian Civil Liberties Association.

Michael Bothe, Visiting Professor of Law, Université de Montréal; co-author, *The Limitation of Human Rights in Comparative Constitutional Law.*

Irving Brecher, Professor of Economics, McGill University.

François Chevrette, Dean and Professor of Law, Université de Montréal.

Roland de Corneille, MP, Human Rights Critic, Official Opposition.

Armand de Mestral, Professor of Law, McGill University; author (with Sharon Williams), *Introduction to International Law.*

The Honourable Alice Desjardins, Justice, Quebec Superior Court.

Nicole Duplé, Professor of Law, Laval University.

The Honourable Roland Durand, Justice Quebec Superior Court.

Bruce Elman, Professor of Law, University of Alberta; author of a forthcoming work on the *Keegsra* trial.

Morris Fish, partner, Yarosky, Fish (Montreal).

Martin Friedland, Professor and former Dean, Faculty of Law, University of Toronto.

The Honourable Alan Gold, Chief Justice, Quebec Superior Court.

The Honourable Charles Gonthier, Justice, Quebec Superior Court.

Leslie Green, University Professor, Faculty of Law, University of Alberta.

The Honourable Irving Halperin, Justice, Quebec Superior Court.

The Honourable Fred Kaufman, Justice, Court of Appeal of Quebec.

The Honourable Guy Kroft, Justice, Manitoba Court of Queen's Bench.

Hélène LeBel, Professor of Law, McGill University.

Harold Levy, Editorial Board, *Toronto Star.*

Jack London, Professor of Law, University of Manitoba.

J. Noel Lyon, Professor of Law, Queen's University.

Joseph Magnet, Professor of Law, University of Ottawa; author, *Constitutional Law.*

Kathleen Mahoney, Professor of Law, University of Calgary.

Morris Manning, constitutional and criminal law specialist.

Stephen Marcus, partner, Covington, Burling (Washington).

Norman May, partner, Fogler, Rubinoff (Toronto); former Professor, Osgoode Hall Law School.

The Honourable Perry Meyer, Justice, Quebec Superior Court; former Professor of Law, McGill University.

Ed Morgan, Professor of Law, University of Toronto.

Joseph Nuss, partner, Ahern, Nuss (Montreal); frequent counsel to commissions of inquiry.

Michel Proulx, partner, Proulx, Barot, Masson (Montreal); author of a Report for the Commision of Inquiry on War Criminals.

Jonathan Richler, legal researcher on war crimes.

Alti Rodal, Director of Research, Commission of Inquiry on War Criminals; author of the "Rodal Report."

Ronald Sklar, Professor of Law, McGill University.

Margaret Somerville, Professor of Law, McGill University; Director, Centre for Medicine, Ethics and Law.

John Sopinka, partner, Stikeman, Elliott (Toronto); Counsel to the Ukrainian-Canadian Committee before the Commission of Inquiry on War Criminals.

Eric Stein, Professor, University of Michigan Law School.

The Honourable Henry Steinberg, Justice, Quebec Superior Court.

Charles Taylor, Professor of Political Science, McGill University.

Stephen Toope, Professor of Law, McGill University.

Harold Troper, Professor of History, University of Toronto.

Daniel Turp, Professor of Law, Université de Montréal.

Ivan Vlasic, Professor of Law, McGill University.

Morton Weinfeld, Professor and Chair, Department of Sociology, McGill University.

Sharon Williams, Professor of Law, Osgoode Hall Law School; author of a Report for the Commission of Inquiry on War Criminals.

Harvey Yarosky, partner, Yarosky, Fish (Montreal); former Counsel, Special Committee on Hate Propaganda.

CONFERENCE ORGANIZING COMMITTEE

Chair: Prof. Irwin Cotler

Prof. Peter Benson	Dean Roderick Macdonald
Prof. Frank Buckley	Prof. Yves-Marie Morissette
Prof. Armand de Mestral	Andrew Orkin
Richard Golick	Prof. Ronald Sklar
Richard Janda	Prof. Stephen Toope
Prof. Rosalie Jukier	Prof. Ivan Vlasic
Sylvia Litvack	Lorianne Weston

The Conference Organizing Committe wishes to express its gratitude
to the following for their financial support of the Conference:

Department of Justice, Government of Canada
Department of Justice, Government of Quebec
Secretary of State, Government of Canada
Canadian Friends of Bar-Ilan University